VOGUE
BOOK OF
MENUS

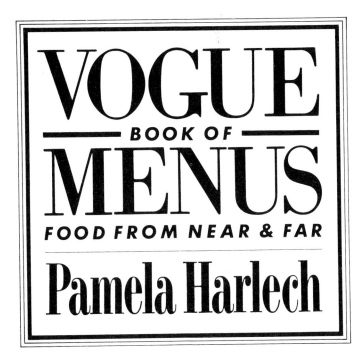

VOGUE
BOOK OF
MENUS
FOOD FROM NEAR & FAR

Pamela Harlech

CENTURY PUBLISHING
LONDON

For Georgina Boosey, a patient
friend for many years

Acknowledgements

I would like to thank many friends and colleagues for allowing me to use their recipes. In particular, Claudia Roden, who taught me Middle Eastern cookery and gave me permission to adapt some of her recipes, and Yan Kit So, who taught me Chinese cookery, and gave me permission to reproduce my favourite recipes from her book, *Classic Chinese Cookbook* (Dorling Kindersley, 1984). I would also like to thank Madhur Jaffrey who gave me valuable advice about Indian ingredients, and Arvind Saraswat and Satish Arora, two brilliant Indian chefs who taught me many dishes while I was in India. Other friends to thank are Nathalie Hambro, Jane Grigson, Cecilia McEwen, Ruth Deeley, Fernanda Neves, Mrs. Srinavasa and my mother, Georgia Colin. Very special thanks to my editor, Gill Edden, whose patience and knowledge, not to mention sense of humour, made the final publication date possible. Steve Lovi and Judy Brittain, with their perfect artistic eyes, brought that special something needed to produce the beautiful photographs. And once again, many, many thanks to Jane Fellowes, who lived through the eternal hours of typing and retyping. Finally, my gratitude to Gail Rebuck who understood what we were all trying to achieve and allowed us to do so.

Copyright © Pamela Harlech 1984

All rights reserved

First published in Great Britain in 1984
by Century Publishing Co. Ltd,
Portland House,
12–13 Greek Street, London W1V 5LE

British Library Cataloguing in Publication Data

Harlech, Pamela
Vogue book of menus
1. Cookery
I. Title
641.5   TX717

ISBN 0 7126 0325 5

Designed by Rose & Lamb Design Partnership

Illustrations by Rob Shone

Photographs by Steve Lovi

Typeset by Servis Filmsetting Ltd, Manchester

Printed in Italy by Imago Publishing Limited

Contents

*Dishes which are marked with an asterisk may be
prepared completely in advance. Metric measures
and American equivalents both of measures and
ingredients are given in brackets. Spoon measures
are level unless otherwise stated.*

'The French are thoroughly alive to
the art of dinner-giving, and they say
good eating is favourable to beauty,
and keeps off the exterior appearance
of old age. It gives brilliancy to the
eyes, freshness to the skin and stays
the depression of the muscles which
cause the wrinkles that are the
enemies of beauty; and that it is
certain that those females who know
how to eat are comparatively ten years
younger in appearance than those that
know not the science; and that
painters and sculptors are aware of the
fact, for they never represent the half-
starved, the bilious, or the pale, from
the malady of badly cooked food, their
blotches, wrinkles, or decrepitude.'

*Dinner and Dinner-Parties, or the
Absurdities of Artificial Life* 1862

Introduction

'Food, beside being an absolute necessity for existence, is one of the few pleasures which span the entirety of the human lifetime. For this reason, the joy of eating is given great importance in China; and cooking, through the decades, has been dreamed and fussed over, in times of want as well as in times of plenty, until it has ceased to be plain cooking, but has grown and developed into an art. Food has been represented through other mediums of art, especially poetry, literature and folklore; and these tales and food beliefs have been handed down, from generation to generation, with ever-increasing glamour. Every aspect of food is analysed, from its palatableness to its texture, from its value to its effectiveness, and from its fragrance to its colourfulness, until, as in other works of art, proportion and balance are instilled in every dish.'

Doreen Yen Hung Feng wrote that thirty-two years ago in her fascinating book, *The Joy Of Chinese Cooking*. It could have been written today, tomorrow or in fifty years time. Although she was referring to Chinese cooking, it can be applied to all forms and cuisines in the world.

Cooking *is* an art form, but let us not be pretentious about it. I mean to say, there is an art in planning a menu, taking into account its variety of taste, texture and colour. A creamy first course should not be followed by a creamy second course. Instead it could be a spicy entrée with crunchy underdone vegetables and for dessert, a tangy fruit sorbet with, perhaps, some sweet biscuits.

The colours should vary from course to course in the same way as texture and taste. I have often heard about people who have given all green or all pink dinners, right down to the table linen and flowers. Personally, I find this terribly tedious and pretentious. It seems to me that the host or hostess is trying to make the guests aware continually of his or her cleverness. This is wrong. The guests are the important people; they shouldn't feel the need to applaud their host or hostess at every course. Colours among the courses, and therefore in table linen and flowers, ought to complement one another subtly, so that the guests may be aware of a pleasant aura of entirety but contrast, without knowing the reason why.

I have discovered that often if you mix cuisines, an almost automatic variety of taste and texture, not to mention colour, will follow. For example, Chinese Pickled Cabbage served with pheasant relieves the tedium of the eternal Brussels sprouts or even red cabbage, both of which I like, but with something else for a change. The sweet and sour crunchy and punchy taste of the cabbage complements, but is a surprise with, the gamey taste of pheasant, without overwhelming it. The same is true when it is served with venison. Again, Spring lamb baked in a jacket of herbs, spices and mustard marries beautifully with a Kashmiri dish of fried aubergines (eggplants), marinated in a tamarind sauce then quickly stir-fried with a bit of dhal.

There is no need to cook an entire Indian or Chinese meal to enjoy their cuisines, although, if you have the time, this is fun to do as a complete change. But quite often, the preparation of one of these feasts will take more time than the cook can spare. Therefore, if you choose one or two courses from these cuisines, which may need a bit of time to prepare, the third could be a plain roasted, grilled (broiled) or poached dish. Even the preparation, if well organized, need not take as long as some think. And dishes such as the Chinese Pickled Cabbage, Chicken Rouxinol, Soufflé Roulé aux Epinards, Tomato and Herb Mousse, Japanese Twice-fried Chicken and many soups can be prepared hours before serving; indeed, some should be. In this way the herbs and spices have time to become infused into the main ingredients.

Sometimes things even out. With Chinese cooking, quite often the preparation takes quite a while, but the cooking itself takes only 2–7 minutes immediately before serving. It is possible and usually essential to chop up the ingredients in advance. Many recipes call for grated or chopped fresh ginger, chopped garlic and chopped spring onions (scallions) or green onions. The white part of the onion, the bulb, should be separated from the green part, because the white part takes longer to cook than the green, and is therefore added right after the ginger and garlic. The green stem is added at the end of cooking the dish, for a colourful garnish. I find that the polystyrene trays which supermarkets use as food containers are extremely useful and inexpensive to use for the prepared ingredients. I put each ingredient on a separate small tray, covered with cling film (Saran Wrap), and put them into the refrigerator until needed. Just before cooking, I remove them from the refrigerator and place them next to the stove, in the order in which they will 'enter the pot', i.e. the wok or frying-pan. The rest is easy and there is no panic.

With Chinese, Indian and Middle Eastern recipes, as with some Western recipes, the food is marinated before cooking. This takes from 30 minutes to 12 hours, so it is important to read the recipe through well in advance so as not to be caught at the last minute with instructions to have marinated the meat the night before. In fact, it is always necessary to read through the recipe well in advance. You do not want to find, again at the last minute, that an important ingredient is lacking in your larder. And *always* try out a new recipe on

yourself, your family or some kind friends, *before* inflicting it upon a dinner party of unsuspecting guests. Even though recipes are checked before publishing, sometimes things are left out by mistake or, more important, you may find that something is too hot for your taste or too bland. All can be corrected, but not during a party.

Ingredients

All the ingredients used in the Chinese recipes in this book are available in Oriental food shops, and some are widely available in supermarkets throughout the world because of the new-found popularity of Chinese cuisine.

Middle Eastern and Indian ingredients are usually to be found in Middle Eastern and Oriental food shops too. I do know, though, that curry leaves are difficult to find in the United States, whereas in Great Britain they are often available in Indian and Thai greengrocers. But do not worry, because curry leaves are usually an optional ingredient in the recipes in this book, and if necessary I find that a pinch of curry powder added at the last minute is not a bad substitute.

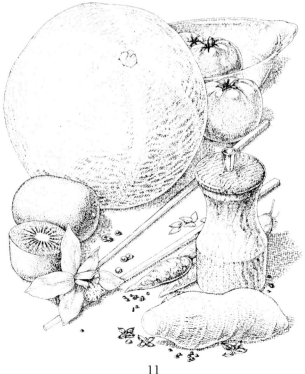

A lot of basic preparation can take place early in the day in Indian cooking. For instance, in many Indian dishes roasted ground cumin and coriander seeds are required. These can be prepared in advance. It is important to use an enamel or non-stick frying-pan for this and for frying mustard seeds, because they have a high acid content, which becomes explosive if it comes in contact, over heat, with metal. Put the seeds in a *dry* (no oil) frying-pan over high heat, and keep shaking the pan until the seeds have turned brown. If roasting mustard seeds with them, cover the pan to prevent the mustard seeds spitting in your face. When adding water to the frying spices, remove the pan from the heat and pour the water along the edges of the pan, otherwise the hot spices may fly up into your face once again. When the cumin seeds and coriander seeds have turned pale brown, remove them from the heat and either grind them with a mortar and pestle or, as I often do with spices, grind them in a small electric coffee grinder, reserved for grinding herbs and spices *only*. These ground spices can then be put into a bowl, covered and put aside for later use. Do not put them into the refrigerator, as this will lessen their pungency.

With garam masala (see page 181), it is better to make it fresh when you need it, but if you haven't the time, make a larger, though not too large, quantity, place it in a screw-top jar and put in a cupboard or on a shelf away from the sunlight. Do not keep it for more than three weeks.

Two or three ingredients are well worth preparing ahead, when you have a free moment, to keep either in the larder or in the refrigerator. The first is tamarind juice. This will keep in the refrigerator for up to 1 month, and you usually need only 2–3 tablespoons (30–45 ml) at a time. It is at its best if you take a 2½-inch (6.3-cm) piece of tamarind (again available in Oriental and Middle Eastern food shops) and soak it overnight in 16 fl oz (475 ml, 2 cups) hot water. Then pour the juice through a sieve into a bowl. Mash the tamarind pulp in the sieve with the back of a wooden spoon, so that the pulp goes through as well. Be sure to scrape all the pulp from the bottom of the sieve. Then pour it into a screw-

top jar and place in the refrigerator. You can make it at the last moment by simmering the tamarind in the water over low heat for 15 minutes, then mashing the pulp as before. However, this method is less satisfactory in the final result.

Garlic oil is another useful ingredient to keep handy, and simple to make. Just put 3–4 crushed garlic cloves into 8 fl oz (225 ml, 1 cup) good olive oil, and allow it to marinate for at least two days before using. Keep in a screw-top jar in the larder.

There is often confusion between chilli powder and chili powder. Many people talk about them as though they are one and the same thing. They are not. Chilli powder derives only from the chilli pepper, and is sometimes known as red pepper or cayenne pepper. It is this unblended powder which is used in the cooking in Eastern countries. To avoid confusion I have referred to it in this book as cayenne pepper. Chili powder, on the other hand, is the ground chilli pepper blended with other spices such as cumin, oregano and garlic; it is used in Central American dishes such as chili con carne. Paprika is a milder spice taken from the various capsicums grown around the Mediterranean area. Spanish paprika has a somewhat earthy, bland flavour, which lends itself as a garnish, as well as a natural food colouring. Hungarian paprika has a stronger though sweeter taste and is used in dishes such as Goulash, see page 111.

Yoghurt
When cooking with commercial yoghurt, a better result will be achieved if you pour it through a muslin or cheesecloth lined sieve to get rid of the excess water. Before adding yoghurt to a dish, beat it as you would egg yolks, so that it will absorb the fat and not separate. After adding it to the dish, do not cover it while it is cooking, and always stir it in the same direction. If you are afraid it might curdle when added to a hot sauce, beat an egg yolk into it before combining it with the sauce.

Cooking rice
Rices prepared in the Italian, Indian, Middle Eastern and Chinese cuisines are not totally

unalike, except that the aimed-for result is usually different. The Italian, Indian and Middle Eastern aim is for a crispy and individual grained rice, whereas the Chinese prefer a more tender, but not mushy, result. All use the long grain rice except in sweet dishes, where the short grain rice is often used.

For special Indian dishes, Basmati, the delicately perfumed, nutty tasting and rather expensive 'king of rices', is perfect. It grows in the foothills of the Himalayan mountains. This rice must be picked over carefully, removing any tiny stones or foreign objects, before cooking. The Italian Arborio rice is particularly good for risottos. Partially prepared or 'easy-cook' rices take less time to cook, but the results are not as good, nor is the taste.

All long grain rices should be washed three to five times, prior to cooking (American rice is the exception), until the water runs clear. And they all benefit from being soaked for 30–40 minutes, after washing and before cooking, to enable the rice to puff up, thus ensuring separate grains at the end of cooking.

These are all hints that I hope will make your life in the kitchen that much easier, and encourage you to try new things. The point is, to *think first and plan ahead*, and that is what this book is meant to help the reader to do. Menus are suggested. However that is not to say that combining a dish from one menu with one from another menu would be a disaster. In fact, it is to be encouraged. The more you try different combinations, the more adventurous, imaginative and fun your cooking will be.

Important Often I use a first course, vegetable or dessert in two or three menus. The number of servings varies sometimes, so you will need to adjust the amount of ingredients.

I have tried to use ingredients such as fish, game, poultry, meat and vegetables which are available throughout the world. If a particular one is not available, a good substitute is, such as guinea hen for pheasant, or blue fish for mackerel. It is for this reason, that I have not suggested such delicacies as soft-shelled crabs or red snapper, which are only to be found in the Americas, or grouse, which are to be found only in Great Britain.

When I suggest a mixed green salad, or one made of radicchio, Belgian endive and watercress, I have not given a recipe, as I assume most people know how to make these salads and have their own favourite vinaigrettes. Equally, I do not think it is necessary to always have three courses. Most people today prefer not to eat too much, so often I will leave out either the first course or the last. Also, as time is a priority in our lives, I think two good courses are better than three hastily put together ones. Dishes which are marked with an asterisk may be prepared completely in advance. Many other dishes can be prepared in advance up to a certain point. This will be indicated within the recipe.

As Doreen Yen Hung Feng reiterates, 'Maximum preparation of ingredients before cooking is absolutely necessary if one desires to keep the peace of mind, remain unflustered, and cook a good meal. The experienced cook will have all the materials well prepared and neatly set out within easy reach; because once the food hits the pot upon the fire, the rest usually follows with cyclonic rapidity.' She is referring specifically to the cooking of a Chinese meal, I, however, say, 'This refers to *all* cooking. Be prepared and the rest is easy.'

Imperial and Metric Weights and Measures

Weight

$\frac{1}{2}$ kg = 500 g

Imperial measures	Approximate metric equivalent
1 oz	25 g
2 oz	50 g
3 oz	75 g
4 oz	100–125 g
5 oz	150 g
6 oz	175 g
7 oz	200 g
8 oz	225 g
9 oz	250 g
10 oz	275 g
11 oz	300 g
12 oz	325–350 g
13 oz	375 g
14 oz	400 g
15 oz	425 g
16 oz (1 lb)	450 g
$1\frac{1}{2}$ lb	700 g
2 lb	900 g
$2\frac{1}{2}$ lb	1.1 kg
3 lb	1.4 kg
$3\frac{1}{2}$ lb	1.6 kg
4 lb	1.8 kg
$4\frac{1}{2}$ lb	2 kg
5 lb	2.3 kg
$5\frac{1}{2}$ lb	2.5 kg
6 lb	2.7 kg
$6\frac{1}{2}$ lb	3 kg
7 lb	3.2 kg
$7\frac{1}{2}$ lb	3.4 kg
8 lb	3.6 kg
$8\frac{1}{2}$ lb	3.9 kg
9 lb	4.1 kg
$9\frac{1}{2}$ lb	4.3 kg
10 lb	4.5 kg

Liquid Capacity

Imperial pint (20 fl oz) measures slightly more than $\frac{1}{2}$ litre – approximately 575 millilitres (ml)
1000 ml = 1 litre (l)

Imperial measures	Approximate metric equivalent
1 fl oz	25 ml
2 fl oz	50 ml
3 fl oz	75 ml
4 fl oz	100–125 ml
5 fl oz	150 ml
6 fl oz	175 ml
7 fl oz	200 ml
8 fl oz	225 ml
9 fl oz	250 ml
10 fl oz ($\frac{1}{2}$ pt)	275–300 ml
20 fl oz (1 pt)	575–600 ml

Metric measures and American equivalents both of measures and ingredients are given in brackets. Spoon measures are level unless otherwise stated.

Oven Temperatures

	Fahrenheit	Celsius (Centigrade)	Gas
Very cool	250°F	130°C	Mark $\frac{1}{2}$
	275°F	140°C	Mark 1
Cool	300°F	150°C	Mark 2
Warm	325°F	170°C	Mark 3
Moderate	350°F	180°C	Mark 4
Fairly hot	375°F	190°C	Mark 5
	400°F	200°C	Mark 6
Hot	425°F	220°C	Mark 7
Very hot	450°F	230°C	Mark 8
	475°F	240°C	Mark 9
	500°F	250°C	Mark 10

To convert Fahrenheit to Celsius or Centigrade: subtract 32, multiply by 5, divide by 9.
To convert Celsius to Fahrenheit: multiply by 9, divide by 5 and add 32.

Conversion of Solid Measures

British	American
5 oz plain flour	1 cup all-purpose or cake flour
1 lb plain flour	$3\frac{1}{2}$ cups all-purpose or cake flour
$1\frac{1}{2}$ oz plain flour	1 tablespoon all-purpose or cake flour
4 oz self-raising flour	1 cup self-raising flour
$\frac{1}{3}$ oz cornflour	1 tablespoon cornstarch
8 oz granulated or caster sugar	1 cup granulated or superfine granulated sugar
$\frac{1}{2}$ oz granulated or caster sugar	1 tablespoon granulated or superfine granulated sugar
6 oz brown sugar	1 cup brown sugar
$\frac{1}{3}$ oz brown sugar	1 tablespoon brown sugar
$4\frac{1}{2}$ oz icing sugar	1 cup confectioners' sugar
1 lb butter, margarine or lard	2 cups butter, margarine or lard
8 oz butter, margarine or lard	1 cup butter, margarine or lard
$\frac{1}{2}$ oz butter, margarine or lard	1 tablespoon butter, margarine or lard
7 oz uncooked rice	1 cup uncooked rice
3 oz fresh breadcrumbs	1 cup fresh breadcrumbs
6 oz dry breadcrumbs	1 cup dry breadcrumbs
13 oz syrup	1 cup syrup
5 oz currants	1 cup currants
5 oz sultanas	1 cup raisins
$5\frac{1}{2}$ oz chopped nuts	1 cup chopped nuts
$3\frac{1}{2}$ oz chopped parsley	1 cup chopped parsley
2 oz rolled oats	1 cup rolled oats
3 oz grated cheese (e.g. Cheddar)	1 cup grated cheese (firm American)
$4\frac{1}{2}$ oz chopped onion	1 cup chopped onion
11 oz clear honey	1 cup clear honey

Conversion of Liquid Measures

British	American
$\frac{1}{4}$ pint (5 fl oz)	$\frac{1}{4}$ pint (4 fl oz or $\frac{1}{2}$ cup plus 2 tablespoons)
$\frac{1}{2}$ pint (10 fl oz)	$\frac{1}{2}$ pint (8 fl oz or $1\frac{1}{4}$ cups)
1 pint (20 fl oz)	1 pint (16 fl oz or $2\frac{1}{2}$ cups)
1 quart (2 pints or 40 fl oz)	5 cups ($2\frac{1}{2}$ pints)
1 gallon (4 quarts or 8 pints)	$1\frac{1}{4}$ gallons (10 pints)

Spring

────── DINNER ──────
SERVES 6

Hot Spinach and Chicken Liver Salad (see page 26)

───────

*Milos Fritos
(Portuguese Lambs' Brains in Batter)
with Molho de Tomate

or

Monkfish Delight

Fried Parsley (see page 79)

*Glazed Carrots (see page 74)

───────

*Sesame Biscuits

───────

The brains may be halfway prepared in advance, leaving only the deep frying to be done at the last minute, at the same time as the parsley. The carrots may also be cooked ahead. The Sesame Biscuits keep well for several days in an air-tight tin.

*Milos Fritos

$2\frac{1}{2}$ lb (1.1 kg) lambs' brains
1 bay leaf
1 small onion
1 small carrot
salt and pepper
2 drops wine vinegar
2 tablespoons (30 ml) lemon juice
2 tablespoons (30 ml) fresh coriander (Chinese parsley) or parsley, chopped finely
1 recipe Massa Vinho (see page 61)
olive oil for frying

To prepare the brains, place them in a medium-sized saucepan in salted cold water to cover for $1\frac{1}{2}$ hours, then remove the membranes and veins. Return the cleaned brains to the saucepan. Add to the cold water the bay leaf, onion, carrot, salt and pepper, and vinegar. Bring to the boil, then simmer for 10 minutes, drain and allow to cool before cooking further.

Season the brains with salt and pepper, lemon juice and chopped coriander (Chinese parsley) or parsley. Coat them with the Massa Vinho batter. Allow to rest on kitchen paper towels for 5 minutes. In a large frying-pan heat the olive oil and fry the brains on both sides until they turn golden brown. Serve with the Molho de Tomate.

Soaking time: $1\frac{1}{2}$ hours
Preparation time: approximately 30 minutes
Cooking time: approximately 30 minutes

Molho de Tomate

4 fl oz (125 ml, $\frac{1}{2}$ cup) olive oil
1 tablespoon (15 ml) unsalted butter
1 medium-sized onion, chopped finely
1 large carrot, peeled and chopped finely
1 large clove garlic, chopped finely
2 lb (1 kg) ripe tomatoes, blanched and peeled, or canned tomatoes
$1\frac{1}{2}$ tablespoons (22.5 ml) plain (all-purpose) flour
pinch of sugar
1 tablespoon (15 ml) dried oregano
salt and freshly ground pepper to taste

In a large saucepan heat the olive oil and butter, then add the onion, carrot and garlic. Cook until the vegetables are tender, approximately 10 minutes, then add the tomatoes and simmer over low heat for 10 minutes. Measure 10 fl oz (300 ml, $1\frac{1}{4}$ cups) water. Mix the flour into about 2 tablespoons (30 ml) of the water, then add the mixture plus the rest of the water to the sauce. Cook for a further 5 minutes, then add the sugar, oregano, salt and freshly ground pepper. Pour the mixture into a food processor or blender and mix well to a smooth sauce. Return it to the saucepan to heat. Serve hot.

Preparation time: 30–40 minutes
Cooking time: approximately 35 minutes

Monkfish Delight

The monkfish is one of the ugliest fish living, with a horrifying mouth – it usually puts off people by its looks. Therefore you will rarely see the whole fish on a fishmonger's stall. The tail is usually cut up into steaks, which then may be used for a variety of dishes. The meat of the tail has the texture of and a somewhat similar taste to a lobster, without the expensive price. Sometimes when scallops are unavailable, I use monkfish as a substitute.

4 oz (125 g, 1 cup) onions, sliced
3 large cloves garlic, sliced
4½ tablespoons (67 ml) butter
1½ lb (700 g) monkfish tail, cut into bite-size pieces
salt and pepper
2 tablespoons (30 ml) chopped dillweed
2 tablespoons (30 ml) fresh coriander (Chinese parsley) chopped finely
3 oz (75 g, ½ cup) dry breadcrumbs
1½ tablespoons (22 ml) grated Parmesan cheese

In a large sauté pan, brown the onion and garlic in the butter. Add the fish, salt, pepper, dillweed and fresh coriander (Chinese parsley). Cover the pan and simmer for 5 minutes, stirring occasionally. Add the breadcrumbs, stir and mix well until all the liquid has been absorbed. Add the cheese and cook for 3 minutes, uncovered. Serve immediately.

Preparation time: approximately 25 minutes
Cooking time: approximately 20 minutes

*Sesame Biscuits

Makes approximately 4 dozen biscuits
(cookies)

7 oz (200 g, 1⅓ cups) plain (all-purpose) flour
1 tablespoon (15 ml) baking powder
1 lb (450 g) granulated sugar
8 oz (225 g, 1 cup) butter, melted
4 oz (125 g, ½ cup) lard, melted
4 eggs, beaten
1 tablespoon (15 ml) anise flavouring
milk, if needed
¾ lb (350 g) sesame seeds

Preheat the oven to 325°F, 170°C, Mark 3.
In a large bowl, blend the flour, baking powder and sugar, then add the butter, lard and eggs. Mix thoroughly with the hands. Add the anise and mix to a smooth dough, adding a bit of milk, if necessary. Roll out the dough on a lightly floured board to about ⅛ inch (0.3 cm) thickness, cut into 1 × ½-inch (2.5 × 1.2-cm) lengths, and roll in the sesame seeds. Bake in the preheated oven for about 20 minutes.

Preparation time: 30–40 minutes
Cooking time: approximately 20 minutes

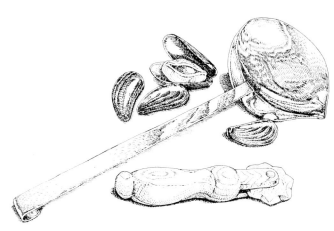

```
┌──────────────────────────────────────┐
│ _____ DINNER _____            │
│         SERVES 6                       │
│                                        │
│     Mozzarella in Carrozza             │
│         ─────────                      │
│                                        │
│  Carne de Porco a Alentejana           │
│   (Portuguese Pork and Clams)          │
│                                        │
│ Onion, Tomato and Cucumber Salad       │
│         ─────────                      │
│                                        │
│ *Cold Almond and Raspberry Pudding     │
│         (see page 39)                  │
└──────────────────────────────────────┘
```

Mozzarella in Carrozza

*12 1-inch (2.5-cm) thick slices of white bread,
  crusts removed*
6 1-inch (2.5-cm) thick slices of Mozzarella cheese
salt and freshly ground black pepper
*8 fl oz (225 ml, 1 cup) 'half and half' milk and
  single (light) cream*
*2 oz (50 g, ⅓ cup) plain (all-purpose) flour, for
  dredging*
3 eggs, lightly beaten
olive oil

For the sauce:
2 oz (50 g, ¼ cup) butter, melted
2-oz (50-g) can anchovies, drained and chopped
juice of 1 lemon
2 tablespoons (30 ml) capers, drained (optional)

Form 6 sandwiches with bread and cheese,
sprinkling a little salt and pepper on the cheese.
The sandwiches may be left whole or cut into
halves or quarters. Dip each sandwich into the
'half and half' mixture, dredge lightly with flour,
then dip into the eggs, letting the excess drip off.
Fry the sandwiches in the hot oil, turning once so
that both sides turn golden brown. Drain them on
kitchen paper towels. Mix together the ingredients for the sauce and serve with the
sandwiches.

Preparation time: 30–40 minutes
Cooking time: 15–20 minutes

Carne de Porco a Alentejana

This dish originated in the Alentejo, the rolling
South-Western region of Portugal, famous for
its herds of pigs which feed on the acorns from
the local corn oaks. Now it has become a
recognized national dish. I ate it in the
Algarve.

*2½ lb (1.1 kg) loin of pork, cut into 1-inch
  (2.5-cm) cubes*
2 tablespoons (30 ml) red wine vinegar
12 fl oz (350 ml, 1½ cups) dry white wine
3 large cloves garlic
1 bay leaf
2 tablespoons (30 ml) parsley, chopped
1 large onion, chopped finely
2 carrots, peeled and grated
1½ teaspoons (7.5 ml) saffron powder
2 sprigs of fresh coriander (Chinese parsley)
salt and freshly ground black pepper
3 tablespoons (45 ml) good olive oil
*1½ lb (700 g) cockles in brine, or canned whole
  clams, well washed*
*fresh coriander (Chinese parsley) or parsley
  leaves, chopped finely for garnish*
slices of lemon

In an earthenware dish or glass bowl, place the
pork cubes and all the ingredients except for the
olive oil, cockles or clams, coriander (Chinese
parsley) and lemon slices. Marinate the meat for
24 hours, then drain, reserving the marinade.
  In a large, deep sauté pan, heat the olive oil and
sauté the pork over a high heat for 10 minutes,
making sure that all the sides of the meat are
browned and well cooked. Lower the heat, add
the cockles or clams, and the reserved marinade.
Taste for seasoning, adding more if necessary.
Cook for a further 10 minutes, covered. Serve on a
heated dish garnished with the fresh coriander
(Chinese parsley) or parsley and slices of lemon.

Preparation time: 15 minutes
Marinating time: 24 hours
Cooking time: 20–25 minutes

Brazilian Hearts of Palm Omelette

Lebanese Baked Fish in Tahini Sauce

or

Trotto al Forno
(Baked Trout with Sardines)

*Lebanese Spiced Rice (see page 86)

*Seviyal Bakala Bath
(Indian Vermicelli pudding) (see page 33)

The bland omelette is followed by a spicy fish and rice dish, ending with a cooling, light touch.

Lebanese Baked Fish in Tahini Sauce

2-lb (1-kg) whole sea bass or striped bass, cleaned
  and scaled
4 fl oz (125 ml, ½ cup) hazelnut or olive oil
1 medium-sized onion, chopped finely
8 fl oz (225 ml, 1 cup) Tahini Sauce (see below)
2 oz (50 g, ¾ cup) fresh coriander (Chinese
  parsley) or parsley, chopped finely
wedges of lemon to garnish

Preheat the oven to 350°F, 180°C, Mark 4.

Rub the sea bass with half the oil, place in a baking pan and bake in the preheated oven for approximately 30 minutes, or until the flesh is flaky. In a frying-pan sauté the onion in the remaining oil until it is transparent. Drain well on kitchen paper towels, then mix in with the Tahini Sauce. Completely coat the fish with this mixture and return the fish to the oven to cook for a further 10 minutes. Serve on a warmed dish. Sprinkle with fresh coriander or parsley and garnish with lemon wedges on the side.

Brazilian Hearts of Palm Omelette

1 tablespoon (15 ml) olive oil
1 onion, chopped finely
1 tomato, peeled and chopped finely
1 fresh hot green chilli pepper, stem removed,
  seeded and chopped finely
10-oz (275-g) can hearts of palm
5 eggs, separated
salt and freshly ground black pepper
grated Parmesan cheese

Preheat the oven to 350°F, 180°C, Mark 4.

In a frying-pan heat the oil and sauté the onion, tomato and hot chilli pepper until they are soft. Add the palm hearts and cook for 3 minutes. Arrange the vegetables in an ovenproof dish big enough to hold them in one layer. Beat the egg yolks in one bowl with the salt and freshly ground black pepper. In another bowl beat the egg whites until they are light and frothy. Fold them into the egg yolks and pour over the vegetables. Sprinkle the grated cheese over the surface and bake in the preheated oven until golden.

*Preparation time: approximately 30 minutes
Cooking time: approximately 15 minutes*

Tahini Sauce

Makes 1 pint (600 ml, 2½ cups)

1 clove garlic, crushed
½ teaspoon (2.5 ml) salt
8 fl oz (225 ml, 1 cup) tahini (bitter sesame paste
  made from raw sesame seeds)
4 fl oz (125 ml, ½ cup) lemon juice
2 oz (50 g, ¾ cup) fresh coriander (Chinese
  parsley) or parsley, chopped finely

In a medium-sized bowl, mix the crushed garlic and salt into a paste. Add the tahini, mix, then add the lemon juice and again mix well. Slowly add water, bit by bit, beating constantly, until the sauce has reached a thick and creamy consistency. Finally, mix in the coriander (Chinese parsley) or parsley. You may find that it needs a little more lemon juice.

*Preparation time: approximately 20 minutes
Cooking time: 40 minutes*

Trotto al Forno

½ lb (225 g) sardines, packed in brine
2–3-lb (900 g–1.4-kg) trout
4 oz (125 g, ½ cup) butter
8 fl oz (225 ml, 1 cup) sour cream
6 water biscuits (oyster crackers), crushed
3 oz (75 g, 1 cup) Pecorino or Cheddar cheese, grated
cayenne pepper

Soak the sardines in fresh water for 1 hour, then drain well. Preheat the oven to 400°F, 200°C, Mark 6. Bone the sardines and chop them finely. In a bowl, mix them with the butter and sour cream. Split the trout and remove the centre bone. Place the trout, skin side down, in an ovenproof baking dish, and cover with the butter, sour cream and chopped sardines. Sprinkle with biscuit (cracker) crumbs, cheese and cayenne pepper, and bake in the preheated oven for 45 minutes. Serve in the same dish.

Preparation time: 1 hour soaking plus 20 minutes
Cooking time: 45 minutes

DINNER
SERVES 8

Deep-fried Camembert Parcels with
Cranberry Sauce

————

Lemon Chicken with Hollandaise Sauce

or

Avial-Malayali
(Vegetable Curry)

Pomodori Ripieni
(Italian Stuffed Tomatoes) (see page 30)

————

*Biscotti di Mandorle
(Almond Biscuits) (see page 78)

Deep-fried Camembert Parcels with Cranberry Sauce

8 oz (225 g, 1¼ cups) plain (all-purpose) flour
1 teaspoon (5 ml) salt
4 tablespoons (60 ml) oil
1 firm 1-lb (450-g) Camembert
6 tablespoons (90 ml) cranberry sauce or Almond Cranberry Sauce (see page 179)
2 eggs, beaten
oil for deep frying
spinach leaves for garnish

Sift the flour and salt into a bowl and make a well in the centre. Add the oil and gradually stir in enough water to make a firm dough. Knead lightly until smooth, then roll out very thinly on a lightly floured surface. Cut the pastry into 24 3½-inch (9-cm) squares

Cut the Camembert into 1-inch (2.5-cm) cubes. Put a little cranberry sauce in the centre of each pastry square and top with a cube of Camembert. Brush the edges of the pastry with beaten egg. Fold the pastry around the cheese, gathering the corners on top and twisting to seal the parcels.

Heat the oil in the deep-fat frying-pan to 375°F (190°C) or until a cube of bread browns in 30 seconds. Fry the cheese parcels, a few at a time, for about 1 minute, until crisp and golden. Drain on kitchen paper towels and keep hot while you cook the rest. Arrange the parcels on individual serving dishes, lined with spinach leaves. Serve immediately.

Preparation time: approximately 45 minutes
Cooking time: 12–15 minutes

Lemon Chicken with Hollandaise Sauce

I was at dinner one night in New York where we were served the most delicious lemon chicken with hollandaise sauce. My friend very kindly gave me the recipe and so I pass it on.

2 3½-lb (1.6-kg) chickens, cut into serving pieces
6 oz (175 g, 1 cup) sultanas (white raisins)
4 tablespoons (60 ml) Cognac
5 tablespoons (75 ml) butter
3 tablespoons (45 ml) vegetable oil
12 small white onions, sliced
rind of 1 lemon
juice of 3 lemons
salt and pepper
Hollandaise Sauce

Soak the sultanas (white raisins) in a mixture of the Cognac and 4 tablespoons (60 ml) water for about 45 minutes. In a casserole melt the butter and oil and sauté the chicken pieces until they turn golden. Remove them to a heated dish.

In the same oil sauté the onion slices until they turn translucent, approximately 5–10 minutes. Then place the chicken pieces on top of the onions, add the soaked raisins, Cognac mixture, lemon rind and lemon juice. Cover with a round piece of buttered parchment, then place the lid tightly on top. Simmer for 45–50 minutes.

Remove the chicken, onions and sultanas (white raisins) to a heated serving dish. Add the cooking liquids to the Hollandaise Sauce and check the seasoning. Pour the sauce over the chicken and serve immediately.

Hollandaise Sauce

Makes approximately 16 fl oz (475 ml, 2 cups)

8 oz (225 g, 1 cup) butter
2 tablespoons (30 ml) white wine vinegar
salt
freshly ground white pepper
3 egg yolks
lemon juice to taste
cayenne to taste

Have the butter, divided into 12 parts, at room temperature. In a small, heavy saucepan combine the white wine vinegar and 2 tablespoons (30 ml) water with ¼ teaspoon (1.25 ml) salt and a few grinds of pepper, and cook over high heat until it is reduced to 1 tablespoon (15 ml). Remove the pan from the heat and add another 1 tablespoon (15 ml) cold water. Add the egg yolks and stir briskly with a wire whisk until the sauce turns thick and creamy. Set the pan over low heat and beat in the butter, one part at a time, lifting the pan occasionally to cool the mixture, otherwise it will curdle. Make sure that each part of butter is completely melted before adding more. Continue to beat the sauce until it is thick and firm. Add lemon juice, salt and cayenne, to taste.

Keep the sauce warm over a shallow pan of warm water until needed. It can be refrigerated for a few days and reheated over hot water, beating constantly. Add a few teaspoons of single (light) cream while reheating if the sauce is too thick.

Preparation time: approximately 45 minutes
Cooking time: 1½ hours

Avial-Malayali

The following recipe was given to me by Mrs Srinavasa, at whose house in Madras we ate the most perfect vegetarian, or any other, dinner I have been fortunate to have been given.

1 medium-sized potato, peeled
1 medium-sized yam, peeled
2 green bananas
$\frac{1}{4}$ lb (125 g) baby marrows (zucchini)
$\frac{1}{4}$ lb (125 g) French beans (string beans), strings removed
2 oz (50 g, $\frac{1}{2}$ cup) green peas, shelled
2–3 teaspoons (10–15 ml) salt
1 tablespoon (15 ml) oil
pinch of asafoetida
$\frac{1}{2}$ teaspoon (2.5 ml) black mustard seeds
1 teaspoon (5 ml) cumin seeds
7 oz (200 g, 2 cups) grated fresh or packaged desiccated coconut
4 green chillies, stems removed, seeded and chopped
8 fl oz (225 ml, 1 cup) plain yoghurt (curds)
1 tablespoon (15 ml) coconut oil
a few curry leaves or fresh coriander (Chinese parsley), chopped finely

In a medium-sized saucepan, cook the potato and the yam with water to cover until they are soft but not mushy. In another saucepan place the other vegetables in boiling salted water and blanch for 3 minutes until they are tender but still crunchy (do not overcook). Drain and cool. Cut all the vegetables, aside from the peas, vertically into long thin julienne strips. Place them all in a large deep sauté pan.

In a small frying-pan heat the oil and put in the asafoetida, then the mustard seeds and cumin seeds. As soon as the mustard seeds begin to pop remove them from the heat. Combine these spices with the grated coconut and green chillies either in a mortar and pestle, or in an electric coffee grinder (kept specifically for grinding spices). Grind the mixture into a smooth paste.

In a bowl, beat the yoghurt until it becomes light and creamy. Add the spice paste to this, and pour over the vegetables, mixing thoroughly. Heat the mixture through, cooking for approximately 3 minutes, but do not allow to boil. Remove from the heat, mix in the coconut oil and place on a dish. Sprinkle with fresh curry or coriander (Chinese parsley) leaves.

Preparation time: approximately 30 minutes
Cooking time: approximately 45 minutes

DINNER
SERVES 6

*Marinated Mushrooms

Veal Chops with Walnut-anchovy Sauce

or

Greek-style Quail with Salsa Victoria

Carciofi Fritti con Salsa
(Italian Artichoke Fritters)

---

*Green Grape and Kiwi Fruit Salad

*Chocolate Biscuits (see page 149) and Coffee

---

*Marinated Mushrooms

4 fl oz (125 ml, $\frac{1}{2}$ cup) white wine vinegar
4–6 fl oz (125–150 ml, $\frac{1}{2}$–$\frac{1}{3}$ cup) olive oil
1 teaspoon (5 ml) dried oregano
1 teaspoon (5 ml) ground cumin
1 clove garlic, minced
$\frac{1}{2}$ teaspoon (2.5 ml) salt
$\frac{1}{2}$ teaspoon (2.5 ml) freshly ground black pepper
$\frac{1}{2}$ teaspoon (2.5 ml) brown sugar
1 tablespoon (15 ml) lemon juice
1 teaspoon (5 ml) prepared mustard
2 teaspoons (10 ml) fresh coriander (Chinese parsley) or parsley, minced
1 small onion, sliced finely
1 lb (450 g) fresh mushrooms, sliced thickly

Combine all the ingredients, *except* the mushrooms, in a saucepan and bring to the boil. Remove the marinade from the heat and cool. Add the mushrooms to the cooled marinade and refrigerate in a tightly covered bowl overnight. Remove the mushrooms from the marinade with a slotted spoon just before serving.

Marinating time: 24 hours
Preparation time: 25 minutes
Cooking time: 5 minutes

23

Veal Chops with Walnut-anchovy Sauce

6 veal chops, boned
1 teaspoon (5 ml) salt
freshly ground black pepper
a few drops of olive oil

For the sauce:
3 canned anchovy fillets, drained and desalted in
  milk
1 clove garlic
5 walnuts, shelled and peeled
$\frac{1}{2}$ teaspoon (2.5 ml) red wine vinegar
8 fl oz (225 ml, 1 cup) olive oil

Put the chops on a dish, sprinkle with salt, freshly ground pepper and a few drops of olive oil and leave for 20–30 minutes. Preheat the grill (broiler). Just before serving, place the chops on a baking tray and grill (broil) them 5 inches (12.5 cm) from the heat for 5 minutes; turn and cook for 5 minutes the other side, making sure not to overcook them. They should be brown on the outside, pink on the inside.

Meanwhile make the sauce. With a mortar and pestle, or food processor or blender, purée the anchovies, garlic and walnuts to a smooth paste. Add the vinegar, then the olive oil, little by little, blending all the time. When the meat is cooked, place it on a heated dish and cover it lightly with the sauce.

Marinating time: 20–30 minutes
Preparation time: 20 minutes
Cooking time: approximately 10 minutes

Greek-style Quail

For the rice:
6 tablespoons (90 ml) butter
2 tablespoons (30 ml) onion, chopped finely
7 oz (200 g, 1 cup) long grain rice, washed
$1\frac{1}{4}$ pints (725 ml, 3 cups) veal or chicken stock
  (broth)
2 generous tablespoons (35 ml) pork sausage meat
2–3 tablespoons (30–45 ml) lettuce, shredded
  finely
3 generous tablespoons (55 ml) peas, shelled
1 tablespoon (20 ml) red pimento, chopped finely

6 plump quail, cleaned and dressed
lemon juice
salt and pepper
4 oz (125 g, $\frac{1}{2}$ cup) butter
6 leaves of lettuce
6 fl oz (175 ml, $\frac{3}{4}$ cup) Salsa Victoria

Preheat the oven to 325°F, 170°C, Mark 3.

Prepare the rice. Melt 2 tablespoons (30 ml) butter in a fireproof casserole, and sauté the onions in it for 1 minute. Do not brown. To this add the rice and cook, stirring constantly, until it takes on a milky colour, then gradually pour in the veal or chicken stock (broth), stirring gently. Cover tightly and set in the preheated oven for 25 minutes without stirring. In a saucepan, melt 2 tablespoons (30 ml) butter and add the sausage meat, shredded lettuce, peas and pimento. Cook over a moderate heat for 8–10 minutes, stirring constantly. Remove the rice from the oven and dot the top with 2 tablespoons (30 ml) butter divided into small bits. Then carefully, stirring very gently so as not to break the grains, add the sausage meat and vegetable mixture. Mix well.

While the rice is cooking, clean the quail and rub them with lemon juice, then with salt and black pepper. Sew and truss them. In a fireproof casserole or Dutch oven, melt 4 oz (125 g, $\frac{1}{2}$ cup) butter over moderate heat and place the quail in it. Cook, turning often to brown the birds on all sides, for 15–20 minutes or until the juice runs clear if their thighs are pierced with a skewer or sharp knife. Meanwhile, place 6 lettuce leaves together with 1 fl oz (25 ml) water and 1 oz (25 g) butter in a saucepan; cover and braise over low heat for 2–3 minutes, no more. Remove the lettuce leaves from the liquid with a slotted spoon and drain on kitchen paper towels. When cooked, put the birds on a heated platter and keep warm.

Arrange the rice, sausage and vegetable mixture on a hot platter. Make 6 little nests with the back of a spoon and place a braised lettuce leaf in each one. Arrange the quail on the lettuce leaves.

Pour 2 tablespoons (30 ml) Salsa Victoria over each bird.

Preparation time: approximately 30 minutes
Cooking time: 40–45 minutes

Salsa Victoria

This Spanish sauce is particularly tasty when used for venison, duck or goose, or game birds. If you make too much, freeze the remainder to use another time.

3 tablespoons (45 ml) blackcurrant jelly
* preferably, if not, redcurrant jelly*
10 fl oz (300 ml 1¼ cups) port or Madeira
10 fl oz (300 ml 1¼ cups) game, duck or goose,
* stock (broth)*
½ teaspoon (2.5 ml) ground cinnamon or 1-inch
* (2.5-cm) stick cinnamon*
3 cloves
salt and freshly ground black pepper
juice and grated rind of 1 orange
pinch of cayenne pepper

In a medium saucepan, melt the jelly over low heat. Add the port or Madeira, the stock (broth), the grated orange rind and the spices and seasoning. Simmer the sauce for 10 minutes; just before serving sieve it into a bowl and add the orange juice and cayenne pepper.

Cooking time: 10 minutes

Carciofi Fritti con Salsa

6 artichokes
salt
4 teaspoons (20 ml) white wine vinegar
1 egg
2½ oz (57 g, ½ cup) plain (all-purpose) flour
1 teaspoon (5 ml) grated onion
½ teaspoon (2.5 ml) dried oregano
¼ teaspoon (1.25 ml) freshly ground black pepper
vegetable oil

Remove the outer leaves and points of the artichokes, then place them in boiling water, to which a pinch of salt and 2 teaspoons (10 ml) vinegar have been added. Cook for 30–40 minutes, depending upon the size of the artichokes, until the leaves pull off easily. Drain. Cool, quarter, and remove the ' choke ', the white fuzzy fibres.

In a bowl, beat the egg and 2 tablespoons (30 ml) water; add the flour gradually, then the onion, 2 teaspoons (10 ml) vinegar, the oregano, ½ teaspoon (2.5 ml) salt and the freshly ground black pepper. Dip the artichokes into the batter, shake off the excess, and in a deep-fat frying-pan, filled 2 inches (5 cm) deep with vegetable oil, fry the quartered artichokes until they turn golden brown. Drain on kitchen paper towels.

Preparation time: 30–40 minutes
Cooking time: approximately 1 hour

DINNER
SERVES 4–6

Hot Spinach and Chicken Liver Salad

———

Tangy Halibut

or

Eel à la Grecque

*Mushroom Pullao (see page 167)

———

Hot Stuffed Peaches with Zabaglione
Sauce (see page 74)

or

Cheese and Biscuits

Hot Spinach and Chicken Liver Salad

*2½ lb (1.1 kg) fresh spinach, washed and spines
removed*
8 large fresh mushrooms, wiped clean and sliced
2 teaspoons (10 ml) granulated sugar
*4 fl oz (125 ml, ½ cup) white wine vinegar or cider
vinegar*
10 slices streaky bacon, rinds removed
*½ lb (225 g) chicken livers, gristle and fat removed,
and sliced*
4 oz (125 ml, ½ cup) brandy
salt and pepper

Place the spinach leaves and mushrooms in a salad bowl, add the sugar and vinegar and toss well. In a frying-pan cook the bacon until it turns crisp, drain, then crumble. Add the chicken livers to the bacon fat in the pan and cook until the livers are brown on the outside and pink on the inside, about 1 or 2 minutes. Return the crumbled bacon to the pan with the livers, pour on the brandy, flame it and pour the mixture over the salad. Toss it well, season and serve immediately.

Preparation time: 30–40 minutes
Cooking time: approximately 20 minutes

Tangy Halibut

Any firm white fish such as haddock, cod or flounder may be used – but not oily fish like mackerel or herring.

1½ lb (700 g) halibut fillets, cut into small pieces
1 oz (25 g, ¼ cup) onion, chopped finely
2 tablespoons (30 ml) unsalted butter
*12 fl oz (350 ml, 1½ cups) sour cream or plain
yoghurt*
½ teaspoon (2.5 ml) salt
½ teaspoon (2.5 ml) paprika
2 egg yolks
½ teaspoon (2.5 ml) dried basil
1½ teaspoons (7.5 ml) lemon juice
salt
*fresh coriander (Chinese parsley) or parsley,
chopped finely for garnish*

In a sauté pan, cook the onions in the butter until they turn golden but not brown. Then add the sour cream or yoghurt, salt and paprika, stir and mix thoroughly but do not allow to boil. Add the fish bit by bit and cook over low heat for 5 minutes until it is flaky. Remove the fish to a warm platter.

Beat the egg yolks in a small bowl, pour some of the sour cream mixture in, mix well and pour the mixture back into the rest of the sauce. Cook over a low heat until the sauce thickens, then add the basil, lemon juice and salt to taste. Pour the sauce over the fish. Sprinkle with fresh coriander (Chinese parsley) or parsley and serve hot.

Preparation time: 20–25 minutes
Cooking time: approximately 25 minutes

Eel à la Grecque

$\frac{1}{2}$ teaspoon (2.5 ml) salt
$\frac{1}{4}$ teaspoon (1.25 ml) freshly ground black pepper
2 lb (900 g) eel, skinned, cleaned and cut into
   2-inch (5-cm) pieces
2 fl oz (50 ml, $\frac{1}{4}$ cup) olive oil
2 cloves garlic, chopped finely
1 teaspoon (5 ml) thyme leaves
juice of $\frac{1}{2}$ lemon
1 lemon, sliced thinly
fresh coriander (Chinese parsley) or parsley,
   chopped finely

Preheat the oven to 375°F, 190°C, Mark 5.

In a small bowl, blend the salt and pepper and sprinkle it over the eel. In a baking pan, heat the olive oil, add the garlic and thyme, then place the pieces of eel on top and sprinkle the lemon juice over them. Bake in the preheated oven for 25–30 minutes. Garnish with lemon slices and chopped coriander (Chinese parsley) or parsley.

Preparation time: approximately 15 minutes, if fishmonger cleans and skins eels, 30–40 minutes
if you do
Cooking time: 25–30 minutes

DINNER
SERVES 6

*Seafood Cocktail

Kashmiri Raan
(Baked Lamb in a Spiced Yoghurt Jacket)

or

Mutton Biryani

Dahi Pakodi
(Spicy Yoghurt)

Pomodori Ripieni
(Italian Stuffed Tomatoes)

Tarte de Amendoa
(Spanish Almond Tart)

---

*Seafood Cocktail

4 tablespoons (60 ml) good olive oil
1 small onion, sliced thinly
$\frac{3}{4}$ lb (350 g) monkfish tail, skinned, boned and cut
   into small strips
4 scallops, cut into bite-sized pieces
2 teaspoons (10 ml) roasted coriander seeds,
   ground
1 teaspoon (5 ml) roasted cumin seeds, ground
$\frac{1}{4}$ pint (150 ml, $\frac{1}{2}$ cup) dry white wine
1 bay leaf
salt and freshly ground black pepper
24 freshly cooked prawns (shrimp), shelled
fresh coriander (Chinese parsley), chopped

In a large frying-pan heat the oil, then add the onion. When the onion has become transparent, stir in the monkfish and scallops together with the spices and white wine. Cook gently for about 10 minutes, then remove the fish and onion with a slotted spoon and place them in a glass or ceramic bowl with the prawns (shrimp).

Reduce the cooking liquid by half over high heat. Discard the bay leaf, adjust the seasoning, then pour the sauce over the fish. Cover and place the bowl in the refrigerator for approximately 2–3 hours, then serve in individual glasses topped with fresh coriander (Chinese parsley).

Preparation time: 30–40 minutes
Cooking time: 15 minutes
Chilling time: 2–3 hours

Kashmiri Raan

Raan means thigh, so the meat should be taken from the top of the thigh, on the bone, preferably of the foreleg.

3–4 lb (1.4–1.8 kg) leg of lamb
4 oz (125 g, ¾ cup) besan (chickpea or gram) flour (available from Middle Eastern grocery stores)
1 tablespoon (15 ml) ginger and garlic paste (fresh ginger and garlic pounded in a mortar with just enough water added to make a paste)
1 teaspoon (5 ml) red chilli paste (cayenne pepper with just enough water added to make a paste)

Spices to be ground together in mortar and pestle:
2 pieces mace
1 nutmeg, freshly ground
2 sticks cinnamon
6 small cardamom pods
2 small cloves
pinch of asafoetida (available from Middle Eastern grocery stores)
1 tablespoon (15 ml) fresh poppy seeds, soaked in water
4 blanched almonds
salt to taste
8 fl oz (225 ml, 1 cup) plain yoghurt

Remove the white fat and membrane from the meat. With a small sharp knife pierce the flesh deeply down to the bone, repeatedly all over the leg. This is the most important part; the spices must be allowed to infuse the meat and the fibres of the meat must be broken and the meat loosened from the bone during the cooking process. Put the besan (chickpea) or gram flour in a bowl, then add the ginger and garlic paste and the red chilli paste. Mix thoroughly and add all the ground spices, mixing again. Add the yoghurt and mix again.

Apply the yoghurt mixture in a thick coat all over the lamb, making sure that it enters all the pierced flesh and seeps into the holes. Prick the lamb again. Cover and leave the meat to marinate for at least 8 hours, more if possible, in a cool place.

Preheat the oven to 400°F, 200°C, Mark 6. Place the lamb on a rack in a roasting pan and bake in the oven for 1 hour, basting the meat with a pinch of asafoetida soaked in 2 tablespoons (30 ml) water. Then lower the oven temperature to 350°F, 180°C, Mark 4. Add 1¼ pints (750 ml, 3 cups) water to the pan to keep the lamb moist and bake for a further 2 hours. When the raan is ready to be served, you should be able to spoon the meat off the bone. (In India they eat the meat with their right forefinger and thumb, picking up the tender meat chunks.)

Preparation time: approximately 45 minutes
Marinating time: 8–12 hours
Cooking time: approximately 3 hours

Mutton Biryani

This delicious and subtle dish was taught to me in Delhi by a brilliant Indian chef, Arvind Saraswat, *chef culinaire* for the northern region of the Taj Hotel group. The dish dates from the 6th century, during the time of Akbar the great Mogul king. Since then it has become a classic Indian dish with many variations.
Important: The bones must be included so that the taste of the marrow is infused into the biryani.

$1\frac{1}{2}$ lb (700 g) Basmati rice, picked over, washed
   and drained 3–4 times
1 teaspoon (5 ml) salt
12 oz (350 g, $1\frac{1}{2}$ cups) ghee or clarified butter
   (ghee can be bought in Middle Eastern grocery
   stores)
6 oz (175 g, $1\frac{1}{2}$ cups) onion, sliced paper thinly
$3\frac{1}{2}$ lb (1.6 kg) lean lamb chops, cut in 1-inch
   (2.5-cm) cubes
12 cardamom pods
8 cloves
2 tablespoons (30 ml) ground coriander
2 teaspoons (10 ml) cayenne pepper
2 teaspoons (10 ml) cumin seeds
6 fl oz (175 ml, $\frac{3}{4}$ cup) plain yoghurt
6 oz (175 g) tomatoes, quartered
1 bunch fresh mint, chopped finely
$\frac{1}{2}$ bunch fresh coriander (Chinese parsley), chopped
2 bay leaves, chopped finely

Bring 2 pints (1.2 litres, $2\frac{1}{2}$ pints) water and the salt to the boil in a large saucepan, then add the rice in a slow thin stream. Cook the rice over high heat, uncovered, stirring constantly for 10 minutes. Drain in a colander and set aside.

In a heavy frying-pan, melt 9 oz (250 g, 1 cup plus 2 tablespoons) ghee or clarified butter, add the sliced onions and fry for about 6–8 minutes or until they turn brown. Remove with a slotted spoon and set aside.

Put the lamb cubes in the ghee remaining in the pan, adding more if necessary, and stir until all the meat has browned on all sides, then add the cardamom pods, cloves, ground coriander, cayenne, cumin seeds and yoghurt. Stir thoroughly and cook, covered, over low heat for 15 minutes then set aside.

Preheat the oven to 375°F, 190°C, Mark 5. Take a casserole and pour the remaining 3 oz (75 g, $\frac{1}{3}$ cup) ghee into the casserole so that the bottom is well coated. Spread half the parboiled rice over the bottom and add half the meat cubes, reserving the cooking liquid. Then spread the remaining rice over the meat; add the remaining meat on top, plus the quartered tomatoes and chopped fresh herbs. Pour the reserved cooking liquid down the sides of the casserole. If there is not enough liquid, melt some saffron threads in $\frac{1}{2}$ pint (300 ml, $1\frac{1}{4}$ cups) boiling water and add to the liquid. Cover the casserole with some aluminium foil, then the lid, and bake in the preheated oven for 20–30 minutes until all the liquid has been absorbed and the meat is tender. To serve, turn out the mixture on to a warm serving dish and sprinkle with the browned onions.

Preparation time: 30–40 minutes
Cooking time: approximately 1 hour

Dahi Pakodi

3 pints (1.2 litres, $3\frac{3}{4}$ pints) plain yoghurt (if
   commercial yoghurt is used, strain it to get rid
   of excess water)
2 teaspoons (10 ml) sugar
salt to taste
6 oz (175 g, 1 cup) besan (chickpea or gram) flour
2 teaspoons (10 ml) cayenne pepper
2 teaspoons (10 ml) ginger and garlic paste (fresh
   ginger and garlic pounded in a mortar with just
   enough water added to make a paste)
pinch of turmeric powder
6 fl oz (175 ml, $\frac{3}{4}$ cup) vegetable oil
1 teaspoon (5 ml) cumin seeds
1 teaspoon (5 ml) black mustard seeds
5 red chillies, stems and seeds removed
1 sprig curry leaves (if available)

In a bowl dissolve the sugar in the yoghurt, then beat in the besan flour, cayenne, ginger and garlic paste and turmeric. In a deep frying-pan heat the oil. Add the cumin seeds, mustard seeds, red chillies and curry leaves. Mix well. Then drop the yoghurt mixture into the hot oil, mix again and cook, stirring constantly in one direction so as not to curdle the yoghurt, until the oil rises to the surface. Pour the mixture into a heated, but not hot, bowl, garnish with curry leaves and serve.

Preparation time: approximately 10 minutes
Cooking time: 10–15 minutes

Pomodori Ripieni

Perfect with raan – or any other roast lamb or chicken dish.

1¼ pints (725 ml, 3 cups) chicken stock or broth
3½ oz (87 g, ½ cup) long grain rice
6 canned anchovy fillets, drained and chopped
freshly ground black pepper
few sprigs of mint, chopped
6 tomatoes
2 tablespoons (30 ml) olive oil
1 large clove garlic, crushed

Preheat oven to 350°F, 180°C, Mark 4. In a saucepan, bring the chicken stock or broth to the boil, then add the rice and cook, covered, for 10–15 minutes, or until the liquid has been absorbed and the rice is tender.

In a large bowl, combine the rice, the chopped anchovies, freshly ground pepper and chopped mint. Remove the tops of the tomatoes and remove the pulp. Add the pulp to the rice, then fill the tomatoes with the mixture. Heat the olive oil and garlic in a small baking dish, place the filled tomatoes in it with a little space between each, and bake in the preheated oven for about 20 minutes, basting the tomatoes with the garlic oil twice. Serve hot.

Preparation time: approximately 25 minutes
Cooking time: approximately 35 minutes

Tarte de Amendoa

This tart can be served with or without a meringue on top. The choice is a purely personal one. The joy is that no matter which sort you choose, either is terribly simple.

1 oz (25 g) unsalted butter
6 eggs
½ lb (225 g, 1 cup) caster (superfine granulated) sugar
½ lb (225 g) blanched almonds, chopped finely
5 oz (150 g, 1 cup) plain (cake) flour
1 tablespoon (15 ml) brandy

For the meringue (optional):
3 egg whites
white wine vinegar
5 oz (150 g, ¾ cup) caster (superfine granulated) sugar

Preheat the oven to 375°F, 190°C, Mark 5. Butter an 8–9 inch (20.3–22.8 cm) shallow flan pan. In a bowl beat the eggs and the sugar with an electric mixer until it becomes a thick and creamy mixture, then add the almonds, the flour and the brandy. Mix well with a spatula or flat wooden spoon, and pour into the buttered flan case. Bake in the preheated oven for 25–30 minutes. Remove from the oven.

If you have chosen to cover it with meringue, turn the oven up to 425°F, 220°C, Mark 7. Beat the egg whites until stiff with a drop or two of the vinegar, then slowly add the sugar, a little at a time, and mix with a spatula. Smooth the mixture over the top of the cooked tart in a thick layer and bake in the preheated oven for a few minutes until the top turns golden brown.

Preparation time: approximately 25 minutes
Cooking time: 30–40 minutes

DINNER
SERVES 6

Barbecued Spicy Fish

or

Chinese Fish with Mandarin Sauce

Garbanzos con Espinacas
(Chickpeas with Spinach)

———

*Seviyal Bakala Bath
(Indian Vermicelli Pudding)

The chickpeas must be soaked the night
before and may be cooking while the fish
is being barbecued. The dessert may be
prepared ahead and cooled, with just the
mustard, chillies and curry leaves poured
over at the last minute.

Barbecued Spicy Fish

1 3½-lb (1.6-kg) fresh sea bass or striped bass,
  cleaned, scaled and gutted
1 3½-inch (8.9-cm) ball of tamarind
1½ teaspoons (7.5 ml) turmeric powder
2 tablespoons (30 ml) cumin seeds
7 slices garlic
1 1½-inch (3.8-cm) piece fresh ginger
6 red chillies, stems and seeds removed
vegetable oil
2½ large onions, sliced thinly
2½ cucumbers, sliced thinly
6 tomatoes, sliced thinly
8 oz (225 g, 1⅓ cups) cashew nuts
2 limes, quartered

Make gashes on both sides of the fish. Cover the
tamarind with 16 fl oz (475 ml, 2 cups) warm
water and simmer for 10 minutes over low heat.
Remove from the heat and pour it through a sieve
into a bowl, mashing the tamarind with the back
of a wooden spoon, so that the pulp goes through
as well. Be sure to scrape the pulp from the
bottom of the sieve. Grind the turmeric, cumin
seeds, garlic, ginger and red chillies in an electric
coffee grinder to a smooth paste and add the paste
to the tamarind juice. Mix thoroughly into a thick
paste. Rub the paste all over the fish, making sure
it enters the slits in the sides. Leave aside for 20
minutes then barbecue over a charcoal fire for 1
hour, basting occasionally with oil, until the fish
is golden brown and the flesh opaque. Serve on a
bed of sliced onions, cucumbers and tomatoes.

In a frying-pan, sauté the cashew nuts in 3
tablespoons (45 ml) oil until they turn light
golden. Sprinkle over the fish and serve with lime
quarters.

Preparation time: 30 minutes
Marinating time: 20 minutes
Cooking time: approximately 1 hour

Chinese Fish with Mandarin Sauce

2 lb (1 kg) firm white fish fillets, such as cod, haddock, halibut or bass
2 tablespoons (30 ml) cornflour (cornstarch)
4 tablespoons (60 ml) groundnut (peanut) oil
2 spring onions (scallions), sliced
2 cloves garlic, chopped finely
2 slices fresh ginger, chopped finely
8 fresh mushrooms, or Chinese mushrooms
10-oz (283-g) can bamboo shoots, drained and sliced thinly
4 fl oz (125 ml, $\frac{1}{2}$ cup) soy sauce
2 tablespoons (30 ml) Shaohsing wine or dry sherry
1 tablespoon (15 ml) brown sugar
1 teaspoon (5 ml) salt
8 fl oz (225 ml, 1 cup) chicken stock (broth)

Dredge the fish fillets in the cornflour (cornstarch) and allow them to rest for 10 minutes. Meanwhile heat a wok or a deep frying-pan until the smoke rises, then add the oil and heat until the smoke rises again. Stir-fry the fillets in the oil until both sides have turned golden brown, then remove them to a warm plate. In the same oil stir-fry the spring onions (scallions), garlic and ginger until they turn light golden, then add the mushrooms and bamboo shoots and cook for 1 minute. In a bowl mix the soy sauce, sherry, sugar and salt and add, along with the stock, to the vegetable mixture. Bring to the boil, add the fish, cover, lower the heat and simmer for 15 minutes. Serve immediately.

Preparation time: 30 minutes
Cooking time: 15 minutes

Garbanzos con Espinacas

1 lb (450 g) chickpeas
1 teaspoon (5 ml) bicarbonate of soda (baking soda)
salt
5 tablespoons (75 ml) olive oil
1 slice white bread, crusts removed
1 medium-sized onion, chopped finely
2 large tomatoes, peeled and chopped
1 tablespoon (15 ml) paprika
1$\frac{1}{4}$ lb (575 g) fresh spinach, washed and sprinkled with salt
2 oz (50 g, $\frac{1}{3}$ cup) almonds, roasted
1 clove garlic

Soak the chickpeas overnight in water to cover, with the bicarbonate of soda (baking soda). Rinse them well, put them in a saucepan with cold water to cover, bring it to the boil, and simmer them for approximately 1 hour, until they are tender; about 10 minutes before they are cooked, add salt to taste. Drain.

In a large saucepan, heat 3 tablespoons (45 ml) oil and fry the bread until it turns golden on both sides. Remove it and in the same oil sauté the onion and tomato until the onion softens. Add the chickpeas.

In a large saucepan, heat the remaining oil, stir in the paprika, then immediately add the spinach. Stir and sauté lightly, then add it to the chickpeas. In a food processor or large mortar pound together the almonds, garlic and fried bread and add them to the chickpeas. Cover and cook the vegetables for about 10–25 minutes over low heat.

Preparation time: 20 minutes
Cooking time: 1$\frac{1}{2}$ hours

Seviyal Bakala Bath

From the Tamil Nadu region of India, I was given this delicious vermicelli pudding on a banana leaf one very hot night in Madras at the home of Mrs Srinavasa. It takes very little time to cook and makes a light finish to a heavy meal. The vermicelli is *sev*, found in Indian grocery shops, and must be very fine. Alternatively, Chinese 'cellophane' noodles, as fine as possible, may be substituted.

9 oz (250 g) very fine sev, broken into small pieces
3 tablespoons (45 ml) corn oil
1½ teaspoons (7.5 ml) salt
8 fl oz (225 ml, 1 cup) curds (plain yoghurt)
8 fl oz (225 ml, 1 cup) milk
1 teaspoon (5 ml) black mustard seeds
2 fresh green chillies, stems and seeds removed, chopped
a few curry leaves, if possible
1 teaspoon (5 ml) peeled and grated fresh ginger

In a medium-sized saucepan fry the vermicelli in 2 tablespoons (30 ml) oil until it turns golden brown. Add 16 fl oz (475 ml, 2 cups) water and the salt. Bring to the boil, then lower the heat, and cook the vermicelli until it softens and thickens. Remove from the heat and cool. Then add the curds (yoghurt) and milk. Up to this point, the dish may be prepared in advance.

In a small frying-pan heat 1 tablespoon (15 ml) oil and add the mustard seeds. As soon as they begin to pop, add the green chillies and curry leaves. Pour this over the vermicelli mixture and mix thoroughly. Sprinkle grated ginger on top and serve.

Preparation time: approximately 20 minutes
Cooking time: 20–25 minutes

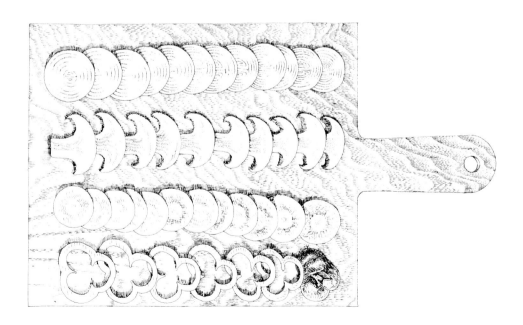

*Clams Madrilène (see page 43)

DINNER
SERVES 8

Herbal Spring Lamb with *Garlic Sauce

Tomato Bath

Fried Bringals
(Indian Fried Aubergines/Eggplants)

*Kulfi (Indian Ice Cream)

It is the contrast in cold, hot, cold, and spicy, spicy, nutty which makes this such an interesting menu. The first and last courses may be prepared ahead, as may the Garlic Sauce and the herbal jacket for the lamb.
The Kulfi, cold with its pistachio and saffron flavour, is in sharp contrast to the spicy Tomato Bath and aubergines (eggplants) marinated in tamarind.

Herbal Spring Lamb with *Garlic Sauce

Because the garlic is cooked whole, you get a subtle sauce rather than an overwhelming garlic taste.

5-lb (2.3-kg) leg or crown of lamb
2 cloves garlic, sliced thinly

For the herbal crust:
5 tablespoons (75 ml) green peppercorn mustard or homemade Basil Honey Mustard (see page 181)
2 cloves garlic, crushed
1 tablespoon (15 ml) ground ginger
2 tablespoons (30 ml) special herbal mixture, consisting of 1 teaspoon (5 ml) dried thyme, 1 teaspoon (5 ml) dried rosemary, 1 ground bay leaf, 1 teaspoon (5 ml) roasted ground cumin, 1 teaspoon (5 ml) roasted ground coriander
1 teaspoon (5 ml) hazelnut oil

For the Garlic Sauce:
2 heads garlic, split into cloves, unpeeled
4 tablespoons (60 ml) unsalted butter
1 tablespoon (15 ml) ground juniper berries and
black peppercorns, mixed
16 fl oz (475 ml, 2 cups) double (heavy) cream
freshly ground salt

Remove all the excess fat from the crown or leg of lamb and make small incisions in odd lines across the flesh. Place a sliver of garlic (sometimes $\frac{1}{2}$ sliver) into each incision. In a small bowl, mix the ingredients for the herbal crust. About 1 hour before roasting, with a pastry brush, paint the entire leg or crown of lamb so that the herbal mixture will have a chance to infuse into the meat.

Preheat the oven to 400°F, 200°C, Mark 6. If cooking a leg of lamb, place it on a rack in a roasting pan in the oven and cook for $1\frac{3}{4}$ hours for pink lamb, 2 hours for more well done. If cooking a crown place it directly in a roasting pan and cook for 20–30 minutes, depending on how well you like it done.

To make the sauce, blanch the garlic cloves for 2 minutes in boiling, salted water. Drain and, when cool enough to handle, peel them. In a large saucepan cook the garlic in the butter over a very low heat for about 20 minutes. Do not let them burn. Add the juniper berries and black peppercorn mix. Heat the cream, then add it to the garlic, bring to the boil and cook for another 1–2 minutes. Remove from the heat and purée the sauce in a food processor or food mill. Strain it through a fine sieve, if necessary, to remove any bits of garlic. Return the mixture to the saucepan and simmer for 1–2 minutes to reheat it. Season with salt and serve with the lamb.

Preparation time: 1–2 hours
Marinating time: approximately 30 minutes
Cooking time: 20–30 minutes or $1\frac{3}{4}$–2 hours

Tomato Bath

9 oz (250 g, $1\frac{1}{4}$ cups) Basmati or long grain rice,
washed and picked over
2 tablespoons (30 ml) salt
6 tablespoons (90 ml) groundnut (peanut) oil
10–12 cashew nuts
1 tablespoon (15 ml) masur pink lentils
1 teaspoon (5 ml) poppy seeds
1 tablespoon (15 ml) coriander seeds
1 teaspoon (5 ml) cumin seeds
2 red chillies, split and stems and seeds removed
1 teaspoon (5 ml) black mustard seeds
1 tablespoon (15 ml) Chenna dhal (large yellow
lentils) or yellow split peas
$\frac{1}{2}$ lb (225 g) tomatoes, peeled and chopped finely

Bring 3 pints (1.8 litres, $3\frac{3}{4}$ pints) water to a rolling boil, add 1 tablespoon (15 ml) salt and then the rice, stir and cover. Then turn the heat very low and cook gently for 30 minutes. Turn off the heat and allow the rice to sit for 10–15 minutes longer, covered.

Meanwhile in a small frying-pan heat 1 tablespoon (15 ml) oil and fry the cashew nuts, masur pink lentils, poppy seeds, coriander and cumin seeds, and the red chillies, until the cumin seeds start popping. Then in a mortar and pestle or electric coffee mill, grind all the spices into a paste.

In a large sauté pan, heat the remaining oil and add the mustard seeds. When they start popping add the Chenna dhal or yellow split peas and cook until the dhal has darkened a bit. Then add the ground paste, and finally the tomatoes and remaining salt. Cook the mixture over low heat for 15 minutes, or until it has reached a thick sauce consistency. Remove from the heat and mix in with the cooked rice.

Preparation time: 10 minutes
Cooking time: 45 minutes

Fried Bringals

2 lb (900 g) small aubergines (eggplants), washed
   and stems removed
2 tablespoons (30 ml) salt
2 tablespoons (30 ml) ground coriander
2 teaspoons (10 ml) cayenne pepper
2 tablespoons (30 ml) thick tamarind juice (see
   below)
corn or groundnut (peanut) oil, for frying

For seasoning:
a small piece of asafoetida
$\frac{1}{2}$ teaspoon (2.5 ml) black gram dhal (urad dhal)
$\frac{1}{2}$ teaspoon (2.5 ml) black mustard seeds

To make the tamarind juice: take a 1-inch (2.5-cm) diameter ball of tamarind pulp or cake and soak it in 2 fl oz (50 ml, $\frac{1}{4}$ cup) boiling water overnight, or if you are in a hurry simmer it over low heat for 10 minutes. Then pour the juice through a sieve into a bowl. Mash the tamarind in the sieve with the back of a wooden spoon, so that the pulp goes through as well as the juice. Be sure to scrape all the pulp from the bottom of the sieve.

In each whole aubergine (eggplant) make 4–5 slits. In a bowl combine the salt, coriander, cayenne pepper and tamarind juice. Mix it to a smooth paste. Fill the slits of the aubergine (eggplant) with this paste. After a while, drain off the excess water which the aubergine (eggplant) has emitted.

In a large frying-pan heat the oil and add the asafoetida. Fry for a minute or two in the oil. Remove the asafoetida and put it in a bowl with a tiny bit of boiling water until it dissolves. Meanwhile, in a small saucepan, boil the black gram (urad) dhal until it just splits; drain. Return the asafoetida to the large frying-pan and add the black mustard seeds. When the mustard seeds start to pop, add the black gram (urad) dhal and stir-fry them over low heat until the dhal turns reddish-brown. Then add the drained aubergines (eggplants) and fry until all the sides are roasted. Serve immediately.

Preparation time: approximately 30 minutes
Cooking time: approximately 15 minutes

*Kulfi

When this dish is made in India, instead of ramekins they use marvellous tiny tubular earthenware pots, which are terribly cheap to buy. I brought some of these back with me to use. It may be my imagination, but these pots lend an added flavour. But it is the saffron plus the pistachios which give this ice cream its pale Chartreuse colour and subtle taste.

2 pints (1.1 litres, 5 cups) creamy milk (you need
   a milk with a high fat content, such as that
   from Jersey cows)
4 oz (125 g, $\frac{1}{2}$ cup) sugar
5 strands saffron
20 pistachios, chopped
20 almonds, blanched and sliced thinly
4 cardamom pods, crushed
10 fl oz (275 ml, 1$\frac{1}{4}$ cups) double (heavy) cream,
   whipped
rose water for flavouring
chopped pistachios for garnish

Put the milk in a large saucepan and slowly simmer it, stirring occasionally until it reaches a thick, creamy consistency. The richer you want the ice cream the more you boil it down. Then add the saffron, pistachios, almonds, cardamom pods and double (heavy) cream, and a dash of rose water. Boil for another 5 minutes, remove from the heat and let it cool.

When the milk mixture is cold, pour it into ramekins and cover first with cling film (Saran Wrap), then aluminium foil. Place the ramekins in the freezer for 4 hours. Serve with chopped pistachios on top.

Preparation and cooking time: approximately 1
hour
Chilling time: 4 hours

Spring or Summer

LUNCHEON ---
SERVES 6

*Cold Salmon or Sea Bass, Sauce
Andalouse

*Tabbouleh (see page 143) and/or
Radicchio, Belgian Endive and
Watercress Salad

---

*Cold Almond and Raspberry Pudding

*Brownies

A meal where everything may be
prepared in advance.

*Cold Salmon, Sauce Andalouse

1 4-lb (1.8-kg) fresh salmon or sea bass
vegetable oil
2 medium-sized onions, sliced
2 bay leaves
salt and freshly ground pepper
juice of 1 lemon
2 fl oz (50 ml, $\frac{1}{4}$ cup) dry white wine
cucumber slices for garnish

For the sauce:
2 medium avocados, peeled, stone removed and
    cut into cubes
2 tablespoons (30 ml) olive oil
2 large eggs
2 teaspoons (10 ml) white wine vinegar
1 teaspoon (5 ml) salt
$\frac{1}{2}$ teaspoon caster (superfine granulated) sugar
2 teaspoons (10 ml) Dijon-type mustard
white pepper
2 tablespoons (10 ml) tomato purée (paste)
2 sweet red peppers, chopped finely

Preheat the oven to 350°F, 180°C, Mark 4. Take a
piece of aluminium foil large enough to wrap the
salmon in, and oil it thoroughly. Place the
salmon in the centre of the foil, with the onions
and bay leaves on top. Sprinkle with salt and
pepper. Holding the foil up on all sides, sprinkle
the lemon juice and white wine over the fish, fold
in the ends of the foil over the head and tail, then
roll up the fish in the rest. Place it on a rack in a
roasting pan and bake in the preheated oven for
approximately 1 hour 40 minutes or until the
flesh flakes. Remove and cool completely, then
remove the skin. Place the fish on a serving dish
and garnish with cucumber slices. Chill it in the
refrigerator for 2 hours.

Make the sauce. Place all the ingredients
except the red pepper in a blender or food
processor and mix until smooth, then stir in the
chopped red peppers. Cover and store in the
refrigerator until needed.

Preparation time: approximately 15 minutes
Cooking time: approximately 1 hour 40 minutes
Chilling time: 2 hours

Cold Almond and Raspberry Pudding

3 egg yolks
4 oz (125 g, ½ cup) caster (superfine granulated) sugar
2 tablespoons (30 ml) plain (all-purpose) flour
10 fl oz (300 ml, 1¼ cups) milk
1 vanilla pod
1 pint (500 ml, 2½ cups) double (heavy) cream, whipped
4 fl oz (125 ml, ¼ cup) eau de vie framboise
1 lb (450 g) raspberries, frozen or fresh
6 oz (175 g, 1 cup) whole blanched almonds, chopped coarsely
Demerara or light brown sugar

In a medium-sized bowl whisk together the egg yolks, caster (superfine granulated) sugar and flour. In a saucepan heat the milk, with the vanilla pod in it, to just below boiling point. Remove the vanilla pod and add the milk to the egg mixture. Pour this into a bain marie set on a stand in simmering water or into the top of a double boiler over simmering water, and stir until the mixture becomes thick and creamy and coats the back of a wooden spoon. Remove from the heat and cool almost completely, then add the whipped cream. Mix the eau de vie framboise into the custard, then pour half the amount into a shallow serving dish, lay the raspberries on top and cover with the rest of the mixture. Sprinkle the almonds over the top, then sprinkle on the brown sugar and chill. Serve chilled.

Preparation time: approximately 15 minutes
Cooking time: approximately 25 minutes
Chilling time: 2 hours

Brownies

Makes about 2½ dozen

4 eggs
1 lb (450 g, 2 cups) granulated sugar
8 oz (225 g, 1 cup) unsalted butter
4 oz (125 g) unsweetened chocolate
5 oz (150 g, 1 cup) plain (all-purpose) flour
6 oz (175 g) chocolate chips

Preheat the oven to 350°F, 180°C, Mark 4. Beat the eggs and sugar until light and thick. Melt the butter and chocolate together, then add to the egg mixture; then add the flour and mix in the chocolate chips. Pour into a greased and floured Swiss roll baking tin 7 × 11 inches (17.8 × 27.9 cm) and bake for 20–30 minutes. Cut into squares when cold.

Preparation time: approximately 20 minutes
Cooking time: 20–30 minutes

— WEEKEND LUNCH OR DINNER —
SERVES 8

*Avocado Mousse

———

Sea Bass with *Sorrel Hollandaise

Potatoes All-i-oli

*Carrot Cosimber

*Pear and Green Peppercorn Sorbet (see page 77)

*Biscotti di Mandorle
(Almond Biscuits) (see page 78)

The creamy but tart avocado mousse is followed by sea bass with a tangy sorrel hollandaise, lightly garlicked potatoes and gently spicy carrots and bean sprouts. To finish, a surprise: subtle pear sorbet with a peppery bite. The sea bass may be prepared in advance up until the moment to bake in the oven.

*Avocado Mousse

3 ripe avocados, peeled and stones removed
6 oz (175 g, 1½ cups) onion, chopped or grated
1 egg, hard-boiled, chopped
2 cloves garlic, crushed
4 tablespoons (60 ml) lemon juice
4 oz (125 g, ½ cup) sour cream
16 fl oz (475 ml, 2 cups) home made mayonnaise
salt and freshly ground black pepper
2 tablespoons (30 ml) powdered gelatine
2 egg whites, beaten
8 slices streaky bacon, cooked to crispiness

Purée the avocados in a vegetable mill, blender or food processor. Pour into a large mixing bowl, then stir in the onion, egg and garlic. In another bowl combine the lemon juice, sour cream and mayonnaise, then gradually beat it into the avocado mixture. Season well. In a small bowl, sprinkle the gelatine over 4 tablespoons (60 ml) warm water. Leave for 2–3 minutes until the gelatine has completely dissolved, then pour into the avocado mixture. Add the beaten egg whites and taste for seasoning. Either pour into individual ramekins or into an 8-inch (20.3-cm) soufflé dish. Cover with cling film (Saran Wrap) and chill for 2–3 hours. Garnish with bits of crispy bacon sprinkled over the top.

Preparation time: approximately 30 minutes
Chilling time: 2–3 hours

Opposite: *Carciofi Forno (Hot or Cold Baked Artichokes), p. 53 Overleaf: (left to right) Kulfi, p. 36; Clams Madrilène, p. 43; Herbal Spring Lamb with Fried Bringals and Garlic Sauce, pp. 34–6; and Lebanese Spiced Rice, p. 86*

Sea Bass with *Sorrel Hollandaise

6-lb (2.7-kg) sea bass, cleaned and scaled
vegetable oil
a sprig of fresh tarragon or 1 teaspoon (5 ml)
  dried tarragon
salt and pepper
juice of 1 lemon
½ pint (300 ml, 1¼ cups) dry white wine

Preheat the oven to 325°F, 170°C, Mark 3. Oil a piece of aluminium foil large enough to wrap the sea bass in. Place the sea bass in the centre of the foil, put the tarragon, salt and pepper inside the belly cavity. Oil both sides of the fish. Holding the foil up on all sides, sprinkle the lemon juice and white wine over the fish, fold the ends of the foil over the head and tail, then roll the fish in the rest of the foil to make a package. Place it on a rack of a roasting pan and put in the preheated oven for 20 minutes per 1 lb (450 g), plus 20 minutes, i.e. 2 hours 20 minutes for a 6-lb (2.7-kg) fish. Serve with sorrel hollandaise on the side. Left in its foil package the fish will keep hot for 15–20 minutes while you prepare the Potatoes All-i-oli.

*Sorrel Hollandaise

9 oz (250 g, 1 cup plus 2 tablespoons) unsalted
  butter at room temperature
2 tablespoons (30 ml) white wine or tarragon
  vinegar
salt
freshly ground white pepper
3 egg yolks, beaten
juice of 1 lemon
cayenne pepper to taste
¼ lb (125 g) sorrel, stems removed, washed and
  shredded

Reserve 2 tablespoons (30 ml) of the butter and divide the rest into 12 portions. In a small heavy saucepan, combine the vinegar and 2 tablespoons (30 ml) water with ¼ teaspoon (1.25 ml) salt and a little pepper. Cook the mixture over high heat until it is reduced to 1 tablespoon (15 ml). Remove the pan from the heat and add a further 1 tablespoon (15 ml) water. Pour the vinegar mixture into the top of a double boiler or bain marie, with hot water in the lower pan, and add the egg yolks, stirring briskly with a wire whisk until the mixture becomes thick and creamy.

Set the pan over low heat and beat in the butter, one portion at a time, lifting the pan occasionally to cool the mixture. Make sure that each portion has melted before adding more. Continue to beat the sauce until it is thick and firm. Add the lemon juice, salt and cayenne to taste. (Note: If a thicker sauce is required, use 4 egg yolks.) Keep the sauce warm in the double boiler, off the heat.

In a saucepan soften the sorrel in the reserved butter for 2 minutes. Then place it in a food processor or blender and mix until it becomes a purée. Add the hollandaise sauce and mix for 10 seconds. Return the sorrel hollandaise to the top of the double boiler until needed. This can be made 2 hours before it is needed and kept, covered, until ready to serve. If the sauce curdles, beat an extra egg yolk in a small bowl, then pour in 2 tablespoons (30 ml) of the hollandaise, mix well, and return the mixture to the sauce, whisking. When reheating, do it slowly and do not make it too hot otherwise it will curdle. Also, do not heat the sauceboat too much as this will make the sauce curdle instantly.

Preparation time: 10 minutes
Cooking time: 2 hours 20 minutes

Opposite: Tabbouleh (Middle Eastern Burghul Salad), p. 143

Potatoes All-i-oli

The 'all-i-oli' referred to in this recipe is garlic and oil, *not* 'aïoli', the garlic mayonnaise.

3 lb (1.4 kg) potatoes, peeled
5 cloves garlic
½ teaspoon (2.5 ml) salt
5 tablespoons (75 ml) olive oil
2 teaspoons (10 ml) fresh breadcrumbs (if necessary)
3 oz (75 g, ⅓ cup) butter, cut into pieces
4 fl oz (125 ml, ½ cup) Tomato Sauce (see page 180)

In a saucepan, boil the potatoes until they are tender.

Make the all-i-oli. Pound the garlic in a mortar and pestle and season with salt. Mash it to a paste, adding the olive oil drop by drop and stirring continuously in the same direction, until you achieve a smooth sauce. If you find that the sauce is not thick enough, or if it gets too thin after making it, pound fresh breadcrumbs in a mortar and add the sauce to it, drop by drop, stirring continuously.

Preheat the oven to 400°F, 200°C, Mark 6. When the potatoes are cooked, rub them through a sieve and mix in the all-i-oli. Press the potato mixture into an ovenproof dish just large enough to take it and press it down well. Top with pieces of butter, cover with tomato sauce and place the dish in the preheated oven for 10 minutes. Serve immediately.

Preparation time: 30 minutes
Cooking time: 25 minutes

Carrot Cosimber

From Madras

¼ lb (125 g) whole mung beans or bean sprouts
1 lb (450 g) carrots, grated finely
2 teaspoons (10 ml) salt
juice of 2 large or 4 small limes
3 fresh green chillies, stems removed, seeded and chopped finely
1 teaspoon (5 ml) grated fresh ginger
½ teaspoon (2.5 ml) large black mustard seeds, or yellow mustard seeds, crushed
2 tablespoons (30 ml) groundnut (peanut) oil

Soak the mung beans or bean sprouts for 15 minutes and strain off the water. Put the grated carrots in a bowl, then add the salt, lime juice, mung beans or bean sprouts and the green chillies and ginger. Heat the oil in a ladle, add the mustard seeds and pour over the vegetables.

Preparation time: approximately 30 minutes

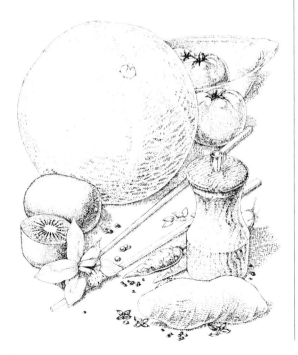

---------------- DINNER ----------------
SERVES 6

*Clams Madrilène
————

*Hyderabad Sheekh Kebabs with Mint
Chutney

or

Murg Tikka
(Barbecued Chicken Cubes)

Paneer Masala
(Indian Cream Cheese with Spicy Sauce)

Spinacci con Limone (see page 91)
————

Songos de Morangos
(Spanish Strawberry Dreams)

*Cardamom Biscuits
————

The Indian kebabs from one of the most
delicious cuisines in the world,
Hyderabad, can be mixed in advance and
chilled. Then they need only to be
barbecued, during which time you can
stir-fry the paneer and cook the spinach.
The strawberries will have been
marinating for 2 hours while the special
batter rests. Then it is a matter of
minutes to deep fry these dreams – a
delicious contrast to the spicy kebabs and
mint chutney.

*Clams Madrilène

I always keep two cans of consommé
madrilène in the refrigerator because it is
terribly good as a last minute basis for making
a quick cold soup. One way is just adding
some lumpfish roe and yoghurt or sour cream.
But a friend in Cape Cod gave me this different
version, particularly useful since another staple
in my cupboard is cans of clams – so useful for
pasta dishes.

2 $14\frac{1}{2}$-oz (411-g) cans consommé madrilène
12-oz (350-g) can clams, drained and chopped
  finely
5 oz (150 g, 1 cup) celery, chopped finely
10 oz (275 g, $1\frac{1}{4}$ cups) plain yoghurt or sour
  cream
fresh coriander (Chinese parsley) or parsley,
  chopped finely

Pour the consommé madrilène into a large
mixing bowl and place in the refrigerator until it
sets. Then fold in the clams and celery. Put back
into the refrigerator until needed. When ready to
serve, pour into soup bowls and top with yoghurt
or sour cream and chopped coriander (Chinese
parsley) or parsley.

Preparation time: 10 minutes, plus chilling

Murg Tikka

2½-lb (1-kg) chicken, boned and cut into 1½-inch
  (3.8-cm) pieces, reserve the wings for another
  use
salt to taste
3 fl oz (75 ml, ⅓ cup) white wine or cider vinegar
2 oz (50 g) dried red chillies
1 oz (25 g) fresh ginger, peeled
1 oz (25 g) garlic, peeled
2 oz (50 g) cashew nuts (kaju)
1 tablespoon (15 ml) garam masala (see page
  181)
3 fl oz (75 ml, ⅓ cup) groundnut (peanut) oil
12 fl oz (350 ml, 1½ cups) plain yoghurt (curds),
  drained of any water
butter, for brushing
2 lemons, quartered, or 4, halved

Put the chicken pieces into a deep earthenware or
glass dish and sprinkle them with the salt and
vinegar. Combine the red chillies, ginger, garlic
and cashew (kaju) nuts in a food processor or
electric coffee grinder and grind into a paste.
Then mix the paste into the chicken. Beat the
garam masala and oil into the yoghurt and pour
it over the chicken, mixing well. Leave to marinate for at least 4 hours.

When ready to cook, either allow the barbecue
to become moderately hot or preheat the oven to
400°F, 200°C, Mark 6. Place the chicken pieces on
skewers and let them drip for 10 minutes. Bake
them on the barbecue or in the preheated oven
for 10 minutes until they are half cooked, then
brush with butter and finish cooking for approximately 10–15 minutes until done. Remove
the pieces from the skewers and serve hot with
lemon wedges.

Preparation time: 20 minutes
Marinating time: 4 hours
Cooking time: 20–25 minutes

*Hyderabad Sheekh Kebabs

Here is a hot and spicy dish we were served in
Kashmir as part of an eight-course dinner on a
houseboat on the beautiful Lake Nageen. It
can be prepared a few hours in advance, the
cooking to be done at the last minute.

1 lb (450 g) lean minced lamb, ground twice
1 tablespoon (15 ml) besan (gram or chickpea)
  flour, roasted
1 2-inch (5-cm) raw papaya (optional)
1 inch (2.5 cm) fresh ginger, peeled
1 small clove garlic
2 oz (50 g, ½ cup) fresh coriander (Chinese
  parsley) leaves
8 fresh mint leaves
2 fresh green chillies, stems and seeds removed
1 teaspoon (5 ml) cumin seeds, roasted and ground
1 teaspoon (5 ml) coriander seeds, roasted and
  ground
1 tablespoon (15 ml) garam masala (see page
  181)
salt
1 tablespoon (15 ml) plain yoghurt
1 egg, beaten
ghee or clarified butter for basting
2 limes, quartered
2 large onions, sliced thinly

In a large mixing bowl put the lamb and the
besan flour. Place the papaya, ginger, garlic,
coriander, mint and chillies in a food processor
and chop finely, then add this mixture to the
lamb. Put in the roasted and ground cumin and
coriander, then the masala, salt and finally the
yoghurt. With your hands mix all the ingredients
well, cover and leave for 1 hour in the refrigerator.

Mix in the beaten egg and from the mixture
make 16 2½-inch (6.3-cm) elongated balls (roughly
the size of a lime). Take 6–8 skewers, heat and
grease them, then shape and press the balls with
your fingers, moulding them into long flat cig-
arettes around the skewers. Either grill (broil)
them over a charcoal fire, or in the oven 5–6
inches (12.7–15 cm) from the heat, basting twice
with ghee or clarified butter, for 15–20 minutes.
Turn them until they are golden brown on all
sides. Remove very carefully by sliding them off
the skewers on to a plate. Serve with lime
quarters, sliced onions and mint chutney.

Preparation time: approximately 30–40 minutes
Chilling time: 1 hour
Cooking time: 15–20 minutes

Mint Chutney

4 oz (125 g, 1 cup) mint leaves
handful fresh coriander (Chinese parsley) leaves
1 shallot, peeled
1 fresh green chilli, stem and seeds removed
1 teaspoon (5 ml) tamarind juice (page 12) or a
  pinch of tamarind
½-inch (1.2-cm) piece fresh ginger, peeled
1 teaspoon (5 ml) sugar
1 teaspoon (5 ml) lime juice
salt to taste

Put all the ingredients into the food processor and mix into a fine paste. *Do not add water.* This is best when made just before serving, otherwise it tends to lose its fresh green colour.

Preparation time: 5–10 minutes

Paneer Masala

It is essential to make your own paneer. You cannot substitute Western cream cheese, as this will separate when cooked.

4 fl oz (125 ml, ½ cup) groundnut (peanut) oil
2 lb (900 g) paneer (see page 54) cut in ¾-inch
  (1.9-cm) cubes
1 teaspoon (5 ml) cumin seeds
7 oz (200 g, 1¾ cups) onions, chopped
1 tablespoon (15 ml) chopped hot green chillies
3 tablespoons (45 ml) fresh ginger, peeled and
  chopped
2 teaspoons (10 ml) red chilli and garlic paste
  (available from Oriental stores)
10 oz (275 g, 2 cups) tomatoes, peeled and chopped
1 teaspoon (5 ml) turmeric powder
2 teaspoons (10 ml) white wine vinegar
1 oz (25 g) sweet green, yellow or red pepper,
  quartered
1 oz (25 g) tomatoes, seeds removed and quartered
1 teaspoon (5 ml) garam masala (see page 181)
salt
1 teaspoon (5 ml) fresh ginger, peeled and
  julienned, for garnish
1 teaspoon (5 ml) fresh coriander (Chinese
  parsley) or parsley, very finely chopped, for
  garnish

In a wok, heat 2 fl oz (50 ml, ¼ cup) oil and stir-fry the paneer (cream cheese) cubes until they are golden brown – then remove them and put them in cold water. Add the remaining oil and the cumin seeds. When they start browning, add the onions and stir-fry until they turn a light golden colour. Add the green chillies and 2 tablespoons (30 ml) chopped ginger and continue to fry for 5 minutes. Mix the red chilli and garlic paste and remaining chopped ginger with 1 teaspoon (5 ml) water and add to the onion mixture. Cook for 3–4 minutes, then add the chopped tomatoes and turmeric powder, cooking until the oil separates and rises to the top. Add the vinegar, cook for 2 minutes, then add quartered sweet peppers. Next drain the cheese cubes and add to the mixture together with the quartered tomatoes. Cook for 5 minutes, then sprinkle in the garam masala and mix. Add salt to taste and serve hot, garnished with the ginger julienne and fresh coriander.

Preparation time: 20 minutes
Cooking time: 15 minutes

Songos de Morangos

Peaches, nectarines and apricots may be prepared in the same manner.

2 lb (900 g) strawberries, just ripe and firm,
  washed and hulled
2 fl oz (50 ml, ¼ cup) port or Madeira
1 teaspoon (5 ml) caster (superfine granulated)
  sugar
1 recipe sweet Massa Vinho (see page 61)
corn oil for frying
icing (confectioners') sugar, for dusting

In a bowl, marinate the strawberries in the port or Madeira and sugar for 2 hours. Immediately make the massa vinho batter and allow it to rest for the same 2 hours. Drain the strawberries and dip them into the massa vinho batter, making sure to coat them thoroughly. In a deep-fat frying-pan, heat the oil to 360°F (184°C) and fry the strawberries quickly until they are pale golden and crisp. Do not allow them to get mushy. Drain them on kitchen paper towels and dip them into the icing (confectioners') sugar. Serve hot, immediately.

Marination and resting time: 2 hours
Cooking time: 15–20 minutes

*Cardamom Biscuits (Cookies)

Makes about 8 dozen biscuits (cookies)

8 oz (225 ml, 1 cup) unsalted butter
8 oz (225 ml, 1 cup) granulated sugar
2 eggs
1¼ lb (575 g, 4 cups) plain (all-purpose) flour
1 tablespoon (15 ml) cardamom seeds, crushed
rind of 1 lemon

Preheat the oven to 325°F, 170°C, Mark 3. In a large bowl cream the butter and sugar, beat in the eggs and fold in the flour and flavourings. Roll out the dough on a lightly floured board, until ⅛ inch (0.3 cm) thick. Cut out as you wish, and bake in the preheated oven for about 12 minutes. Cool and store in an air-tight tin.

Preparation time: approximately 30 minutes
Cooking time: approximately 12 minutes

```
──────── DINNER ────────
        SERVES 6

      Sopa de Marisco
   (Spanish Seafood Soup)
         ────────
Barbecued Chicken with Garlic and Herbs

    *Riso al Sugo d'Arancia
    (Spanish Orange Rice)

  Zucchini Frittata en Uova
(Italian Fried Courgettes, Zucchini, in
              Egg)
         ────────
    *Pasticcio di Fragola
(Cold Italian Strawberry Pudding)

        *Koulourakia
(Greek Easter Biscuits, Cookies)

The contrast in colour in this menu gives
  a fresh, summery feeling: pale pink for
 the first course; brown, green and orange
  in the main course; finishing with pale
       pink again for the dessert.
```

Sopa de Marisco

This soup should be made with uncooked prawns (shrimp), *not canned*, because the shells lend an important taste to the soup. If only cooked ones are available, then use fish stock or clam juice instead of water.

2 lb (900 g) uncooked prawns (shrimp) in their
* shells*
3 small onions or 6 shallots, chopped finely
3 tablespoons (45 ml) olive oil
1¾ pints (1 litre, 2¼ pints) dry white wine
2 tablespoons (30 ml) tomato purée (paste)
8 fl oz (225 ml, 1 cup) single (light) cream
freshly ground white pepper
¼ teaspoon (1.25 ml) saffron powder
fried croûtons

If you are using uncooked prawns (shrimp), then boil them in 1¾ pints (1 litre, 2¼ pints) unsalted water for 1 minute, and reserve the water for use later in the recipe. Remove the shells from 12 prawns (shrimp) and reserve the prawns (shrimp) for garnish. In a deep sauté pan, fry the onions or shallots in the olive oil over low heat for 5 minutes, or until they become soft and transparent. Add the remaining unshelled prawns (shrimp) and cook for a further 5 minutes, then pour in the wine and prawn water (or fish stock or clam juice). Mix well. In batches, purée the prawn (shrimp) mixture in a food processor or blender, then rub the purée through a sieve with a wooden spoon into a large saucepan so as to leave any bits of shell behind. Place the purée over a low heat and stir in the tomato purée (paste), then the cream. Add the reserved peeled prawns (shrimp) and season with freshly ground white pepper and saffron powder. Top with hot fried croûtons.

Preparation time: approximately 15 minutes
Cooking time: 15–20 minutes

Barbecued Chicken with Garlic and Herbs

2 2½–3½-lb (1.1–1.6-kg) chickens, quartered
1 teaspoon (5 ml) chopped fresh tarragon or ½
    teaspoon (2.5 ml) dried tarragon
1 teaspoon (5 ml) fresh parsley, chopped
4 cloves garlic, crushed
1 teaspoon (5 ml) coarsely ground black pepper
juice of 2 lemons
12 fl oz (350 ml, 1¼ cups) olive oil or safflower oil
1 loaf French or Italian bread

Herb butter:
4 oz (125 g, ½ cup) butter
1 clove garlic, crushed
1 tablespoon (15 ml) mixed fresh herbs (basil and
    coriander/Chinese parsley are delicious)

Mix the herbs, garlic and seasonings in a bowl, then add the lemon juice. Slowly pour in the oil, stirring constantly to make a thick marinade. Wash and dry the chicken pieces and place them close together in a shallow pan. Spoon the marinade over them and allow to stand, basting occasionally, until you are ready to grill (broil) or barbecue. Cook the chicken, basting occasionally, until cooked through.

Meanwhile, slice a loaf of French or Italian bread diagonally to make rather long slices. Cream the butter in a bowl with the garlic and herbs and spread the slices with the herb butter. Heat the slices near the edge of the fire until they are hot and partially toasted. When the chicken is done, serve the quarters on the pieces of the bread so that none of the juices are lost.

Preparation time: approximately 30 minutes
Cooking time: approximately 20–25 minutes

*Riso al Sugo d'Arancia

This dish is a particularly good substitute for potatoes, served with ham or poultry. It can be prepared in advance and reheated by steaming it in a colander over water.

3 tablespoons (45 ml) butter, or chicken or duck
    fat
2 oz (50 g, ⅔ cup) finely chopped celery with leaves
2 tablespoons (30 ml) onion, chopped finely
2 tablespoons (30 ml) grated orange rind
8 fl oz (225 ml, 1 cup) orange juice
1¼ teaspoons (6.25 ml) salt
½ teaspoon (2.5 ml) dried thyme
7 oz (200 g, 1 cup) long grain rice

In a large saucepan, melt the butter or fat and cook the celery and onion until the onion is soft, but not brown. Add 12 fl oz (350 ml, 1½ cups) water, the orange rind, orange juice, salt and thyme and bring to the boil. Add the rice slowly, bring back to the boil, reduce the heat and simmer over low heat for 25 minutes or until the rice is soft and fluffy and the liquid is all absorbed.

Preparation time: approximately 30 minutes
Cooking time: approximately 30 minutes

Zucchini Frittata en Uova

1½ lb (700 g) courgettes (zucchini), sliced
1 egg, well beaten
3 oz (75 g, 1 cup) dried breadcrumbs
1 oz (25 g, ¼ cup) grated Parmesan cheese
1 large clove garlic, crushed
1 teaspoon (5 ml) dried oregano
salt and freshly ground black pepper
4 fl oz (125 ml, ½ cup) vegetable or olive oil

Dip the slices of courgette in the beaten egg, and then into a mixture of breadcrumbs, grated cheese, garlic, oregano, salt and freshly ground black pepper to taste. In a large frying-pan heat the oil, then fry the courgettes, slowly, on both sides.

Preparation time: approximately 25 minutes
Cooking time: approximately 20 minutes

*Pasticcio di Fragola

4 egg yolks
4 fl oz (125 ml, ½ cup) unsalted butter
10 oz (275 g, 2 cups) icing (confectioners') sugar
juice and grated rind of 1 lemon
6 egg whites, beaten stiffly
1 lb (450 g) fresh strawberries, washed and hulled
3 oz (75 g, ½ cup) flaked almonds, chopped
8 fl oz (225 ml, 1 cup) whipping cream, whipped

Preheat the oven to 350°F, 180°C, Mark 4. In the top of a double boiler or bain marie, over hot water, combine the egg yolks, butter, sugar, lemon juice and rind. Cook, stirring constantly, until the custard becomes thick and smooth and covers the back of a wooden spoon. Remove the mixture from the heat and gently fold in the beaten egg whites, with a metal spoon so as not to break down the air bubbles. Stir in the strawberries and almonds and pour the pudding into a soufflé dish or glass ovenproof dish. Bake in the preheated oven for 20–25 minutes, or until the pudding becomes firm. Cool, chill for 2 hours and serve with whipped cream.

Preparation time: approximately 20 minutes
Cooking time: 40–55 minutes
Chilling time: 2 hours

*Koulourakia

Makes 100 biscuits (cookies)

½ lb (225 g, 1 cup) unsalted butter at room temperature
8 oz (225 g, 2 cups) icing (confectioners') sugar
3 eggs
4 egg yolks, beaten
2 lb (900 g) plain (cake) flour
2 teaspoons (10 ml) vanilla essence (extract)
2 teaspoons (30 ml) baking powder
½ teaspoon (2.5 ml) salt
6 fl oz (175 ml, ¾ cup) whipping cream
2 fl oz (50 ml, ¼ cup) cold strong coffee

For the topping:
1 egg, beaten
1 teaspoon (5 ml) milk
sesame seeds

Preheat the oven to 350°F, 180°C, Mark 4. In a large mixing bowl use an electric mixer to cream the butter and sugar together until light and fluffy. Then add the whole eggs, one at a time, beating well, then the egg yolks. Mix well.

In another bowl, mix together half the flour, the vanilla essence (extract), baking powder and salt. In another bowl mix the whipping cream and coffee. Add the flour mixture and coffee cream alternately to the creamed butter mixture. Mix well and add the remaining flour. Mix until it forms a soft dough.

Pinch a piece of dough about the size of a walnut and roll it on a pastry board until you have a piece about 10 inches (25.4 cm) long, then fold it in half and plait (braid) it. Repeat this until all the dough is used. Place the biscuits (cookies) on a baking sheet, spaced wide enough apart to allow for expansion. Brush the tops of each koulouraki with a mixture of the beaten egg and milk. Top with the sesame seeds and bake in the preheated oven for about 30 minutes.

Preparation time: 30–35 minutes
Cooking time: 30 minutes

———— DINNER ————
SERVES 8

Sweet Melon Soup
————
Kerala Hot and Spicy Prawns (Shrimp)

or

Red Mullet alla Livornese

*Raita
(Indian Cucumber in Yoghurt Salad)

*Baked Aubergines
(Eggplants)
————
*Mango and Kiwi Sorbet

Using the fresh produce of the season, for a change start with a hot sweet soup, to be followed by spicy prawns (shrimp) and tangy baked aubergines (eggplants). Then to cool down there is the cold cucumber Raita and to finish a cold sweet and sour sorbet, to clear the palate. It is only the soup and the prawns (shrimp) which need to be made just before dinner. The aubergines (eggplants) can be prepared in advance and put under the grill for 2 minutes just before serving.

Sweet Melon Soup

Charles Carter devised this recipe in 1732. I discovered that if one flavoured the basic recipe with some spices and apricot jam or chutney, it adds a lovely tangy taste.

4 small Ogen or 2 small cantaloupe melons, halved
4 oz (125 g, ½ cup) butter
4 tablespoons (60 ml) plain (all-purpose) flour
2 teaspoons (10 ml) ground cumin
1 teaspoon (5 ml) crushed cardamom
2 tablespoons (30 ml) apricot jam or apple chutney
2 pints (1.1 litres, 5 cups) single (light) cream

Carefully scoop out the flesh from the melons, reserving the shells to use as soup bowls and 8 small melon slices. Dice the remaining flesh. In a medium-sized saucepan melt the butter and lightly sauté the melon in it until the pieces turn a light golden colour. Stir in the flour and cook for 1 minute.

In a bowl mix the spices and apricot jam or apple chutney. Add the cream and blend well. Then pour into the melon mixture, and cook until the soup has thickened slightly. Pour into the melon shells and garnish with the melon slices.

Preparation time: 15–20 minutes
Cooking time: 20–25 minutes

Kerala Hot and Spicy Prawns (Shrimp)

This dish is from the Northern region of India – Delhi. Rice would be one side dish to serve with it, but I prefer a cool raita and baked aubergines (eggplants).

40 large prawns (shrimp), uncooked
salt
1 tablespoon (15 ml) turmeric powder
1 2½-inch (6.3-cm) piece tamarind or 5 tablespoons (75 ml) tamarind juice
1 teaspoon (5 ml) fenugreek seeds
1 teaspoon (5 ml) black mustard seeds
2 tablespoons (30 ml) coriander seeds
4 red chillies, stems and seeds removed, chopped
4 fresh green chillies, stems and seeds removed, chopped
1-inch (2.5-cm) piece fresh ginger, peeled
4 cloves garlic, sliced finely
½ lb (225 g) onions, chopped finely
5 tablespoons (75 ml) vegetable oil
4 fresh curry leaves
fresh coriander (Chinese parsley) leaves, for garnish

Shell the prawns (shrimp), then make a slit down the back of them and remove any intestine or roe. Wash them well and pat dry with kitchen paper towels. Then toss them, in a bowl, in salt to taste and turmeric powder and set aside for at least 30 minutes, but this can be done as early as 24 hours ahead if you wish.

If you haven't a stock of tamarind juice in the refrigerator, take a saucepan and in it cover the piece of tamarind with 16 fl oz (475 ml, 2 cups) hot water. Either leave it overnight, if you have the time, or if not simmer it over low heat for 10 minutes. Then pour the juice through a sieve into a bowl. Mash the tamarind in the sieve with the back of a wooden spoon, so that the pulp goes through. Be sure to scrape all the pulp from the bottom of the sieve.

In a dry, heavy-bottomed frying-pan, roast the fenugreek, mustard and coriander seeds until they start to pop and turn pale brown. Grind them together in a mortar and pestle and set aside.

In a food processor or blender, chop the chillies, ginger, garlic and onions. In a large frying-pan, heat the oil and fry the onion mixture and the curry leaves lightly for 2 minutes, then mix in the prawns (shrimp), ground spices and 5 tablespoons (75 ml) tamarind juice. Cook over low heat, stirring constantly for approximately 10–15 minutes, until the prawns (shrimp) are tender and the liquid has been absorbed. Serve hot, garnished with coriander (Chinese parsley) leaves.

Preparation time: 45 minutes
Cooking time: 10–15 minutes

Red Mullet alla Livornese

4 oz (125 g, ½ cup) butter
2 small onions, chopped finely
8 small red mullet, cleaned
1½ bulbs fennel with leaves, chopped finely
salt
3 tablespoons (45 ml) tomato purée (paste)
fresh coriander (Chinese parsley) or parsley,
*   chopped finely*
lemon slices for garnish

In a frying-pan large enough to hold the fish in one layer, melt the butter and brown the chopped onion. Put in the mullet close together on top of the onion, then sprinkle the chopped fennel over them and salt to taste. Cook over a low heat for 7–8 minutes, then remove the pan from the heat, allowing the fish to cool a bit before turning them over. This will help to prevent the mullet from breaking.

Dissolve the tomato purée (paste) in 10 fl oz (300 ml, 1¼ cups) warm water. Return the pan to the heat and add the tomato mixture. Cook for another 5–6 minutes. Remove the fish to a heated serving dish and pour the hot sauce over them. Sprinkle with fresh coriander (Chinese parsley) or parsley and garnish with lemon slices.

Preparation time: approximately 20 minutes
Cooking time: approximately 25 minutes

*Raita

This delicious cool side dish can be made with any of the following other vegetables:

¼ *lb (125 g) potatoes (alu) – boil, peel and chop finely. Add to the yoghurt.*
½ *lb (225 g) okra (ladies' fingers) – wash and slice thinly. In a frying-pan sauté them in very little oil. Cool, and add to the yoghurt.*
¼ *lb (125 g) aubergine (eggplant) – either roast or steam it whole. When it is soft, squeeze out the pulp, throw away the skin, and mix the pulp into the yoghurt.*
¼ *lb (125 g) Palak (spinach) – wash and remove the stems and spines, leaving only the leaves, which then should be chopped finely. In a little bit of oil, sauté the leaves lightly, then mix with the yoghurt.*
3 medium mooli (white radish) – wash, scrape then grate the radish and mix it into the yoghurt.
4 medium pyaz (onions) – peel and grate the onion, then mix it into the yoghurt.

1 lb (450 g) plain yoghurt
1 teaspoon (5 ml) sugar
2 medium cucumbers, peeled
½ *teaspoon (2.5 ml) black mustard seeds*
½ *teaspoon (2.5 ml) cumin seeds*
1 teaspoon (5 ml) coriander seeds
a pinch of asafoetida
½ *teaspoon (2.5 ml) ground ginger*
salt
cayenne pepper
½ *fresh green chilli, stem and seeds removed, chopped finely (optional)*
fresh coriander (Chinese parsley) leaves, for garnish

In a medium-sized bowl, with a balloon whisk, whip the yoghurt together with the sugar until it reaches a creamy consistency. Grate the cucumber into a separate bowl. Then press all the liquid out of it, by squeezing it in your hand. Add the pulp to the yoghurt. Then in a dry, heavy-bottomed frying-pan roast the black mustard seeds, cumin seeds, coriander seeds and the asafoetida until the mustard seeds start to pop and the cumin and coriander turn pale brown. Then crush the spices in a mortar and pestle and pour them into the yoghurt. Add the ground ginger, salt and cayenne to taste, as well as the chopped green chilli, if you wish. Mix thoroughly and sprinkle with fresh coriander (Chinese parsley). Serve cold.

Preparation time: 20 minutes

*Baked Aubergines (Eggplants)

2 large aubergines (eggplants), peeled and sliced
8 fl oz (225 ml, 1 cup) vegetable oil
1 onion, chopped finely
2 green peppers, chopped finely
4 slices bacon, fried to crispness, broken into bits
8 fresh tomatoes, peeled and chopped, or 14-oz (400-g) can Italian plum tomatoes
12 oz (350 g, 2 cups) cashew nuts, chopped
3 oz (75 g, 1 cup) fresh breadcrumbs, fried in oil
$\frac{1}{2}$ teaspoon (2.5 ml) paprika
1 teaspoon (5 ml) dried oregano
1 teaspoon (5 ml) salt
$\frac{1}{2}$ teaspoon (2.5 ml) freshly ground black pepper
3 oz (75 g, 1 cup) grated Parmesan cheese

Preheat the oven to 350°F, 180°C, Mark 4. In a frying-pan brown the sliced aubergine (eggplant) lightly in the oil, then place the slices in a layer on the bottom of a gratin dish. In the same oil brown the onion and the green pepper lightly, then mix them with the bacon, tomatoes and half the nuts and spread the mixture over the aubergine (eggplant). In a bowl, mix the remaining nuts with the breadcrumbs and seasonings and set aside. Up to this point the dish may be prepared in advance. Sprinkle the nut mixture over the vegetables, cover with grated cheese and bake in the preheated oven for about 40 minutes, or until the top is brown and bubbly.

Preparation time: approximately 30 minutes
Cooking time: approximately 1 hour

*Mango and Kiwi Sorbet

1 ripe mango, peeled, stone removed and sliced
7 kiwi fruit, peeled and sliced
10 fl oz (300 ml, $1\frac{1}{4}$ cups) simple sugar syrup (see page 78)
4 teaspoons (20 ml) fresh orange, lemon or lime juice

In a food processor, blender or vegetable mill purée the mango and kiwis. Add the sugar syrup and fruit juice and blend well. Either place the sorbet mixture in an electric ice cream machine or sorbetière and proceed according to the manufacturer's instructions, or take an ice tray and pour the mixture into that. Place in the freezer for approximately 1 hour or until it begins to harden. Remove, mix in the food processor, or with a fork, then return it to the freezer until it freezes hard.

Preparation time: approximately 10 minutes
Freezing time: approximately 20 minutes, if using an electric ice cream machine or sorbetière; approximately 2–3 hours, if using ice trays

*Carciofi Forno
(Hot or Cold Baked Artichokes)
————
Barbecued Fish Kebabs with *Mint
Hollandaise Sauce

or

Filetto di Sogliola Marinato
(Fillets of Sole in Vinegar Sauce)

Palak Paneer
(Spinach and Onions with Homemade
Cream Cheese)
————
*Strawberries in Wine

*Almond Crisps

An easy and quick menu, with the first course, the herb hollandaise and the marinated strawberries in wine with sweet almond biscuits (cookies) all prepared in advance. Only the kebabs and spinach have to be prepared at the last minute.

*Carciofi Forno

4 medium artichokes, stems and sharp tips of
  leaves removed
2 cloves garlic
1 teaspoon (5 ml) parsley, chopped finely
salt and freshly ground pepper
6 tablespoons (90 ml) olive oil

Loosen the artichoke leaves slightly. In a bowl, crush the garlic, mix it with the parsley, salt and pepper to taste and place the mixture between the loosened leaves. Place the artichokes in a fireproof enamel dish. Pour 1½ tablespoons (22 ml) olive oil over each artichoke and add 8 fl oz (225 ml, 1 cup) water to the dish. Cover and simmer over low heat for 40 minutes or until the leaves and bottom are tender, adding more water if necessary. Meanwhile preheat the oven to 400°F, 200°C, Mark 6. When the artichokes are tender, uncover and place the dish in the oven for 5 minutes to crisp up. Serve hot or cold.

Preparation time: approximately 30 minutes
Cooking time: approximately 45 minutes

Barbecued Fish Kebabs

4 cloves garlic, crushed
1 teaspoon (5 ml) red chilli peppers, stems and
  seeds removed, skins crushed
1 teaspoon (5 ml) sweet paprika
1 tablespoon (15 ml) salt
4 fl oz (125 ml, 1½ cups) white wine vinegar
2 bay leaves, crushed
2 lb (900 g) fillets of haddock, cod, halibut or bass

In a bowl combine all the ingredients except the fish with 8 fl oz (225 ml, 1 cup) water. Put the fish in a shallow dish in a single layer. Pour over the marinade and leave, covered, in the refrigerator overnight, turning the pieces once.

When ready to cook, drain the fish, reserving the marinade, and cut the fillets into long strips 1 inch (2.5 cm) wide. Roll up, push a skewer through the roll, and place this on a grill over the hot coals. Grill (broil) the fish, turning often and basting with the marinade, for about 15 minutes, or until the fish is opaque and light golden brown. Serve with Mint Hollandaise Sauce.

Preparation time: 20–30 minutes
Marinating time: 24 hours
Cooking time: approximately 15 minutes

*Mint Hollandaise Sauce
For grilled meat or fish

2 spring onions (scallions), chopped finely
2 tablespoons (30 ml) tarragon vinegar
4 egg yolks
4 tablespoons (60 ml) butter
1 tablespoon (15 ml) chicken or fish stock (broth)
  (depending on whether serving with meat or
  fish)
¼ teaspoon (1.25 ml) paprika
2 teaspoons (10 ml) finely chopped mint leaves
1 teaspoon (5 ml) finely chopped parsley
¼ teaspoon (1.25 ml) salt

In a medium-sized saucepan add the onions (scallions) to the vinegar and bring to the boil. Simmer until reduced to 1 tablespoon (15 ml). Strain and cool. Add egg yolks one at a time to the vinegar, whisking continuously. Cook over low heat until smooth and thick. Gradually stir in the butter, the stock (broth), paprika, mint, parsley and salt to taste.

Preparation time: approximately 15 minutes
Cooking time: approximately 15–20 minutes

Filetto di Sogliola Marinato

2 fl oz (50 ml, $\frac{1}{4}$ cup) olive oil
2 medium-sized onions, chopped finely
2 lb (900 g) fillets of sole
flour
salt and freshly ground pepper
1 tablespoon (15 ml) raisins
1 tablespoon (15 ml) pine nuts (pine kernels)
4 fl oz (125 ml, $\frac{1}{2}$ cup) white wine vinegar

In a frying-pan heat the olive oil and brown the onions. Remove to a plate. Sprinkle the sole with seasoned flour and brown it on both sides in the same olive oil. Remove the fish to a plate. Lower the heat and return the onions to the pan, place the fish on top of the onion, add the raisins and nuts (pine kernels), and cook for 5 minutes. Add the vinegar and simmer for about 20 minutes or until the flesh turns opaque.

Preparation time: approximately 15 minutes
Cooking time: approximately 45 minutes

Palak Paneer

It is essential to make your own paneer. Do not substitute any Western cream cheese, as this will disintegrate when it is fried.

1$\frac{1}{2}$ lb (700 g) fresh spinach, cleaned and spines
*   removed, or 2 lb (900 g) frozen leaf spinach*
2 tablespoons (30 ml) fenugreek powder or
*   pounded fenugreek seeds*
12 oz (350 g) paneer (home made cream cheese)
3 tablespoons (45 ml) groundnut (peanut) oil
1 medium-sized onion, chopped finely
2 cloves garlic, chopped finely
2 teaspoons (10 ml) ground coriander
salt and pepper to taste
pinch of cayenne pepper (optional)

In a saucepan, over low heat, add the minimum of water to the fresh spinach and wilt it together with the fenugreek. If you are using frozen spinach, no water need be added. Then put it all into a blender or food processor. Cut the paneer into 1-inch (2.5-cm) cubes and heat the oil in a wok. Stir-fry the paneer until it turns just golden in colour. Lift out the cheese with a perforated spoon, leaving the oil behind, and drain it on kitchen paper towels.

To the oil left in the wok, add the onion, garlic, ground coriander, salt and pepper and, if you wish, a pinch of cayenne. Mix until the vegetables soften, then add the spinach purée and mix thoroughly. At the last minute add the fried paneer and serve.

Preparation time: approximately 30 minutes, if the fresh paneer has been made
Approximately 1$\frac{1}{2}$ hours, if paneer is not yet made
Cooking time: 25–30 minutes

Paneer, Panir, or Chenna

This is a soft cheese, somewhat like our own cream cheese. But whereas the Western cream cheese separates when fried, paneer will hold its shape. It is used to make Indian sweets, and some vegetable dishes. Use within 2 days as it must be fresh.

2 pints (1.1 litres, 5 cups) whole milk
juice of 3 lemons

In a large saucepan, bring the milk to the boil, stirring constantly to prevent a skin forming. Remove from the heat and add the lemon juice. This will curdle the milk and separate the curds and whey. Keep stirring until the separation process has completed. Line a strainer with some muslin (cheesecloth), leaving the four corners to hang over the side. Pour in the milk mixture and allow it to drain for a minute or two. Gather up the corners of the muslin (cheesecloth) and squeeze more whey from the curds. Tie the corners together and hang the muslin (cheese-cloth) on a hook over a bowl or the sink for approximately 30 minutes (I hang mine on a wooden dish rack over the sink). Squeeze the remaining whey from the muslin (cheesecloth) and do one of two things: either knead it with the palm and heel of your hand as you would ordinary pastry, or place the cheese in its bag between two plates with a weight on top. In either case, when the cheese has become hardened and elastic, it can be used.

Preparation time: approximately 1 hour

*Strawberries in Wine

1½ lb (700 g) strawberries, hulled
2 oz (50 g, ¼ cup) granulated sugar
4 fl oz (125 ml, ½ cup) dry white wine

Sprinkle the strawberries with sugar, cover with wine and chill for 2 hours.

Chilling time: 2 hours

*Almond Crisps

Almond paste keeps well in the refrigerator so it is well worth making a large quantity at a time. The recipe given here makes about 3 lb (1.4 kg). Makes about 2½ dozen biscuits (cookies).

½ lb (225 g) almond paste
6 oz (175 g, ¾ cup) granulated sugar
6 oz (175 g, ¾ cup) unsalted butter
4 egg whites
½ teaspoon (2.5 ml) vanilla essence (extract)
5 oz (150 g, 1 cup) plain (all-purpose) flour
¼ teaspoon (1.25 ml) salt
blanched almonds

For almond paste:
6 oz (175 g, 1 cup) almonds, blanched
5 egg yolks
8 oz (225 g, 2 cups) icing (confectioners') sugar
1 lb (450 g) plain (cake) flour
12 oz (350 g, 1½ cups) butter
1 egg
grated rind of 1 lemon

To make the almond paste place the almonds in a food processor, add 4 egg yolks and 1 tablespoon (15 ml) of the sugar and pulverize them into a paste. Sift the flour and the remaining sugar on to a pastry board. Make a well in the centre and add the butter, almond paste, whole egg and the remaining egg yolk together with the lemon rind. Mix well, with your hands, until the paste reaches a stiff consistency. Allow it to rest, covered, in the refrigerator for 1 hour before using.

To make the biscuits, preheat the oven to 325°F, 170°C, Mark 3. In a bowl work the almond paste and the sugar with a spoon until they are blended well. With an electric hand mixer, cream the butter in a large bowl. Add the almond paste and blend until the mixture becomes light and fluffy. Then add the egg whites and beat well. Add the vanilla essence (extract), flour and salt and mix. Take a lightly greased baking sheet and drop the batter on it by the spoonful, about 4 inches (10 cm) apart. Flatten each with a spoon and place a whole almond in the centre of each crisp. Bake in the preheated oven for 10–15 minutes. Then while they are still warm, roll a wooden spoon handle over each biscuit (cookie) to curl the edges.

Preparation time for almond paste: 20–30 minutes
Resting time for almond paste: 1 hour
Preparation time for biscuits (cookies): approximately 40 minutes
Cooking time: 10–15 minutes

Summer

SPECIAL LUNCHEON
SERVES 8

*Lobster Mousse with Lobster Chunks and Pungent Dressing

Large Mixed Green Salad (Rocket Salad (Arrugala), Belgian Endive, Cos, Romaine)

---

*Strawberries in Wine (see page 55)

*Lemon Squares

Everything in this menu can be prepared in advance. The Pungent Dressing is better made the day before, as are the Lemon Squares.

---

*Lobster Mousse with Lobster Chunks

If you feel like really lashing out on a first course with a simple and inexpensive entrée, or a luncheon dish, then you can make this lobster mousse with lobster chunks. In the summer, lobsters are quite reasonable in price, rich and filling. Make the Pungent Dressing the day before it is to be used so that the ingredients are well absorbed.

5 1½-lb (750-g) lobsters, using tail and claw meat
2 tablespoons (30 ml, 2 envelopes) powdered gelatine
8 fl oz (225 ml, 1 cup) tomato juice
4 fl oz (125 ml, ½ cup) tomato sauce, fresh (see page 180) or canned
juice of 1 large lemon
1 tablespoon (15 ml) Worcestershire sauce
2 fl oz (50 ml, ¼ cup) dry white wine
2 tablespoons (30 ml) prepared horseradish
1 large onion, chopped
3 oz (75 g, 1 cup) celery, chopped finely
1½ oz (37 g) green pepper, chopped finely
2 spring onions (scallions), chopped finely
fresh coriander (Chinese parsley) or parsley, chopped finely
2 cloves garlic, crushed
salt, black pepper and cayenne
croûtons for garnish
Cos lettuce for garnish

Pungent Dressing:
1 clove garlic, chopped very finely
½ teaspoon (2.5 ml) salt
½ teaspoon (2.5 ml) dry mustard
1 teaspoon (5 ml) Worcestershire sauce
3 tablespoons (45 ml) tarragon vinegar
2 tablespoons (30 ml) anchovy paste
3 tablespoons (45 ml) grated onion
3 oz (75 g) fresh coriander (Chinese parsley) or parsley
8 fl oz (225 ml, 1 cup) mayonnaise
4 fl oz (125 ml, ½ cup) yoghurt
freshly ground pepper to taste

Make the Pungent Dressing the day before serving the lobster mousse. Combine all the ingredients in a bowl, cover and refrigerate.

Cook lobsters the day they are to be used. Plunge them into boiling water and cook for 20 minutes until the shell turns bright red. Cool, remove the meat from the shells and cut into bite-sized pieces, keeping the meat of 1 lobster aside to place in the centre of the mousse mould.

Heat 4 fl oz (125 ml, ½ cup) water to lukewarm and soften the gelatine in it. In a large saucepan heat the tomato juice, then add the softened gelatine to it and mix well. Add the lobster meat and the remaining ingredients. Pour the mixture into a well-buttered 2-pint (1.1-litre, 2½-pint) ring mould and chill for 3 hours.

To serve, run a sharp knife round the outer and inner edges of the mould to loosen the mousse. Place a plate on top of the ring mould, then overturn the mould so that the mousse falls out on to the plate. Take the reserved lobster chunks and make a mound of them in the centre of the mousse. Pour the Pungent Dressing over the chunks and top with croûtons. Garnish with lettuce leaves.

Preparation time: 1 hour
Cooking time: approximately 20 minutes
Chilling time: 24 hours for the dressing
3 hours for the mousse

*Lemon Squares

Makes approximately 32 squares

8 oz (225 g, 1 cup) unsalted butter
3 oz (75 g, ½ cup) icing (confectioners') sugar
10 oz (275 g, 2 cups) plain (all-purpose) flour

For the topping:
grated rind of 1 lemon
4 eggs, well beaten
1 lb (450 g, 2 cups) granulated sugar
½ teaspoon (2.5 ml) salt
6 tablespoons (90 ml) lemon juice (3 lemons)
1 teaspoon (5 ml) baking powder
4 tablespoons (60 ml) flour

Preheat the oven to 350°F, 180°C, Mark 4. Cream the butter and icing (confectioners') sugar in a food processor, then add the flour. Press the mixture into 2 ungreased 9-inch (22.8-cm) Swiss roll tins and bake in the preheated oven for 10 minutes.

Meanwhile prepare the topping. Combine the remaining ingredients in a food processor and pour the mixture over the half-cooked crust. Bake for a further 30 minutes. Dust with icing sugar and cut into squares.

Preparation time: approximately 15 minutes
Cooking time: approximately 40 minutes

LUNCHEON
SERVES 6

*Gaspacho à Alentejana
(Portuguese Gazpacho)

Chinese Chicken Salad

Blueberry Buckle

---

*Gaspacho à Alentejana

This soup, a cousin to the Spanish gazpacho, derives from the region southwest of Lisbon which continues down to the Spanish border.

Whereas the Spanish gazpacho is usually made up of chopped vegetables in thin soup, the Portuguese version uses puréed vegetables and chopped 'chorizo', or 'presunto', a smoked ham. Parma ham or the Spanish 'jambon serrano' are good substitutes for the latter.

14-oz (425-g) can tomato juice
2 large tomatoes, skins removed and chopped
1 large cucumber, peeled and chopped
2 green peppers, deseeded and chopped
1 shallot, peeled and chopped
2 large cloves garlic, crushed
2 tablespoons (30 ml) paprika
2 teaspoons (10 ml) roasted cumin seeds, crushed
  (see page 12)
salt
3 tablespoons (45 ml) red wine vinegar
1 tablespoon (15 ml) good olive oil
2 oz (50 g) chorizo, presunto, or smoked ham,
  chopped finely
1 heaped tablespoon (20 ml) fresh coriander
  (Chinese parsley), chopped finely

Into a large mixing bowl pour the tomato juice and 2¾ pints (1.75 litres, 3½ pints) cold water. Add the chopped tomatoes, cucumber, green peppers and shallot. Mix, then ladle the chopped vegetables in batches, with some of the liquid, into a food processor or blender to purée the vegetables. Return the purée to the tomato liquid and mix well. Add the garlic, paprika and crushed cumin seeds, and salt to taste. Then add the vinegar, mix and place in the refrigerator covered with foil or cling film (Saran Wrap) to chill for 4 hours.

Just before serving, add the olive oil, mix and ladle into chilled soup bowls. Top with the chopped chorizo and coriander (Chinese parsley).

Preparation time: approximately 20 minutes
Chilling time: 4 hours

Chinese Chicken Salad

1 4-lb (1.8-kg) chicken, cleaned
1 medium-sized onion, chopped
3 carrots, chopped
1 leek, sliced
2 stalks celery, scraped and chopped
4 stalks fresh coriander (Chinese parsley) or parsley
salt and freshly ground pepper
3 sprigs fresh thyme
½ head Cos or Romaine lettuce
light soy sauce
sesame oil
10 spring onions (scallions), cut in fine strips
¼ lb (125 g) mangetout (snow peas), topped and tailed and cut into fine strips
1 tablespoon (15 ml) peeled and finely chopped fresh ginger
5 tablespoons (75 ml) groundnut (peanut) oil

In a large saucepan place the whole chicken, onion, carrots, leek, celery, coriander (Chinese parsley) or parsley, salt, freshly ground pepper and water to cover. Bring the water to the boil and cook for 10 minutes. Lower the heat and simmer the chicken for 1 hour, approximately, until it is cooked but juicy. Remove the chicken and use the liquid, boiled down with the chicken bones, for stock.

Line a large serving dish with the crisp lettuce. Remove the meat from the bird, making bite-sized pieces, and place them in a mound on top of the lettuce. Dribble some soy sauce over the chicken, then do the same with the sesame oil. Place the spring onions (scallions) over the chicken, then the mangetout (snow peas) over them. Sprinkle salt, to taste, over the vegetables, then the fresh ginger. Dribble some more soy sauce and sesame oil over the salad. In a small saucepan, heat the groundnut (peanut) oil over high heat until the oil just smokes, then pour the hot oil over the entire salad and serve immediately.

Preparation time: 20 minutes
Cooking time: approximately 1½ hours

Blueberry Buckle

10 oz (275 g, 2 cups) plain (all-purpose) flour
2 teaspoons (10 ml) baking powder
½ teaspoon (2.5 ml) salt
2 oz (50 g, ¼ cup) butter
6 oz (175 g, ¾ cup) granulated sugar
1 teaspoon (5 ml) vanilla essence (extract)
1 large egg
4 fl oz (125 ml, ½ cup) milk
15-oz (425-g) can blueberries or 1 lb (450 g) fresh blueberries

For the topping:
4 oz (125 g, ½ cup) granulated sugar
1½ oz (37 g, ⅓ cup) plain (all-purpose) flour
½ teaspoon (1.5 ml) ground cinnamon
2 oz (50 g, ¼ cup) soft margarine

Preheat the oven to 375°F, 190°C, Mark 5. Sift together the flour, baking powder and salt. Cream the butter, sugar and vanilla. Add the egg and beat well. Stir in the sifted ingredients in 3 lots, alternating with the milk. Fold in the fresh or drained canned blueberries and turn the mixture into a floured and greased loaf pan.

Combine the topping ingredients until crumbly. Sprinkle on top of the batter and bake in the preheated oven for 40 minutes. If there is any left over, serve it for tea and eat it cold.

Preparation time: approximately 25 minutes
Cooking time: 40 minutes

------ LIGHT LUNCHEON ------
SERVES 6

Almeijoas à Moda de Portimão
(Clams or Cockles Portimão style)

Tomato, Onion, Cucumber and Sweet
Green Pepper Salad

Hot Stuffed Peaches with Zabaglione
Sauce (see page 74)

------ LUNCHEON ------
SERVES 4

*Hot Green Pepper Soup

Ameijoas Fritos
(Portuguese Fried Clams)

or

Sgombro con Salsa di Basilico
(Mackerel with Basil Sauce)

Fried Parsley (see page 79)

*Cucumber, Tomato and Onion Salad
------
*Pana Montata

Almeijoas à Moda de Portimão

Years ago we used to take a house in Monchique in the Algarve for two or three weeks each summer. It was in the hills just 45 minutes above the sea town of Portimão. The delicious *almeijoas* served in the restaurants of this town beckoned to us with ferocity, so that almost every other day we would lunch on these tiny clams. In England, cooked cockles or cockles in brine are a good substitute but in America buy little neck clams.

6 lb (2.7 kg) smallest little neck clams, or 2 10-oz (275-g) cans whole clams, or 1½ lb (700 g) shelled cockles
2 tablespoons (30 ml) olive oil
2 sweet green peppers, deseeded and chopped finely
3 small onions, chopped finely
3 large cloves garlic, chopped finely
1 bay leaf
1 heaped tablespoon (20 ml) fresh coriander (Chinese parsley) or parsley, chopped finely

If using little neck clams, put them in a saucepan with *no* water, cover and place over a low heat, shaking the pan until the clams open. Discard any clams which have not opened.

In a sauté pan heat the olive oil and cook the peppers for 15 minutes, then add the onions, garlic and bay leaf, and cook for a further 5 minutes. Add the clams or cockles, cover and cook for 2 or 3 minutes. Serve either in heated earthenware soup bowls or individual gratin dishes, topped with coriander (Chinese parsley) or parsley.

Preparation time: approximately 30 minutes
Cooking time: approximately 25 minutes

*Hot Green Pepper Soup

2 medium-sized green peppers, chopped
1½ oz (40 g, ¼ cup) chopped onion
2 tablespoons (30 ml) unsalted butter
16 fl oz (475 ml, 2 cups) chicken stock (broth)
¼ teaspoon (1.25 ml) dried oregano
1 tablespoon (15 ml) plain (all-purpose) flour
¼ teaspoon (1.25 ml) salt
8 fl oz (225 ml, 1 cup) milk

Reserve some of the green pepper for garnish. Sauté the rest with the onion in 1 tablespoon (15 ml) butter, in a saucepan, until the onion turns golden. Add the chicken stock (broth) and oregano and simmer for 10 minutes. Purée the soup in a food processor or blender for a few seconds.

In another saucepan, melt the remaining butter and stir in the flour and salt. Cook the roux for a minute or two to take away the raw taste of the flour, then gradually stir in the milk. Cook, stirring constantly, until the mixture becomes thick and smooth. Stir in the green pepper purée, thoroughly integrating the two mixtures. Remove from the heat. This soup may be served hot or cold. If you are going to serve it cold, cool it down then chill in the refrigerator for 1–2 hours. In any case, hot or cold, serve sprinkled with the reserved chopped green pepper.

Preparation time: 20 minutes
Cooking time: 30 minutes
Chilling time: 1–2 hours

Almeijoas Fritos

6 lb (2.7 kg) clams, well cleaned
4 fl oz (125 ml, ¼ cup) lemon juice
4 fl oz (125 ml, ¼ cup) dry white wine
salt and pepper
1 bunch of fresh coriander (Chinese parsley) or
*   parsley, chopped finely*
3 times the recipe for Massa Vinho
corn oil for deep frying
lemon quarters
fried parsley (see page 79)

Put the clams in a large saucepan, with no water; cover and place over a medium-high heat, shaking the pan until the clams open. Remove the clams from their shells and discard the shells. In a bowl marinate the fish in a mixture of the lemon juice and white wine, salt and pepper to taste, and fresh coriander (Chinese parsley) or parsley for 30 minutes, tossing them occasionally to make sure all the clams are marinated. Drain them and dip them in the massa vinho batter, then deep fry them in hot oil. Serve with Fried Parsley.

Massa Vinho

This batter can be used for fish, meat and vegetables, and for desserts as well but then you must add 1 tablespoon (15 ml) sugar to the ingredients.

8 oz (225 g, 1¾ cups) plain (all-purpose) flour
3 tablespoons (45 ml) olive oil
½ teaspoon (2.5 ml) salt
3 tablespoons (45 ml) dry white wine or beer
2 egg yolks, beaten
3 egg whites

Into a food processor or blender, sieve the flour. Then pour in the oil, salt, wine or beer and 3 tablespoons (45 ml) water. Mix at high speed, until the batter becomes smooth. Add the egg yolks, mix, then pour into a bowl, cover and allow to rest for 2 hours.

In another bowl beat the egg whites together with a pinch of salt until they make stiff peaks. Fold them into the batter with a large metal spoon. The batter is now ready for use.

Preparation time: approximately 15 minutes plus
2 hours resting time for batter
Cooking time: approximately 20 minutes

Sgombro con Salsa di Basilico

This dish is extremely easy to make, but the special quality of taste depends upon using fresh basil, although if it is unavailable, you can use dried basil.

4 fl oz (125 ml, ½ cup) chicken stock (broth)
4 fl oz (125 ml, ½ cup) red wine
½ teaspoon (2.5 ml) dried oregano
2 tablespoons (30 ml) finely chopped fresh basil or 1 tablespoon (15 ml) dried basil
2 egg yolks, beaten
2 lb (900 g) fresh mackerel
salt and freshly ground black pepper
3 tomatoes, sliced
2 tablespoons (30 ml) snipped chives

Preheat the oven to 350°F, 180°C, Mark 4.

In a saucepan heat the chicken stock (broth), wine, oregano and basil, then add the beaten egg yolks and cook until the sauce has thickened. Season the fish and lay it in a greased ovenproof baking dish. Place the tomato slices on top of it, pour the sauce over them and sprinkle with chives. Bake in the preheated oven for 40 minutes.

Preparation time: approximately 15 minutes
Cooking time: 40 minutes

*Pana Montata

1 pint (600 ml, 1¼ pints) double (heavy) cream
2 oz (50 g, ¼ cup) caster (superfine granulated) sugar
1 teaspoon (5 ml) ground cinnamon
4 fl oz (125 ml, ½ cup) orange flower water, or vanilla essence (extract)

Pour the cream into a copper bowl, if you have one, otherwise an ordinary mixing bowl. Whip the cream until it resembles snow and holds peaks. Add the sugar, cinnamon and orange flower water or vanilla essence (extract). Beat again for 15 minutes. Then pour into a glass dish, or individual glass dishes and chill before serving.

Preparation time: approximately 25 minutes
Chilling time: approximately 2 hours

*Tomato and Herb Mousse

*1-lb (450-g) can Italian plum tomatoes
4 spring onions (scallions), including the green
  part, chopped finely
2 tablespoons (30 ml) chopped fresh basil leaves, if
  not available use fresh mint
juice of 1 lemon
10 fl oz (300 ml, 1¼ cups) double (heavy) cream,
  whipped
1 tablespoon (15 ml, 1 envelope) powdered gelatine
2 fl oz (50 ml, ¼ cup) port or Madeira
Tabasco sauce to taste
1 tablespoon (15 ml) salt, or to taste
freshly ground black pepper
fresh basil or mint leaves to garnish*

In a blender or food processor combine the tomatoes, spring onions (scallions), basil or mint, lemon juice and whipped cream and mix well. In a small saucepan, heat the Madeira or Port and sprinkle the gelatine into it. Add to the tomato mixture together with the Tabasco sauce, salt and pepper to taste. Mix well. Rinse a 1¼-pint (725-ml, 3-cup) mould with cold water and pour the tomato mixture into it. Cover with cling film (Saran Wrap), then aluminium foil and chill for at least 6 hours.

When ready to serve, run a knife around the edge of the mould to release the mousse. Invert a plate on the open end of the mould, then turn the mould upside down, and the mousse should come out easily. Sometimes a tap on the top of the mould helps. Decorate with fresh basil or mint leaves.

*Preparation time: approximately 20 minutes
Chilling time: 6 hours or more*

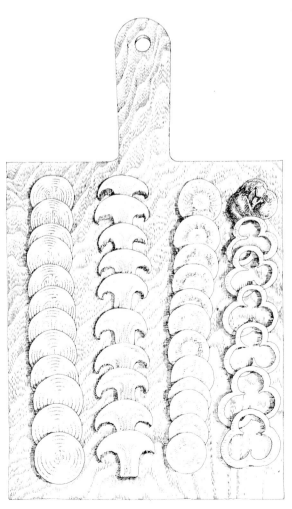

Chicken Gougère

For choux paste:
2 oz (50 g, $\frac{1}{4}$ cup) butter
salt and pepper
2$\frac{1}{2}$ oz (65 g, $\frac{1}{2}$ cup) unbleached flour, sifted
2 eggs

For the filling:
2 onions, chopped finely
2 tablespoons (30 ml) oil
2 tablespoons (30 ml) butter
4 tomatoes, quartered
1 tablespoon (15 ml) tomato purée (paste)
1 teaspoon (5 ml) juniper berries, crushed
1 teaspoon (5 ml) ground cumin
1 tablespoon (15 ml) chopped fresh coriander
    (Chinese parsley) or parsley
2 tablespoons (30 ml) dry sherry
$\frac{1}{2}$ lb (225 g) cooked chicken, cut into long strips
4 tablespoons (60 ml) grated Cheddar cheese

Preheat the oven to 425°F, 220°C, Mark 7. Make the choux pastry. In a large heavy saucepan bring $\frac{1}{4}$ pint (150 ml, $\frac{5}{8}$ cup) water to the boil over moderate heat, then add the butter and salt and pepper. When the butter has melted, remove the pan from the heat and pour in the flour, all at once. Beat the dough until the mixture pulls away from the sides of the pan and forms a ball. Add the eggs, one by one, beating each into the dough until it is well blended before adding the next. When all the egg has been completely absorbed, the mixture should be thick and glossy.

Grease an 8-inch (20.3-cm) diameter round ovenproof dish and flour it. Place heaped table-spoonfuls of the mixture, one against the other, in the shape of a ring on the greased dish. Bake in the preheated oven for 25–30 minutes, or until the gougère is puffed and golden in colour.

In a medium-sized sauté pan, fry the chopped onion in the oil and butter until it turns light golden. Add the tomatoes, the tomato purée (paste), the juniper berries, cumin, fresh cori-ander (Chinese parsley), sherry and finally the chicken strips. Cook the mixture for 6–8 minutes, mixing well. Remove the cooked gougère from the oven and spoon the chicken mixture into the centre of it. Sprinkle the grated cheese over everything and serve hot.

Preparation time: approximately 30 minutes
Cooking time: approximately 45 minutes

Pineapple Moddulu

A tasty vegetable curry from Southern India.

1 large pineapple, skinned and cut into cubes
1 teaspoon (5 ml) salt
2 teaspoons (10 ml) cumin seeds
4 red chillies, stems removed, seeded and chopped
$\frac{1}{2}$ teaspoon (2.5 ml) fenugreek seeds
2 tablespoons (30 ml) grated fresh coconut, or
    packaged desiccated coconut
1 tablespoon (15 ml) oil
$\frac{1}{2}$ teaspoon (2.5 ml) black mustard seeds
1 teaspoon (5 ml) black gram dhal

In a medium-sized saucepan cook the pineapple in water to cover with the salt, until it is tender but not mushy. Set aside. In a frying-pan dry fry, without oil, the cumin seeds, chillies, fenugreek seeds and grated fresh coconut until they are just brown, not burnt, and the cumin seeds are jumping up from the pan. Pour them all into a mortar and pestle and make a *coarse* paste. Mix this in with the pineapple cubes in a serving dish.

Then heat a little oil in the same small frying-pan and fry the mustard seeds until they begin to pop. Add the black gram dhal, mix and cook until the dhal turns reddish-brown. Pour over the pineapple and serve.

Preparation time: approximately 20 minutes
Cooking time: 35–40 minutes

---SPECIAL SUNDAY DINNER---
FOR TWO
(After the Guests have left)

*Tomato and Herb Mousse (left over from luncheon) (see page 63)

Cantonese Lobster

or

Lobster Marsala

Stir-fried Mangetout (Snow Peas) with Toasted Sesame Seeds

---

*Ginger Ice Cream

This is eating the leftovers at their best. The tangy Tomato and Herb Mousse with its bouquet of basil is the starter for a luxurious lobster dish. And to finish, the coolness of Ginger Ice Cream.

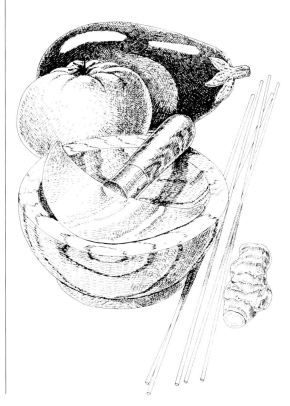

Cantonese Lobster

$1\frac{1}{2}$-lb (700-g) live lobster
$\frac{1}{4}$ lb (125 g) boneless loin pork, minced
1 teaspoon (5 ml) salt
$\frac{1}{4}$ teaspoon (1.25 ml) freshly ground black pepper
1 teaspoon (5 ml) sugar
1 tablespoon (15 ml) cornflour (cornstarch)
2 tablespoons (30 ml) fermented black beans (dowsee)
3 tablespoons (45 ml) groundnut (peanut) oil or corn oil
1 clove garlic, chopped very finely
16 fl oz (475 ml, 2 cups) fish stock (broth) or clam juice
2 eggs, beaten

Plunge the lobster into boiling water for 2 minutes until dead but not cooked. Remove and leave until cool enough to handle. Chop off the claws and legs, chop them at their joints, and crack the claw shells. Then split the lobster lengthways and discard the stomach and intestines. Chop the lobster meat *in its shell* into bite-sized pieces.

In a bowl put the minced pork and add the salt, pepper, sugar, $\frac{1}{2}$ teaspoon (2.5 ml) cornflour (cornstarch), fermented black beans and 1 tablespoon (15 ml) oil; mix well and let stand for 15 minutes. Heat the wok, then add the remaining oil. When it smokes, put in the garlic and allow it to colour pale golden. Add the pork mixture and stir-fry for 1 minute. Next drop in the pieces of lobster in their shell and stir-fry for another minute. Pour in the fish stock (broth) or clam juice, cover and simmer for 10 minutes until the lobster is cooked.

Meanwhile add the remaining cornflour (cornstarch) to 2 tablespoons (30 ml) cold water and mix thoroughly. Make a well in the lobster mixture. Pour in the cornflour (cornstarch) mixture slowly, cook for 1 minute, then bring in the ingredients from the side. Simmer until the gravy thickens. Remove from the heat and stir in the beaten eggs. Pour into a serving dish and serve immediately.

Preparation time: approximately 25 minutes
Cooking time: approximately 20 minutes

Lobster Marsala

For garlic oil, soak 3 peeled and crushed cloves of garlic in 1 pint (600 ml, 2½ cups) olive oil.

1 2½-lb (1.1-kg) or 2 1½-lb (700-g) cooked lobsters, cut in half
3 tablespoons (45 ml) garlic oil
salt and freshly ground black pepper
2 tablespoons (30 ml) fresh coriander (Chinese parsley) or parsley, chopped finely
4 fl oz (125 ml, ½ cup) Marsala
3 oz (75 g, ½ cup) dry breadcrumbs
3 tablespoons (45 ml) grated Cheddar or Pecorino cheese

Preheat the grill (broiler). Remove the lobster meat, including that from the claws, from the shells without breaking the main shell, and clean off the orange coral and green intestines. Cut the meat into bite-size pieces. Heat the garlic oil in a sauté pan and brown the lobster pieces in it, then add salt, pepper and coriander (Chinese parsley) or parsley. Cover and simmer for 20 minutes, then add the wine and simmer for a further 3 minutes. Fill the lobster shells with the mixture and sprinkle with breadcrumbs and cheese. Put on a rack in a baking pan and place under the grill (broiler) for a few minutes until it has turned golden brown. Serve immediately.

Preparation time: approximately 30 minutes
Cooking time: approximately 30 minutes

Stir-fried Mangetout (Snow Peas) with Toasted Sesame Seeds

¼ lb (125 g) mangetout (snow peas), topped and tailed
2 tablespoons (30 ml) sesame seeds
1 tablespoon (15 ml) vegetable oil

When you have trimmed the mangetout (snow peas) put them in a bowl of iced water to crisp. They can be kept in this until just before cooking.

In a small frying-pan, *with no oil or butter*, toast the sesame seeds, continually shaking the pan so they do not burn. When they have turned a light golden colour, remove them from the heat and pour them into a bowl.

Just before serving, heat the vegetable oil in a wok or frying-pan, drain the mangetout (snow peas) then stir-fry in the oil for 2–3 minutes, until they are *just* tender but still crunchy. Remove them from the wok with a slotted spoon and put in a heated dish. Sprinkle the toasted sesame seeds over the vegetable and serve immediately.

Preparation time: approximately 25 minutes
Cooking time: 2–3 minutes

*Ginger Ice Cream

The spicy, tangy ice cream is a perfect finish to a Chinese or Indian dinner. This quantity serves 8, but will keep in the freezer for quite a long while.

1 tablespoon (15 ml) ground ginger
¼ teaspoon (1.25 ml) salt
8 oz (225 g, 1 cup) caster (superfine granulated) sugar
12 fl oz (350 ml, 1½ cups) milk
12 fl oz (350 ml, 1½ cups) double (heavy) cream, whipped
1 tablespoon (15 ml) vanilla essence (extract)
preserved ginger and juices (optional)

In a large bowl mix the ground ginger, salt and sugar, then add the milk and stir until the sugar has completely dissolved. Finally stir in the whipped cream and vanilla. Pour the mixture into the bowl of an electric ice cream making machine, and freeze it according to the manufacturer's instructions until almost solid. Remove and place in a plastic container and freeze for 1 hour. Or turn the mixture into ice trays, freeze until almost firm; remove from the freezer and beat with an electric mixer until it becomes fluffy, then return to the ice trays and freeze until nearly firm. Beat once more before finally freezing. Serve with some preserved ginger and its juices poured over the top, if you wish.

Preparation time: 10 minutes
Freezing time: 20 minutes in an electric ice cream machine or 3 hours, minimum, in ice trays

---
DINNER

SERVES 8

*Sorrel Soup
———

Barbecued Prawns (Shrimp) with *Salsa
Picante

or

Victoria's Veal Canigo

Victoria's Catalan Broad Beans
———

*Torta di Nicciole Ciocolata
(Chocolate Nut Torte)

Here you have the tangy soup, then the
barbecued prawns (shrimp) with a spicy
sauce, and broad beans with the chewy
chorizo. Finish with crisp pastry and a
sweet filling. Since the first and last
courses are cold, they can be made well
in advance, as can the Salsa Picante,
with only the prawns (shrimp) and the
broad beans to do at the last minute.

*Sorrel Soup

1 lb (450 g) fresh sorrel, stems removed, leaves
*   washed and shredded*
2 teaspoons (10 ml) salt
2 tablespoons (30 ml) sugar
2 tablespoons (30 ml) lemon juice
3 egg yolks
2 tablespoons (30 ml) milk
8 fl oz (225 ml, 1 cup) plain yoghurt or sour
*   cream*
6 slices streaky bacon, cooked and chopped finely

Place the shredded sorrel leaves in a heavy
enamel saucepan (do not use aluminium or
stainless steel as it will discolour the sorrel). Add 4
pints (2.4 litres, 2½ quarts) water and the salt;
bring the mixture to the boil and cook it over low
heat for 30 minutes. Add the sugar and lemon
juice and cook for an additional 10 minutes.

In a small bowl, beat the egg yolks together
with the milk. Pour 8 fl oz (225 ml, 1 cup) of the
hot soup into the egg and milk mixture, stir and
return the mixture to the saucepan, stirring
constantly. Remove the pan from the heat and
allow the soup to cool. In a bowl, lighten the
yoghurt or sour cream with 4 fl oz (125 ml, ½ cup)
of the cooled soup and return it, stirring, to the
saucepan. If you are going to serve the soup hot,
slowly heat it, but do not allow it to boil otherwise
the yoghurt or sour cream will separate. If
serving cold, chill the soup in the refrigerator for
2 hours. Serve in either hot or chilled soup bowls,
depending, and sprinkle the soup with bacon bits.

Preparation time: 20 minutes
Cooking time: 45 minutes
Chilling time: 2 hours

Barbecued Prawns (Shrimp)

3 lb (1.4 kg) uncooked prawns (shrimp)
14 oz (400 g, 1¾ cups) butter, melted
hot pepper sauce, to taste
paprika, to taste
salt and pepper
3 limes or lemons, sliced
pinch of dried oregano
2 tablespoons (30 ml) chilli sauce
14 fl oz (400 ml, 1¾ cups) dry white wine
3 cloves garlic, crushed

Take off the heads of the prawns (shrimp) and, with a very sharp knife, slice them down the back just enough to remove the black vein. Leave the shells and tails on. In a bowl combine the rest of the ingredients. Place the prawns (shrimp) in a shallow pan and pour over the marinade. Leave them to marinate for 1½ hours or more. Grill (broil) the prawns (shrimp) over charcoal for about 7 minutes or until they turn pink, turning them and basting them often with the marinade. Serve with any remaining sauce or with Salsa Picante.

Preparation time: approximately 30 minutes
Marinating time: 1½ hours
Cooking time: 7–10 minutes

*Salsa Picante

This can be used also with cold chicken or as a spicy salad dressing.

1 medium-sized onion, grated
2 cloves garlic, crushed
1 teaspoon (5 ml) dried rosemary, crushed
coarse sea salt to taste
1 small dried red chilli pepper
6 fl oz (175 ml, ¾ cup) good olive oil
3 fl oz (75 ml, ⅓ cup) red wine vinegar
6 fl oz (175 ml, ¾ cup) red wine

In a food processor or mortar and pestle mix or pound the onion, garlic, rosemary, salt and red chilli to a paste. Remove and put in a bowl. Slowly add the oil, mixing well. Mix the vinegar and wine together in a separate small bowl, then add the oil mixture, stirring well, and leave to stand for a few hours.

Preparation time: approximately 20 minutes
Standing time: 2 hours

Victoria's Veal Canigo

3 lb (1.4 kg) fillet of veal
8 tablespoons (120 ml) olive oil
juice of 2 lemons
4 cloves garlic, sliced
2 tablespoons (30 ml) dried oregano
6–8 sprigs of parsley or fresh coriander (Chinese parsley), chopped
4 oz (125 g, ½ cup) unsalted butter
salt and freshly ground pepper
2 egg yolks
2 lb (900 g) potatoes, peeled, sliced finely and cut into fine straws
vegetable oil

Put the whole piece of veal in a glass or earthenware dish, sprinkle it well with 4 tablespoons (60 ml) olive oil, the lemon juice, slices of garlic, oregano and chopped parsley or coriander (Chinese parsley). Leave the meat to marinate in this dressing for at least 2 hours.

In a medium-sized frying-pan, melt the butter with the remaining olive oil, remove the meat from the dressing, season it with salt and freshly ground pepper to taste, and sauté it over moderate heat for 10 minutes so that it is brown on the outside, but underdone, pink, on the inside.

Meanwhile, remove half the garlic and the parsley or coriander (Chinese parsley) from the dressing and pound it, either in a mortar or in a food processor; add the egg yolk and blend so that it turns into a smooth paste. Add the dressing juice drop by drop, stirring continuously so that it makes a thick mayonnaise sauce.

Carve the meat into thin slices and place them on a heated dish with foil covering it, in a warm oven. Gradually add the fat from the meat to the sauce and pour the sauce over the meat. Keep warm while you make the potato straws.

Heat the vegetable oil in a deep-fat frying-pan until it reaches 360°F (184°C) and fry the potato straws in it until they turn golden. Drain on kitchen paper towels, salt and place around the sliced veal. Serve very hot.

Marinating time: 2–3 hours
Preparation time: 30–40 minutes
Cooking time: approximately 20 minutes

Victoria's Catalan Broad Beans

For this dish lima beans may be substituted.

9 lb (4.1 kg) fresh young broad beans (lima beans)
2 oz (50 g, ¼ cup) lard or unsalted butter
2 fl oz (50 ml, ¼ cup) vegetable or olive oil
¼ lb (125 g) fat salt pork, diced
¼ lb (125 g) chorizo, sliced
1 medium-sized onion, chopped finely
3 cloves garlic, chopped finely
¼ lb (125 g) tomatoes, peeled and chopped
2 sprigs fresh mint
2 tablespoons (30 ml) paprika
4 fl oz (125 ml, ½ cup) dry white wine
salt
1 teaspoon (5 ml) sugar

Shell the beans and keep them in water so that they don't dry out. In a large saucepan, melt the fat in the oil and lightly fry the salt pork and the chorizo for 2–3 minutes. Add the onion, garlic, tomatoes, mint, paprika and wine. Mix carefully. Then cook for 3–4 minutes, until the onions and garlic soften, but do not allow them to brown. Drain and add the beans and salt to taste, then the sugar, stirring gently and shaking the saucepan from time to time so that all the ingredients cook evenly. Cover and cook over low heat for 5–10 minutes or until the beans are tender.

Preparation time: 30–45 minutes
Cooking time: 15–20 minutes

*Torta di Nicciole Ciocolata

To skin hazelnuts easily, put them on a baking tray in an oven preheated to 350°F, 180°C, Mark 4 for 4–5 minutes. Remove, allow to cool slightly and rub off the skins.

6 eggs, separated
8 fl oz (225 g, 1 cup) granulated sugar
3 oz (75 g, 1 cup) semi-sweet chocolate, grated
6 tablespoons (90 ml) dry breadcrumbs, sifted
4 oz (125 g, 1 cup) hazelnuts, skinned and grated
2 teaspoons (10 ml) baking powder
¼ teaspoon (1.25 ml) salt
1 teaspoon (5 ml) vanilla essence (extract)
sweetened whipped cream to taste

Preheat the oven to 350°F, 180°C, Mark 4. In a large bowl beat the egg yolks with an electric hand mixer until they turn thick and light. Add the sugar slowly, stirring constantly, then the chocolate, breadcrumbs, grated nuts, baking powder, salt and vanilla essence (extract). Beat until the mixture is smooth. Beat the egg whites until stiff in another bowl, then fold into the chocolate mixture.

Butter 2 8-inch (20.3-cm) round cake tins, pour in the chocolate mixture and bake them in the preheated oven for about 30 minutes. Remove and cool on cake racks. Spread whipped cream between the two layers and on the top.

Preparation time: approximately 30 minutes
Cooking time: approximately 30 minutes

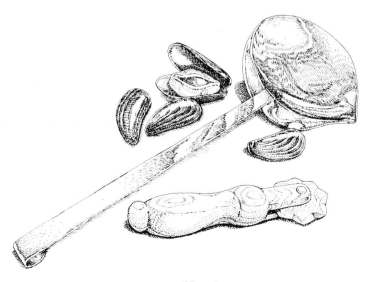

DINNER
SERVES 8

*Carciofi Forno
(Cold Baked Artichokes) (see page 53)

Baked Sea Bass with Mussels or Clams
and *Green Sauce

Fennel in Anchovies with Vinegar Sauce

Spanish Creamed Potatoes

Apricot Fritters

All the new summer products are used in
this menu, with its contrast of sweet and
sour.

Baked Sea Bass with Mussels or Clams

*1 dozen mussels (in England) or hard-shelled
   clams (in America), scrubbed well and beards
   removed*
*1 4½-lb (2-kg) whole sea or striped bass, cleaned
   and boned*
1 teaspoon (5 ml) salt
*½ teaspoon (2.5 ml) dried basil, or 1 teaspoon
   (5 ml) fresh basil, chopped finely*
¼ teaspoon (1.5 ml) freshly ground pepper
2 oz (30 ml) parsley, chopped finely
1 medium-sized onion, sliced thinly
2 celery stalks with leaves, chopped
1 clove garlic, halved
2 bay leaves
4 fl oz (125 ml, ½ cup) dry white wine
4 fl oz (125 ml, ½ cup) melted butter

Preheat the oven to 350°F, 180°C, Mark 4. *Make
sure that any mussels or clams which will not close
are discarded.* Take a large, shallow baking dish
and place the bass in it. Sprinkle the cavity of the
fish with salt, basil, freshly ground pepper and
parsley, then put in half the onion slices.

Place the mussels or clams, onion, celery,
garlic and bay leaves around the fish, and pour
the white wine and butter over the fish. Cover the
dish with foil and bake in the preheated oven for
approximately 50 minutes or until the fish flakes
easily. The mussels and clams should all be open
– discard those which have not opened, along
with the garlic and bay leaves. Serve with Green
Sauce.

Preparation time: 15 minutes
Cooking time: 50 minutes

*Green Sauce

1 bunch fresh coriander (Chinese parsley) or
    parsley, chopped finely
2 stalks celery, chopped finely
½ small onion, chopped finely
1 teaspoon (5 ml) capers
½ teaspoon (2.5 ml) dried oregano
½ teaspoon (2.5 ml) dried basil
1 egg yolk, hard-boiled and chopped
2 tablespoons (30 ml) lemon juice
olive oil

In a bowl or a food processor, combine the parsley, celery, onion, capers, herbs and egg yolks. Then pour in the lemon juice, and finally olive oil, a little at a time, until you have a thick sauce. You may have to add a little more lemon juice, according to taste.

Preparation time: 20 minutes

Fennel in Anchovies with Vinegar Sauce

6 tablespoons (90 ml) olive oil
6–8 canned anchovy fillets, rinsed and minced
8 bulbs Florentine fennel, trimmed and quartered
freshly ground black pepper
½ teaspoon (2.5 ml) powdered mustard
12 fl oz (350 ml, 1½ cups) white wine vinegar
Tabasco sauce (optional)

Heat the olive oil in a large frying-pan and mash the minced anchovies into this. Take the pieces of fennel and cook them slowly in this mixture. Sprinkle them with freshly ground black pepper, to taste. Dissolve the mustard in the vinegar and add it to the fennel mixture. Cover the pan and continue to cook over moderate heat until the fennel is tender, about 15–20 minutes. If you like an added sharpish taste, add a few drops of Tabasco.

Preparation time: approximately 25 minutes
Cooking time: 30–40 minutes

Spanish Creamed Potatoes

3 lb (1.4 kg) potatoes, peeled, washed and cut into
    round slices, ½ inch (1.2 cm) thick
3 tablespoons (45 ml) olive oil or vegetable oil
1½ tablespoons (22 ml) plain (all-purpose) flour
salt to taste
3 cloves garlic, chopped finely
4 tablespoons (60 ml) parsley, chopped finely
juice of 1 lemon
2 eggs, beaten

In a large saucepan, heat the olive oil, then blend in the flour and cook for 1–2 minutes, to eliminate the raw taste of flour. Add the potatoes and cook for 5 minutes. Pour in just enough water to cover the potatoes, season with salt, add the garlic and 2 tablespoons (30 ml) parsley and cook for a further 5–10 minutes, stirring from time to time, making sure not to break the potatoes. When the potatoes are cooked, remove from the heat, add the lemon juice and egg. *Mix very carefully*, turn out on to a heated dish, sprinkle with the remaining parsley and serve.

Preparation time: 25 minutes
Cooking time: approximately 20 minutes

Apricot Fritters

Makes 24 fritters

12 fresh ripe apricots, halved and stones removed
2 tablespoons (30 ml) brandy
sugar, to taste
8 oz (225 g, 1½ cups) plain (all-purpose) flour
½ pint (275 ml, 1¼ cups) milk
2 eggs, separated
1 tablespoon (15 ml) olive oil
safflower or corn oil, for frying
pinch of salt
icing (confectioners') sugar

Sprinkle the halved apricots with brandy and sugar to taste. In a food processor or blender, mix the flour, milk, 2 egg yolks, olive oil and a pinch of salt, then pour the batter into a mixing bowl, cover and leave for 2 hours.

Heat the oil in a deep frying-pan to 360°F (184°C). Beat the egg whites until very stiff and fold them into the batter. Dip each apricot half into the batter, deep fry it until it turns golden in colour, then drain it on kitchen paper towels, and sprinkle it with icing (confectioners') sugar. Keep the fritters warm in a low oven with the door open while you are cooking the rest of them.

Preparation time: 15–20 minutes
Batter resting time: 2 hours
Cooking time: approximately 30 minutes

DINNER

SERVES 6

Asparagi all'Aglio
(Asparagus with Garlic)

Salmon or Sea Bass with Crabmeat Stuffing and *Cucumber and Dill Sauce

or

Petto di Anatra
(Breast of Duck)

*Glazed Carrots

New Potatoes and Mint

Hot Stuffed Peaches with Zabaglione Sauce

In this menu, I try to use all the fresh produce of the summer, the warm asparagus with a piquant garlic sauce, new young salmon with a light crabmeat stuffing and tangy cucumber and dill sauce. To finish there are fresh peaches stuffed with almonds and a cold sweet egg sauce. The carrots and potatoes should be cooked until *just* tender, then reheated slowly. The peaches can be cooking while you are eating the salmon.

Opposite: *Kerala Hot and Spicy Prawns (Shrimp), p. 50*
Overleaf: *(left to right) Ginger Ice Cream, p. 66;*
Tomato and Herb Mousse, p. 63; Cantonese Lobster and
Stir-fried Mangetout (Snow Peas) with Toasted Sesame
Seeds, pp. 65–6

Asparagi all'Aglio

3 lb (1.4 kg) asparagus, tough stems and scales
  removed
hot garlic olive oil (olive oil in which garlic cloves
  have been soaking for 2 days)
salt and pepper
2 oz (50 g, $\frac{1}{2}$ cup) Parmesan cheese, grated

Tie the asparagus into small bunches. Stand in 2
inches (5 cm) rapidly boiling, salted water. Cover
tips with the inverted half of a double boiler.
Steam for 15 minutes. Drain, serve with hot garlic
oil as a dressing, season and sprinkle with the
cheese.

Preparation time: approximately 20 minutes
Cooking time: 15 minutes

Salmon or Sea Bass with Crabmeat Stuffing

This dish may be either baked in the oven or
grilled (broiled), in a double layer of foil on a
barbecue for 1 hour, turning once.

6–8-lb (2.7–3.6-kg) fresh salmon or sea bass,
  cleaned and scaled
salt
$2\frac{1}{2}$ oz (62 g, $\frac{1}{2}$ cup) celery, chopped finely
$2\frac{1}{2}$ oz (62 g, $\frac{1}{2}$ cup) onions, chopped finely
2 oz (50 g, $\frac{1}{4}$ cup) butter
$\frac{1}{2}$ teaspoon (2.5 ml) dried sage
$\frac{1}{2}$ teaspoon (2.5 ml) pepper
$7\frac{1}{2}$-oz (212-g) can white crabmeat, or fresh white
  crabmeat, picked over
6 oz (175 g) fresh bread cubes
vegetable oil

Preheat the oven to 350°F, 180°C, Mark 4. Rinse
the salmon, pat it dry, sprinkle salt on the inside
and outside and lay it aside. In a sauté pan cook
the celery and onion in butter until they are just
tender. Add 1 teaspoon (5 ml) salt, the sage,
pepper and crabmeat. Mix well, then add the
bread cubes and toss together. Fill the salmon
cavity with this mixture and fasten with skewers.
Coat the outside of the fish with oil.

Place the fish in a shallow pan and bake in the
preheated oven for 1–1$\frac{1}{2}$ hours, or until the fish
flakes easily with a fork. Baste with the dripping
twice during the baking. Serve with Cucumber,
Dill and Caper Sauce.

Preparation time: 20–25 minutes
Cooking time: 1$\frac{3}{4}$ hours

*Cucumber and Dill Sauce

5 oz (150 g, 1 cup) cucumber, seeded and diced
white wine
2 tablespoons (30 ml) butter
2 tablespoons (30 ml) plain (all-purpose) flour
2 teaspoons (10 ml) lemon juice
1 teaspoon (5 ml) grated lemon rind
1 teaspoon (5 ml) grated onion
$\frac{1}{2}$ teaspoon (2.5 ml) salt
few grains of pepper
1 tablespoon (15 ml) fresh dill, chopped finely
1 tablespoon (15 ml) capers

Cook the cucumber in 4 fl oz (125 ml, $\frac{1}{2}$ cup) water
until it becomes tender. Drain and measure the
cooking water. Add wine to make up to 8 fl oz
(225 ml, 1 cup). In a saucepan make a white roux
by melting the butter and mixing in the flour,
then add the cooking water. Mix thoroughly and
cook, stirring, until the sauce turns smooth and
thickens. Add the remaining ingredients and the
cooked cucumbers. Serve warm.

Preparation time: 20–25 minutes
Cooking time: approximately 25 minutes

Opposite: *Pear and Green Peppercorn Sorbet, p. 77*

Petto di Anatra

3 ducks
3 eggs, beaten
6 oz (175 g, 1 cup) dry breadcrumbs
4 tablespoons (60 ml) bacon dripping or lard, or
 groundnut (peanut) oil
1 teaspoon (5 ml) salt
2 bay leaves
2 cloves garlic, chopped finely
4 whole cloves
freshly ground black pepper
2 fl oz (50 ml, ¼ cup) red wine vinegar
1 bouquet garni: thyme and parsley
4 fl oz (125 ml, ½ cup) tomato ketchup (catsup)
4 fl oz (125 ml, ½ cup) red wine
12-oz (350-g) jar redcurrant jelly

Fillet the breasts of the duck and cut them lengthwise into 3 pieces each. Use the rest of the bird for soup. Dip the strips of breast into the beaten eggs, then into the breadcrumbs so that they have a thin layer of the breadcrumbs on both sides. Allow to rest on kitchen paper towels.

In a deep sauté pan heat the bacon dripping or lard, add the salt, bay leaves, garlic, whole cloves and freshly ground black pepper. Mix well, then brown the duck fillets in this mixture. In a bowl mix the vinegar, bouquet garni and tomato ketchup (catsup), and pour over the duck. Cover and allow it to simmer over low heat for 1 hour. Ten minutes before the end of the cooking time, add the red wine and redcurrant jelly and stir in thoroughly. Serve hot.

Preparation time: 30–40 minutes
Cooking time: approximately 1¼ hours

*Glazed Carrots

2 lb (900 g) new young carrots, sliced thinly
2 fl oz (50 ml, ¼ cup) clear honey
2 tablespoons (30 ml) butter
2 tablespoons (30 ml) fresh coriander (Chinese
 parsley), minced

In a medium-sized saucepan place the honey and 8 fl oz (225 ml, 1 cup) water; mix together, then add the carrots. Cook the vegetable over a high heat for 7 minutes or until the carrots are just tender. Pour away all but about 2 fl oz (50 ml, ¼ cup) of the liquid. Add the butter and leave covered until needed. When ready to serve, heat up and stir while the butter is melting. Then drain and sprinkle the carrots with the fresh coriander (Chinese parsley).

Preparation time: approximately 20 minutes
Cooking time: approximately 7 minutes

Hot Stuffed Peaches with Zabaglione Sauce

3 fresh just ripe peaches or nectarines, cut in half,
 peeled and stones removed
3 tablespoons (45 ml) almond flakes, chopped
 finely
3 tablespoons (45 ml) cake crumbs
granulated sugar
4 fl oz (125 ml, ½ cup) dry white wine or medium
 dry sherry

Preheat the oven to 350°F, 180°C, Mark 4. Take a baking dish, place the peach or nectarine halves in it, cavity side up. Fill the cavities with almonds and cake crumbs, sprinkle sugar on top, then cover with the white wine or sherry and bake in the preheated oven for 15–20 minutes. Serve hot with cold zabaglione sauce.

Zabaglione Sauce

This sauce may also be served on its own as a dessert, in tall glasses.

6 eggs
¼ teaspoon (1.25 ml) salt
4 tablespoons (60 ml) icing (confectioners') sugar
6 tablespoons (90 ml) sweet sherry

In the top of a double boiler, combine the eggs, salt and sugar, then place it over hot water on low heat and beat constantly with a wire whisk, for 8–10 minutes. Then gradually whisk in the sherry and continue beating until the mixture is thick enough to stand a spoon up in it. Serve hot or cold.

Preparation time: 15–20 minutes
Cooking time: 15–20 minutes

DINNER

SERVES 6

*Wild Mushroom Soup

*Japanese Twice-fried Chicken and
Beansprouts

or

Stufato di Pesce al Forno
(Baked Stuffed Haddock)

Small Whole Beetroot Sautéd in Butter
and Chives

*Pear and Green Peppercorn Sorbet

*Biscotti di Mandorle
(Almond Biscuits, Cookies)

It is preferable to use the wild field
mushrooms available in the summer, but
cultivated ones may be used for this very
'mushroomy' soup. The tang of the
gingery chicken and beansprouts (which
may be prepared ahead up to the last
'fry') is brought into perspective when
you taste the surprise of a sweet pear
sorbet with a peppery bite.

*Wild Mushroom Soup

Makes about 3 pints

*1 lb (450 g) fresh wild mushrooms, or any
   cultivated ones*
juice of $\frac{1}{2}$ lemon
1 medium-sized onion, chopped finely
1$\frac{3}{4}$ pints (950 ml, 2 pints) chicken stock (broth)
$\frac{1}{4}$ lb (125 g, $\frac{1}{2}$ cup) unsalted butter
6 tablespoons (90 ml) plain (all-purpose) flour
1 pint (600 ml, 1$\frac{1}{4}$ pints) milk, scalded
8 fl oz (225 ml, 1 cup) double (heavy) cream
salt and white pepper
Tabasco sauce
2 tablespoons (30 ml) dry sherry (optional)

Wipe any dirt off the mushrooms and cut off the
stems. Slice 6 caps and reserve. Chop the remaining stems (discarding any dried ends) and caps
very finely and sprinkle with lemon juice. Place
the chopped mushrooms in a deep saucepan, add
the chopped onion and cover with the stock or
broth. Simmer for 30 minutes. In a small saucepan melt 1 tablespoon (15 ml) butter and sauté
the reserved mushroom caps until they turn light
golden. Sprinkle with lemon juice and reserve.

In a large saucepan, melt the remaining butter,
stir in the flour with a wire whisk until it turns
into a smooth white roux. Add the scalded milk,
whisking continuously over low heat until the
mixture becomes smooth and thick. Remove
from the heat and add the cream. Combine the
mushroom-broth mixture with the cream sauce
and season to taste with salt, white pepper and
Tabasco. Reheat the soup and add the sherry, if
you wish, just before serving. Pour into heated
soup bowls and garnish with the reserved sliced
mushrooms.

Preparation time: approximately 30 minutes
Cooking time: approximately 1 hour 10 minutes

*Japanese Twice-fried Chicken and Beansprouts

Kara-age is the Japanese method of 'dry frying' which means that although the meat or fish is dredged in cornflour (cornstarch) it is not dipped in a batter. Therefore this thin outer coating seals the surface but the oil is allowed to seep through to cook the food.

The food is deep fried twice, some cook it on a lower temperature first, then raise the heat. I prefer doing it the other way round. Also I find that you can do the first deep frying in a wok about 1 hour before serving, leaving it covered with kitchen paper towels. Then if you have an electric deep fryer, cook it at a lower heat for 10 minutes in that, because inevitably, it will take a larger amount of food than the wok. Also you can be eating the first batch while the second is cooking. I find that everyone eats much more of this than of a Western roast chicken.

3–3½-lb (1.4–1.6-kg) frying chicken, boned and
    cut into large bite-sized pieces, with the skin on
3 fl oz (75 ml, ⅓ cup) sake or dry sherry
3 fl oz (75 ml, ⅓ cup) Japanese soy sauce or
    Chinese thin soy sauce (the Japanese soy sauce
    is lighter than the Chinese)
1½ inches (3.8 cm) fresh ginger, peeled and very
    finely chopped
2 large cloves garlic, very finely chopped
4 oz (125 g, ⅘ cup) plain (all-purpose) flour
2 oz (50 g, ½ cup) cornflour (cornstarch)
kona sansko (Japanese fragrant pepper) or hua
    chiao salt
groundnut (peanut) oil
sesame oil
1 lb (450 g) beansprouts
4 spring (green) onions, chopped into tiny rings,
    white and green parts separated
1 tablespoon (15 ml) oyster sauce
lemon quarters

Hua chiao salt:
1 tablespoon (15 ml) Szechuan peppercorns
2 tablespoons (30 ml) sea salt

If using hua chiao salt, make that first. In a wok or frying-pan, without stirring, dry fry the peppercorns until they turn to a brownish colour. Do not allow them to burn. Remove them and put them in a mortar, or an electric coffee grinder. Then repeat the process with salt until it turns a reddish brown. Pour into the mortar or electric coffee grinder with the Szechuan peppercorns. Grind the two together. If you do not use it all, keep it in an airtight container for a few weeks, no longer, otherwise it loses its fragrance.

For the chicken, in a shallow baking dish, mix together the sake or dry sherry, soy sauce, chopped ginger and garlic. Put the chicken pieces into the marinade and turn once so that both sides are well coated. This may be done 1 hour before, or as I often do, in the morning for use in the evening. Whichever you do, make sure that you turn the pieces fairly frequently.

About 1 hour before serving, place the flour, cornflour (cornstarch) and either Japanese fragrant pepper or hua chiao salt in a flat dish or plate. Dip the pieces of chicken in this mixture, coating them well but shaking off any excess flour. Then place on a piece of paper and allow them to rest for about 5 minutes. Reserve the marinade for the beansprouts.

In a wok, heat enough groundnut (peanut) oil to cook 4 or 5 pieces of chicken at a time to 350°F (180°C). Add a few drops of sesame oil for fragrance. Then slide in 4 or 5 pieces of chicken and, turning them, cook them for about 1 minute until they turn light brown. Repeat until all the pieces have been cooked. Drain them well on kitchen paper towels. Then cover them with another piece of paper towel.

When ready to serve, reserve the oil in the wok for the beansprouts and heat up fresh oil in an electric deep fryer to 325°F (170°C), adding a few drops of sesame oil at the last minute. Place in the frying basket as many chicken pieces as will lie in one layer, and cook for 10 minutes. When ready the chicken should be deep brown and crispy.

While the chicken is in its second frying process, stir-fry the beansprouts. Strain and reserve the marinade liquid, and keep the ginger and garlic separately. Drain off two-thirds of the oil from the wok, and heat the rest until a haze of smoke rises. Then add the ginger and garlic and stir-fry until they colour slightly. Add the spring (green) onions, then the beansprouts. Stir-fry them, continually tossing them in the oil, ginger, garlic and onion for 2½–3 minutes, so they are tender but crisp. Remove them with a wire scoop so that the oil is left behind, and place them in the centre of the serving dish. Add the oyster sauce to

76

the remaining chicken marinade, mix and pour over beansprouts just enough to give a delicate taste but not to drown the beansprouts.

When the first batch of chicken is cooked either eat it immediately or place it in a heated serving dish in a low oven with the door open. Repeat with the remaining chicken. Serve with the beansprouts and lemon wedges, to squeeze over the chicken.

Preparation time: approximately 30 minutes
Marinating time: 1–24 hours
Cooking time: approximately 30 minutes

Stufato di Pesce al Forno

olive oil
2 oz (50 g, ½ cup) celery, chopped finely
2 tablespoons (30 ml) green pepper, chopped finely
2 tablespoons (30 ml) onion, chopped finely
6 oz (175 g, 2 cups) fresh breadcrumbs
2 tablespoons (30 ml) grated Cheddar or Pecorino cheese
1 teaspoon (5 ml) salt
freshly ground black pepper
¼ teaspoon (1.25 ml) saffron
3-lb (1.4-kg) haddock or cod, cleaned and gutted

Preheat the oven to 375°F, 190°C, Mark 5. In a small sauté pan heat 3 tablespoons (45 ml) olive oil and cook the celery, green pepper and onion until they have turned a golden brown. In a large bowl mix the breadcrumbs, cheese and seasonings. Add the cooked vegetables and mix well. Stuff the haddock with this mixture and close the opening with skewers. Place the fish on a rack in a baking pan, brush it with olive oil and bake it in the preheated oven for 25 minutes.

Preparation time: approximately 30 minutes
Cooking time: 25 minutes

Pear and Green Peppercorn Sorbet

2 large pears, peeled, cored and chopped
3 tablespoons (45 ml) lemon juice
6 fl oz (175 ml, ¾ cup) simple sugar syrup (see page 78)
2 tablespoons (30 ml) dried green peppercorns (not in brine)

In a food processor, blender or vegetable mill, purée the pears, then mix in the lemon juice to prevent them from discolouring and also to bring out their taste. Mix in the sugar syrup. Place the sorbet mixture either in a sorbetière and proceed according to the manufacturer's instructions, or in an ice tray and place in the freezer for approximately 1 hour or until it begins to harden. Take out and mix in a food processor or with a fork. Return it to the freezer.

Whether using an ice tray or sorbetière, mix in the green peppercorns *just before the sorbet totally freezes, mixing them evenly, so that they remain whole throughout the sorbet.* In this way, when you eat the sorbet the first taste is a delicate one of pear, then when you bite a peppercorn, there is a surprise spicy taste.

Preparation time: 10 minutes
Cooking time: If freezing in an electric ice cream machine 20–30 minutes
If freezing in ice trays 1–3 hours

*Simple Sugar Syrup

Makes 1¾ pints (1 litre, 1 quart)

2 lb (900 g) granulated sugar

Dissolve the sugar in 1¾ pints (1 litre, 1 quart) water, bring to the boil and remove from the heat. Cool. Use as needed. This syrup will keep in well corked bottles in the refrigerator for 1 month.

*Biscotti di Mandorle

Makes about 4 dozen biscuits (cookies)

7 oz (200 g, 1⅓ cups) plain (cake) flour, sifted
¼ teaspoon (1.25 ml) baking powder
pinch of salt
4 oz (125 g, ½ cup) butter
4 oz (125 g, ½ cup) granulated sugar
2 eggs, well beaten
¼ teaspoon (1.25 ml) lemon essence (extract)
3 oz (75 g, ½ cup) unblanched almonds, chopped finely

In a medium-sized bowl combine the sifted flour with the baking powder and salt. Sift again. In a large bowl cream the butter with the sugar, until it turns light and foamy; add 1 egg and the lemon essence (extract), and mix well. Mix the sifted dry ingredients into the creamed mixture, then fold in the almonds. Allow the dough to rest in the refrigerator for 30 minutes.

Preheat the oven to 425°F, 220°C, Mark 7. Roll the dough out on a lightly floured board to about ⅛ inch (0.3 cm) thick. Cut into any shape you like, place on ungreased baking trays, brush with beaten egg and bake in the preheated oven for 8–10 minutes.

Preparation time: approximately 30 minutes
Dough resting time: 30 minutes
Cooking time: 8–10 minutes

— SUNDAY NIGHT SUPPER —
SERVES 6

Austrian Eggs Czernin

Fried Parsley

---

*Cold Veal with Pimento Sauce

or

Polpette alla Napolitana with *Agro Dolce Sauce
(Sweet and Sour Meatballs)

Fagioli Bolliti all'Aglio
(Kidney Beans with Garlic)

Coffee and *Boals de Figo
(Fig and Almond Delight)

Austrian Eggs Czernin

6 rounds of bread, 2½ inches (6.3 cm) thick
6 eggs, separated
6 oz (175 g, 1½ cups) Cheddar or Gruyère cheese, grated
salt and freshly ground black pepper
freshly ground nutmeg
oil for shallow and deep frying

In a shallow frying-pan, fry the bread rounds on *one side only* until they are lightly browned. Drain and leave to cool.

In a bowl beat the egg yolks, then mix in the grated cheese until it turns into a very thick, sticky paste. Season with salt, pepper and ground nutmeg to taste. In a separate bowl beat the egg whites until they hold stiff peaks. In a deep-fat frying-pan heat the oil until it reaches 375°F (190°C). Just before serving, pile the egg and cheese mixture on to the *cooked* side of the bread round, then top with lots of the egg white and quickly deep fry the whole mixture until the bread is brown on the under-side. You can check this by lifting it out with a flat spatula or fish slice from time to time. Serve immediately surrounded by Fried Parsley.

Fried Parsley

1½ large bunches of parsley
vegetable oil for deep-fat frying
soy sauce to taste
2 small cloves garlic, very finely chopped
½ teaspoon (2.5 ml) caster (superfine granulated)
    sugar

Wash and drain the parsley and divide it into
small bunches. Trim the stems short and dry the
bunches thoroughly. Heat the oil to 390°F
(200°C), then plunge the parsley, a few bunches
at a time, into the very hot oil for 30–40 seconds,
or until they are crisp. Drain on kitchen paper
towels. Warm the soy sauce, chopped garlic and
sugar together in a small saucepan. Place the
fried parsley around the Eggs Czernin and
sprinkle the parsley with the sauce.

Preparation time: 35–40 minutes
Cooking time: 20–25 minutes

*Cold Veal with Pimento Sauce

I ate this distinctive summer dish years ago in
Spain.

1½ lb (700 g) fillet of veal
2 fl oz (50 ml, ¼ cup) olive oil
1 bay leaf
2 sprigs thyme
1 clove
2 tablespoons (30 ml) medium dry sherry
12 black peppercorns
salt to taste

Pimento Sauce:
2½-oz (65-g) can red pimentos, drained
1 egg yolk
pinch of salt
olive oil
juice of ½ lemon

In a casserole, heat the olive oil and brown the
meat on all sides. Add the remaining ingredients
and enough water to cover the meat. Cover and
cook over low heat for 1½ hours until the meat is
tender but still pink inside.

In a large mortar and pestle, or a food processor
or blender, purée the pimento, then add the egg
yolk, salt and olive oil, little by little, stirring
constantly as you would with mayonnaise until
you achieve a creamy, thick sauce. Finally add
the lemon juice and mix again.

When the meat is cooked, cool it in the liquid
then remove it, reserving the liquid as a stock for
soup, and slice it quite thinly. Pour a little
pimento sauce over each slice and serve.

Preparation time: approximately 25 minutes
Cooking time: approximately 1¼ hours

Polpette alla Napolitana

1 lb (450 g) cooked minced meat
¼ lb (125 g) fresh or commercial suet, chopped
    finely
5 oz (150 g, 1 cup) currants
3 oz (75 g, ½ cup) almonds, chopped finely
grated rind of 1 lemon
1 teaspoon (5 ml) ground mixed spice
2 oz (50 g, ½ cup) icing (confectioners') sugar
4 oz (125 g, 1¼ cups) fresh breadcrumbs
4 fl oz (125 ml, ½ cup) milk
4 egg yolks
3 egg whites
3 oz (75 g, ½ cup) dry breadcrumbs
¼ lb (125 g, ½ cup) butter
caster (superfine granulated) sugar
Agro Dolce Sauce (see page 80)
fresh coriander (Chinese parsley) or parsley,
    chopped

In a large bowl mix together the minced meat,
chopped suet, currants, chopped almonds, lemon
rind, mixed spice and icing (confectioners')
sugar. Soak the breadcrumbs in the milk for 5
minutes, then strain and put them in the same
bowl, mixing well. In a small bowl beat the egg
yolks and 2 egg whites together and pour on to
the meat mixture where it must be incorporated
thoroughly.

Make small, round flat cakes, approximately 2
inches (5 cm) diameter, dip in the remaining egg
white and roll in dry breadcrumbs. In a large
frying-pan, melt the butter, bring it to the bubble
and sauté the polpette in it until the breadcrumbs
become light golden in colour. Remove to a
heated serving dish, sprinkle with sugar and
serve with Agro Dolce Sauce separately. Garnish
with fresh coriander (Chinese parsley) or parsley.

Preparation time: 30–40 minutes
Cooking time: 20–25 minutes

*Agro Dolce Sauce

4 oz (125 g, $\frac{1}{4}$ cup) icing (confectioners') sugar
15 fl oz (425 ml, scant 2 cups) white wine vinegar
2 oz (50 g, $\frac{1}{3}$ cup) almonds, chopped finely
2 oz (50 g, $\frac{1}{3}$ cup) currants
1 oz (25 g, $\frac{1}{3}$ cup) chocolate Meunier (semi-sweet
  chocolate), grated

In a small saucepan, dissolve the sugar in the vinegar. Add the rest of the ingredients and cook over low heat, stirring with a wooden spoon until it just comes to the boil. Serve hot or cold.

Cooking time: approximately 10 minutes

Fagioli Bolliti all'Aglio

If you can find the Italian white kidney beans, cannellini, either dried or canned, they are the best.

1 lb (450 g) kidney beans, dried or canned
3 tablespoons (45 ml) olive oil
2 cloves garlic, chopped finely
2 tablespoons (30 ml) fresh coriander (Chinese
  parsley) or Italian parsley, chopped finely
$\frac{1}{2}$ teaspoon (2.5 ml) dried marjoram
$\frac{1}{4}$ teaspoon (1.25 ml) cayenne pepper
salt to taste

If you are using dried beans, soak them overnight in water, then drain. Then cook the beans, soaked or canned, in boiling water until tender. Drain, then sauté them in hot olive oil with the garlic, fresh coriander (Chinese parsley) or parsley, marjoram and cayenne. Season with salt to taste. Serve hot.

Soaking time: 12 hours
Preparation time: approximately 20 minutes
Cooking time: approximately 30 minutes

*Boals de Figo

If using dried figs in this recipe, remove the hard stalks. These little delights are particularly good served with coffee.

10 oz (275 g, 1$\frac{1}{4}$ cups) caster (superfine
  granulated) sugar
rind of 1 orange, chopped finely
10 oz (275 g) figs, fresh or dried, chopped finely
10 oz (275 g) almonds, blanched and chopped
  finely
2$\frac{1}{4}$ oz (55 g) unsweetened chocolate, chopped finely
caster (superfine granulated) sugar

In a medium-sized saucepan combine the sugar with 4 fl oz (125 ml, $\frac{1}{2}$ cup) water and boil them for 3 minutes, or until the mixture becomes slightly syrupy. Add the orange rind, figs, almonds and chocolate. Pour the mixture on to a plate to cool, then shape it into small balls and roll them in caster (superfine granulated) sugar.

Preparation time: approximately 25 minutes
Cooking time: approximately 3 minutes

Autumn

── SPECIAL DINNER PARTY ──
SERVES 6

*Soufflé Roulé aux Epinards
with *Fresh Coriander Cream Sauce

Barbecued Devilled Pheasants or Guinea
Hens

*Jerusalem Artichoke Chips

*Yan Kit's Chinese Pickled Cabbage,
Peking-style

*Flaming Fruit with Brandy Sauce (see
page 107)

The first course may be prepared 1–2
days ahead of the party and the pickled
cabbage is much better when prepared a
day in advance. The artichoke chips may
be deep fried 1 hour in advance and kept
warm in an oven _with the door open_, to
prevent them from becoming soggy. Only
the pheasant or guinea hen need be
cooked at the last minute.

*Soufflé Roulé aux Epinards

(adapted from Nathalie Hambro's _Particular
Delights_)

$1\frac{1}{2}$ lb (750 g) fresh spinach, or 1 lb (450 g) frozen
 leaf spinach
3 oz (75 g, $\frac{1}{3}$ cup) butter
3 oz (75 g, $\frac{1}{2}$ cup plus 1 tablespoon) plain (all-
 purpose) flour
$\frac{1}{2}$ pint (300 ml, $1\frac{1}{4}$ cups) hot milk
mace, nutmeg
salt and freshly ground black pepper
2 eggs, separated
2–3 thin slices smoked salmon, cut into narrow
 strips
2–3 large green outside leaves of spring cabbage

For the filling:
1 large or 2 small smoked trout
$3\frac{1}{2}$-oz (100-g) jar red lumpfish roe
4 tablespoons (60 ml) sour cream (do not
 substitute yoghurt)
1–2 tablespoons (15–30 ml) grated horseradish or
 2–3 tablespoons (30–45 ml) very strong
 commercial horseradish cream

Preheat the oven to 400°F, 200°C, Mark 6. Strip
the spines off and wash the fresh spinach
thoroughly. Drain, but not completely, leaving a
little water clinging to the leaves. In a saucepan,
cook the spinach, without extra water, for 5
minutes, stirring with a wooden spoon until the
spinach has wilted, but is still bright green and
rather dry. Alternatively, chop the thawed frozen
spinach, squeezing out the water.

Make a white sauce. Melt the butter in a large
saucepan, stir in the flour until the mixture is
smooth, then gradually add the hot milk.
Simmer, stirring continually, until the sauce
thickens. Add freshly grated nutmeg and mace to
taste, then the spinach and the 2 beaten egg
yolks. Whisk the egg whites until stiff. Fold them
carefully into the spinach mixture, with a metal
spoon so as not to break them. Take a baking tray
(the Swiss roll type is best) about 12 × 16 inches
(30 × 40 cm) and line it with foil, generously
greased (this is important as otherwise the soufflé
will stick). Spread the mixture evenly and bake
for 20 minutes in the preheated oven. Meanwhile
prepare the filling: remove the skin and bones
from the trout and flake the flesh into a bowl, stir
in the red lumpfish roe, horseradish and sour
cream; reserve.

Have ready a slightly damp cloth and overturn
the soufflé on to it. Carefully peel off the foil with

the aid of a small knife to loosen it. Trim the edges neatly and leave to cool slightly. Now spread the filling lengthwise down the centre of the soufflé. Lifting the edge of the towel, lift and fold one side, then the other over the middle so that the roll is the same length as the original soufflé, but a third of the width. Place a new piece of buttered foil on top of the roll and turn it upside down. Now slide a baking tray underneath to carry it more easily and remove the cloth. Decorate the soufflé with the strips of smoked salmon, making a trellis pattern. Wrap the roll tightly in the foil and leave to rest in the refrigerator for at least 2 hours, but it can be made up to 2 days ahead (this helps the roll to keep its shape).

When ready to serve, preheat the oven to 350°F, 180°C, Mark 4. Then place the roll, still wrapped to keep it moist, in the oven for 20 minutes. Place the spring cabbage leaves on an unheated plate, remove the foil from the heated roll, transfer it to the lined dish and serve with Fresh Coriander Cream Sauce.

As an alternative filling, a less expensive one, you can use 8 oz (225 g) chopped cooked ham, 4 tablespoons (60 ml) sour cream and 2 tablespoons (30 ml) French-type mustard or to taste. Decorate with 3 slices of ham in the same trellis pattern.

*Fresh Coriander Cream Sauce

1 bunch fresh coriander (Chinese parsley)
2 tablespoons (30 ml) very strong commercial
_   horseradish cream_
5 fl oz (150 ml, ⅔ cup) sour cream

Mince the coriander (Chinese parsley) in a food processor, then stir in the remaining ingredients. Chill until needed.

Preparation time: approximately 30 minutes
Cooking time: approximately 1 hour

Barbecued Devilled Pheasants

3 pheasants or guinea hens cut in half
6 tablespoons (90 ml) good French green
_   peppercorn mustard_
1 teaspoon (5 ml) cayenne pepper
6 oz (175 g, 1 cup) dry breadcrumbs
4 oz (125 g, ½ cup) butter, melted

For the sauce:
4 tablespoons (60 ml) red wine vinegar
10 black peppercorns
3 shallots, chopped finely
1 pint (600 ml, 1¼ pints) Brown Sauce (see page
_   180)_
1½ teaspoons (7.5 ml) French peppercorn mustard
1½ teaspoons (7.5 ml) Worcestershire sauce
salt and cayenne pepper
2 tablespoons (30 ml) butter

Coat the pheasants with a mixture of green peppercorn mustard and cayenne pepper. Roll the pheasants in the breadcrumbs and press them tightly on with a palette knife. Drip the melted butter over the birds and barbecue them on a grill over hot charcoal for 1 hour, or under a grill (broiler) for 30 minutes.

Meanwhile make the sauce. In a small saucepan, combine the vinegar, peppercorns and shallots and cook until the liquid has been reduced to 1 tablespoon (15 ml). Add the Brown Sauce, the mustard and Worcestershire sauce, salt and cayenne pepper to taste. Finish it off by whisking in the butter. Serve the sauce separately in a sauce boat.

Preparation time: 20–25 minutes
Cooking time: 30–60 minutes

*Jerusalem Artichoke Chips

1½ lb (700 g) Jerusalem artichokes, cleaned and
  peeled
vegetable oil
salt and freshly ground pepper

On the thin slicer of a food processor or a
mandoline, slice the artichokes as you would for
game chips (potato chips). Put them in cold water
for a few minutes, then dry them with a clean
cloth. Heat the oil in a deep-fat frying -pan with a
basket until it reaches 360°F (184°C). Put the
artichoke slices into the basket and fry them in
the oil until they turn a light brown. When
cooked, remove them and put them in a low oven
on a dish lined with kitchen paper towels to drain
and dry; leaving the door slightly ajar. Sprinkle
them with salt and freshly ground black pepper.

Preparation time: 15 minutes
Cooking time: approximately 20 minutes

*Yan Kit's Chinese Pickled Cabbage, Peking-style

2 lb (900 g) white cabbage, quartered and cored
2 tablespoons (30 ml) salt
½–¾ inch (1–2 cm) fresh ginger, peeled and cut
  into silky threads
5 tablespoons (75 ml) sugar
2½ tablespoons (37.5 ml) groundnut (peanut) or
  corn oil
2½ tablespoons (37.5 ml) sesame oil
3 dried red chillies, seeded and chopped
1 teaspoon (5 ml) Szechuan peppercorns
5 tablespoons (75 ml) rice vinegar

Shred the cabbage as finely as possible either in a
food processor or with a knife. Put into a very
large mixing bowl, sprinkle with the salt and mix.
Leave to stand at room temperature for 2–3
hours; the cabbage will decrease in bulk having
released some of its water content. Take a
handful at a time and, using both hands, squeeze
out the excess water but leave damp. Transfer to
a serving bowl.

Place the ginger threads in a bunch on top of
the cabbage in the centre of the bowl. Sprinkle in
the sugar, taking care not to put it over the
ginger. Heat the groundnut (peanut) oil and
sesame oil in a small saucepan over a high heat
until smoke rises. Remove from the heat and then
add the chillies and peppercorns. Pour the mixture over the ginger first and then the surrounding cabbage in the bowl. The sizzling oil partially
cooks the ginger, enhancing the flavour. Add the
vinegar and mix well. Leave to stand at room
temperature for 2–3 hours before serving.

Marinating time: 3 hours
Preparation time: approximately 30 minutes
Additional marinating time: 3 hours

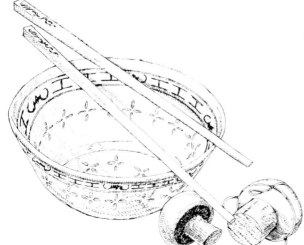

——— DINNER FOR A ———
SPECIAL OCCASION
SERVES 8

*Crabmeat and Avocado Bisque

———

Pheasant in Brandy

*Lebanese Spiced Rice

Braised Cabbage à la Grecque

———

*Chocolate Mousse Meringues

This is a very rich menu, but for a really
special dinner party it is perfect. The joy
of it is that only the pheasant and
cabbage must be prepared during dinner.
The pheasant can be put to cook just
before everyone sits down, then the
spiced rice can also be finished off in the
same oven, and the cabbage cooked.

*Crabmeat and Avocado Bisque

2 avocados, peeled and stones removed
3 tablespoons (45 ml) lemon juice
2 dashes of Tabasco sauce
large pinch each of celery salt and ground cumin
salt
6 oz (175 g, ¾ cup) butter
3 onions, minced
2 stalks celery, minced
3 oz (75 g, ¾ cup) plain (all-purpose) flour
2 pints (1.1 litres, 2½ pints) fish stock (broth) or
    bottled clam juice
2 6½-oz (185-g) cans minced clams, drained
10 oz (275 g) king crabmeat, white only, cooked,
    flaked and picked over
10 fl oz (300 ml, 1¼ cups) double (heavy) cream
large pinch of cayenne pepper
freshly ground white pepper to taste

In a bowl mash the avocado with a silver fork, so
that it doesn't turn brown, until it is almost
smooth, then stir in the lemon juice, Tabasco,
ground cumin, celery salt and salt to taste. In a
heavy saucepan cook the onion and celery in the
butter over low heat, stirring, for 5 minutes, or

until the vegetables are translucent. Add the flour
and cook the roux, stirring, for 5 minutes. Stir in
the fish stock (broth) or clam juice and minced
clams. Simmer the mixture, stirring occasionally,
for 10 minutes. *Up to this point the soup may be
prepared in advance.*

Add the cooked crabmeat, cream, a pinch of
cayenne and freshly ground white pepper to
taste. Place the soup over moderate heat until it
has heated through, but do not allow it to boil.
Ladle the soup into heated bowls and stir 1
heaped tablespoon (20 ml) of the avocado mixture into each serving. Serve immediately.

Preparation time: approximately 20 minutes
Cooking time: approximately 30 minutes

Pheasant in Brandy

8 oz (225 g, 1 cup) butter
4 pheasants, cleaned and cut in half
1 lb (450 g) mushrooms, cleaned and stems
    removed
4 tomatoes, peeled and quartered
16 fl oz (475 ml, 1 pint) dry white wine
8 fl oz (225 ml, 1 cup) pheasant or beef stock
3 tablespoons (45 ml) brandy, or to taste
salt and freshly ground black pepper
fresh coriander (Chinese parsley) or parsley,
    chopped
snipped fresh chives

In a casserole, melt the butter and brown the
pheasant halves over a high heat, turning them
often. Lower the heat to medium and add the
mushrooms and tomatoes. Cook for 5 minutes,
then add the white wine, stock and brandy.
Season with salt and freshly ground black pepper
and cook for an additional 20 minutes.

Remove the pheasant pieces to a hot dish, and
add the fresh coriander (Chinese parsley) or
parsley and chives to the sauce. Reduce it a little
over high heat, then pour the sauce over the
pheasants and serve very hot.

Preparation time: approximately 20 minutes
Cooking time: 50–55 minutes

*Lebanese Spiced Rice

2 teaspoons (10 ml) black peppercorns
2 teaspoons (10 ml) cardamom seeds
1½ teaspoons (7.5 ml) whole cloves
1 lb (450 g) long grain rice, washed
2 fl oz (50 ml, ¼ cup) groundnut (peanut) oil
salt
3 tablespoons (45 ml) lemon juice
2 oz (50 g) cashew nuts
desiccated coconut
fresh coriander (Chinese parsley) leaves, chopped
    finely

Preheat the oven to 350°F, 180°C, Mark 4. In a frying-pan combine the peppercorns, cardamom seeds and cloves and cook dry over high heat, shaking the pan continually so that the spices do not burn. When they start 'popping', remove them and grind in either a mortar and pestle, or in a small electric coffee grinder.

In an ovenproof saucepan combine the rice and spice mixture and sauté it in the groundnut (peanut) oil until the oil has been completely absorbed by the rice. Stir in 1½ pints (900 ml, 3¾ cups) boiling water and salt to taste and cook the rice for 5 minutes or until most of the water has been absorbed; transfer the saucepan to the pre-heated oven and bake the mixture, covered, for 15 minutes, or until the rice is tender. Add the lemon juice, toss the rice with a fork and serve on a warm dish topped with the cashew nuts, coconut and chopped coriander (Chinese parsley).

Preparation time: 15 minutes
Cooking time: approximately 30 minutes

Braised Cabbage à la Grecque

2 oz (50 ml, ¼ cup) olive oil
2 medium-sized onions, chopped finely
1–2 stalks celery, chopped
2 tomatoes, peeled and chopped
2 small carrots, sliced thinly
salt and freshly ground pepper
1 teaspoon (5 ml) ground cumin
2 oz (50 g, ½ cup) parsley, chopped finely
1 large white cabbage, or spring cabbage, chopped
    in 8 pieces, outer leaves and stalks discarded
1 tablespoon (15 ml) capers

In a saucepan heat the oil and cook the onions until they turn transparent. Add the celery, tomatoes, carrots, salt and pepper to taste, cumin, parsley and finally the cabbage. Add just enough water to prevent the vegetables from burning. Cook over low heat for 10 minutes, then add the capers and continue to cook until the cabbage is *just* tender.

Preparation time: approximately 30 minutes
Cooking time: approximately 20 minutes

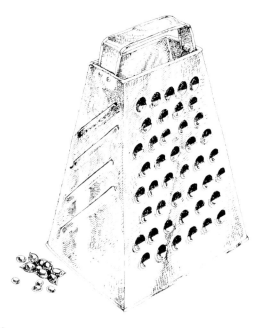

*Chocolate Mousse Meringues

If you like really rich desserts, this is the one. It came about one day when my then eight-year-old daughter had made dozens of meringues. I had run out of ideas on how to use them up, when on making a crunchy chocolate mousse which has long been a favourite of my family and friends, I decided to put the two desserts together. The result, a huge success. The added joy of this dish is that both the meringues and the mousse can be made in advance, then put together either a few hours earlier or at the last minute. You are aiming at chewy meringues, so the oven will be slightly hotter than usual.

For the meringues:
4 egg whites
⅛ teaspoon (0.6 ml) cream of tartar
1 teaspoon (5 ml) vanilla essence (extract)
5 oz (150 g, 1 cup) icing (confectioners') sugar, sifted

For the mousse:
½ lb (225 g) Meunier or Bournville plain (semi-sweet) chocolate
5 egg yolks
1 teaspoon (5 ml) vanilla essence (extract)
1½ tablespoons (22 ml) Cognac or rum
2 oz (50 g, ⅓ cup) blanched almonds, chopped coarsely
5 egg whites, beaten until stiff
1 oz (25 g, ⅛ cup) ground almonds

Preheat the oven to 275°F, 140°C, Mark 1. For fluffier and stiffer egg whites rub the inside of a copper bowl with half a lemon, but stainless steel or glass bowls can also be used. Beat the egg whites and cream of tartar with an electric mixer, then add the vanilla and beat some more. While beating continually, add the sugar, 1 tablespoon (15 ml) at a time, until the mixture stands in stiff peaks, even on the beater.

Take a baking sheet and line it with parchment or rice paper. With a spatula scoop out some meringue and place it on the baking sheet. Shape it with the bowl of a tablespoon into a 3½-inch (8.9-cm) nest. Shape the remaining 7 meringues in the same manner and bake in the preheated oven for about 1 hour. Crush the bottoms lightly by pressing them with your finger. Turn off the oven, leave the door open and allow them to cool for a few hours. Remove them from the baking sheet. Store the meringues immediately in a tightly covered tin. *Do not freeze them.*

To make the mousse chop the chocolate into small pieces, keeping a small handful in reserve. Over simmering water melt the chocolate in the top of a double-boiler with 2 fl oz (50 ml, ¼ cup) water. Stir the melting chocolate until it is smooth and set aside to cool. In a medium-sized bowl beat the egg yolks with the vanilla essence (extract), adding either rum or Cognac according to taste. Then add this to the melted chocolate, mix well and return to the bowl, adding the reserved chocolate bits and the chopped almonds. Carefully but thoroughly fold in the egg whites with a metal spoon and pour the mixture into an 8-inch (20.3-cm) soufflé dish. Chill for at least 3 hours.

Just before serving, take each meringue and fill with a round mound of the chocolate mousse. Sprinkle with ground almonds.

Total preparation and cooking time: 1½ hours
Cooking and chilling time: 2–4 hours

───── DINNER ─────
SERVES 2

Poached Eggs in Avocado, *Sauce
Béarnaise
─────
Perdiz a Ribatejo
(Partridges with Oranges and Grapes)

Karamkalla
(Kashmiri Cabbage)

*Jerusalem Artichoke Chips (see page 84)
─────
Cheese and Biscuits

Poached Eggs in Avocado, *Sauce Béarnaise

8 fl oz (225 ml, 1 cup) béarnaise sauce
1 avocado, just ripe
2 very fresh eggs
salt and freshly ground pepper
2 1-inch (2.5-cm) thick slices of French bread

Make the béarnaise sauce and keep it warm in the top of a double boiler. *Do not leave over direct heat.* Cut the avocado in two lengthwise, remove the stone and any of its outer skin that clings to the cavity. Place the two halves in a pan of warm water over a moderate heat and bring it to simmering point. If the avocado is not quite ripe, leave it to simmer for several minutes, then drain on a clean cloth.

Lightly poach the eggs in water with a little vinegar. Drain on kitchen paper towels and trim with scissors so as to fit the avocado. Then spoon 1 tablespoon (15 ml) béarnaise sauce into each avocado, slide the egg on top, season with salt and freshly ground pepper and coat with another tablespoon (15 ml) of the sauce. Place each avocado half on a piece of French bread with the centre scooped out. Serve the rest of the sauce in a small sauceboat.

*Béarnaise Sauce

Makes 16 fl oz (475 ml, 2 cups)

8 oz (225 g, 1 cup) butter
3 sprigs tarragon, chopped finely
2 teaspoons (10 ml) chervil, chopped finely
2 shallots, chopped finely
4 crushed white peppercorns
4 tablespoons (60 ml) tarragon vinegar
4 tablespoons (60 ml) dry white wine
3 egg yolks
salt and cayenne pepper
1 teaspoon (5 ml) tarragon, chopped finely, to finish
1 teaspoon (5 ml) chervil, chopped finely, to finish

Have the butter, divided into 12 parts, at room temperature. In a small, heavy saucepan combine the tarragon, chervil and shallots, the peppercorns, vinegar and white wine. Cook the mixture over high heat until the liquid has been reduced to 1 tablespoon (15 ml). Add 1 tablespoon (15 ml) cold water and strain, if desired. Pour the mixture into the top half of a double boiler or bain marie, and add the egg yolks. Stir the mixture briskly with a wire whisk until it is thick and creamy. Set the pan over low heat so that the water in the lower half of the double boiler becomes warm. Beat in the butter, one part at a time, lifting the pan occasionally to cool the mixture. Make sure that each part of butter is completely melted before adding more. Continue to beat the sauce until it is thick and firm. Season it with salt and cayenne to taste and add the remaining tarragon and chervil to finish.

Preparation time: approximately 20 minutes
Cooking time: 35–40 minutes

Perdiz a Ribatejo

2 oz (50 g, ¼ cup) unsalted butter
plain (all-purpose) flour, for dredging
salt and freshly ground pepper
2 partridges
2 large oranges, peeled and sliced into segments
¼ lb (125 g) seedless green grapes
juice of 3 oranges
Calvados (optional)

In a large frying-pan, heat the butter. Dredge the partridges in seasoned flour, shake off the excess flour and brown them on all sides in the butter. Transfer them to a casserole just large enough to hold them, and add the oranges and grapes. Pour the orange juice into the butter in the frying-pan, stir and heat. If you wish, pour in a dash of Calvados. Mix and pour this sauce over the partridges. Cover and cook for about 1 hour, or until the juices running out of the thigh, when pricked, are yellow.

Preparation time: 20 minutes
Cooking time: 1¼ hours

Karamkalla

4 fl oz (125 ml, ½ cup) mustard oil or vegetable oil
a pinch of asafoetida
1 teaspoon (5 ml) cumin seeds
½ teaspoon (2.5 ml) fenugreek seeds
1-inch (2.5-cm) piece fresh ginger, peeled and
*   crushed*
1 fresh green chilli, stem and seeds removed,
*   chopped finely*
1 teaspoon (5 ml) ground ginger
1 small cabbage, outer leaves removed, quartered
salt and cayenne pepper
1 teaspoon (5 ml) sugar
1 teaspoon (5 ml) turmeric powder (optional)
1 teaspoon (5 ml) ground coriander
fresh coriander (Chinese parsley) leaves, chopped
*   finely*

In a saucepan, heat the oil, then add the asafoetida, cumin seeds, fenugreek seeds, ginger, green chilli and ground ginger and fry for a few seconds, stirring constantly. Add the cabbage, salt and cayenne to taste, sugar and turmeric powder, if wished. Stir and shake the saucepan, making sure the ingredients are well mixed. Add 2 tablespoons (30 ml) water and cook over low heat, adding more water if necessary, until the cabbage is tender but still crunchy.

Add the ground coriander and toss the ingredients again. Serve in a heated dish, sprinkled with fresh coriander (Chinese parsley).

Preparation time: 20 minutes
Cooking time: 15–20 minutes

——— DINNER FOR A ———
SPECIAL OCCASION
SERVES 4

Carciofi Ripieni
(Italian Stuffed Artichokes)

———

Pheasant or Guinea Hen Stuffed with
Foie Gras

*Wild Rice and Mushrooms

Spinacci con Limone

———

Cheese and Biscuits

The pheasant can be cooked while you
are eating the first course, while the wild
rice may be prepared in advance, then
mixed in with the mushrooms and baked
at the same time and in the same oven
as the pheasant, so that they will be
ready at the same moment. Cook the
spinach at the last minutes, just before
everything comes out of the oven. There
is no dessert because everything else is
quite rich. A really good Brie or blue Brie
will finish off a perfect dinner.

Carciofi Ripieni

4 artichokes, stems and pointed ends of leaves
removed
12 anchovy fillets, in oil
6 cloves garlic
3 large onions, chopped finely
3 carrots, chopped finely
2 tablespoons (30 ml) parsley, chopped finely
1 stalk celery, chopped finely
$\frac{1}{4}$ teaspoon (1.25 ml) dried oregano
$\frac{1}{4}$ teaspoon (1.25 ml) dried basil
$\frac{1}{4}$ teaspoon (1.25 ml) dried marjoram
salt and freshly ground black pepper
4 strips bacon
4 tablespoons (60 ml) olive or vegetable oil

Boil the artichokes in salted water for 20–30
minutes, depending upon their size, until they are
slightly tender but still quite firm; drain
thoroughly and remove the centre leaves and the
choke.

In a mortar, pound the anchovies and garlic
together and fill the artichokes with the mixture,
or pound them in a small electric herb grinder if
you prefer. In a bowl mix the onions, carrots,
parsley, celery, dried herbs, salt and freshly
ground black pepper to taste. Put the vegetable
mixture on the bottom of a saucepan, arrange the
artichokes on top with a strip of bacon over each
artichoke. Add the oil and 3 tablespoons (45 ml)
water, cover and simmer gently for 45 minutes,
basting occasionally. To serve, remove the bacon,
chop it up, arrange an artichoke with some
vegetables surrounding it on each plate, sprinkle
some chopped bacon over it and strain some
sauce over.

Preparation time: approximately 45 minutes
Cooking time: 65–75 minutes

Pheasant Stuffed with Foie Gras

1 lb (450 g) foie gras, duck or goose
8 fl oz (225 ml, 1 cup) medium dry sherry
salt and freshly ground black pepper
4 truffles, sliced
2 pheasants or guinea hens, cleaned and dressed
butter
8 fl oz (225 ml, 1 cup) pheasant, game or chicken
   stock (broth)

Preheat the oven to 350°F, 180°C, Mark 4. In a bowl soak the foie gras in the sherry with a pinch of salt and freshly ground black pepper to taste for 4 hours. Drain, reserving the liquid. Add the truffle slices to the soaked foie gras and stuff the birds with it. Roast in the preheated oven for 30 minutes, basting frequently with butter.

Place the pheasants with their gravy and the stock (broth) in a deep casserole together with the sherry left over from the foie gras. Place a piece of aluminium foil over the dish, then cover it with a lid and simmer over low heat for 15 minutes. When ready to serve, bring the pheasants to the table in the casserole to preserve the perfume and flavour.

Marinating time: 4 hours
Preparation time: 15 minutes
Cooking time: approximately 45 minutes

*Wild Rice and Mushrooms

This is particularly delicious served with any game birds, but as wild rice is very expensive save this dish for a special occasion to serve with pheasant or, if you are particularly lucky, a grouse.

4 oz (125 g, $\frac{1}{3}$ cup) wild rice
1 teaspoon (5 ml) white wine vinegar
2 oz (50 g, $\frac{1}{4}$ cup) butter
1$\frac{1}{2}$ large onions, chopped
$\frac{1}{2}$ green pepper, chopped
1 stalk celery, chopped
$\frac{1}{4}$ lb (125 g) fresh mushrooms, sliced
1 teaspoon (5 ml) salt

Preheat the oven to 350°F, 180°C, Mark 4. Rinse the rice under cold water in a bowl, changing the water 3 or 4 times, until the water runs clear. Cook the rice according to the instructions on the package, adding the vinegar to the water.

In a frying-pan, sauté the onions in the butter until they turn transparent, then add the green peppers, celery and mushrooms, and cook until light brown. Combine the rice and the vegetables and place in a casserole. Cover and bake in the preheated oven for 30 minutes.

Preparation time: approximately 30 minutes
Cooking time: approximately 1$\frac{1}{2}$ hours

Spinacci con Limone

1 lb (450 g) spinach, or any green leaf vegetable,
   washed and spines removed
salt
2 tablespoons (30 ml) olive oil
freshly ground black pepper
juice of 1 lemon

Place the washed spinach in a saucepan with salt to taste and the minimum amount of water to prevent burning. The water on the spinach leaves is almost enough. Cook for 5–10 minutes, stirring from time to time. Drain thoroughly, and chop up the spinach roughly. Return it to the pan, add the olive oil, freshly ground black pepper to taste and lemon juice.

Preparation time: 10 minutes
Cooking time: 5–10 minutes

DINNER

SERVES 6

*Smoked Fish Soup
___

Partridges alla Lombarda, *Sauce alla
Cacciatora

or

Brazilian Pork Kebabs

Cavoli con Castagne
(Cabbage with Chestnuts)

*Carrots in Orange Liqueur (see page
103)
___

*Ksheer Annam
(Indian Rice Pudding)

The hot creamy smoked fish soup may be
prepared up to a point, then reheated
and finished off just before dinner. The
partridges go into the casserole 15
minutes before dinner and the spicy
sauce has only to be reheated at the
same time as the carrots. Only the pork
kebabs, if you are cooking them instead
of the partridges, and the cabbage have
to be cooked at the last minute.

---

*Smoked Fish Soup

2 small onions, chopped finely
2 carrots, chopped finely
1 large potato, peeled and chopped finely
2 tablespoons (30 ml) unsalted butter
2 pints (1.1 litres, 2½ pints) fish stock (broth) or
 bottled clam juice
1½–2 lb (700–900 g) smoked haddock or any other
 smoked fish, cut into 4 pieces
1 bunch fresh coriander (Chinese parsley) or
 parsley, chopped finely
1 bay leaf
1 sprig fresh thyme
8 fl oz (225 ml, 1 cup) double (heavy) cream
freshly grated nutmeg

In a deep saucepan, cook the onions, carrots and
potato in the butter. Add the fish stock (broth) or
clam juice, the haddock and the herbs and simmer for 15–20 minutes, or until the fish has
turned opaque. Remove the fish to a plate, skin

and bone it, flake it and return the fish to the
saucepan over low heat. *Up to this point the soup
may be prepared in advance.*

Stir in the cream, mix thoroughly and slowly
heat the soup through. Do not allow it to boil.
Pour the soup into heated soup bowls and
sprinkle freshly grated nutmeg on top. Serve hot.

*Preparation time: 20–30 minutes
Cooking time: 25–30 minutes*

Partridges alla Lombarda, Sauce alla Cacciatora

8 oz (225 g, 1 cup) butter
6 partridges, cleaned and trimmed
18 slices streaky (lean) bacon
grated rind of 2 lemons
3 bay leaves
salt and freshly ground black pepper
10 fl oz (275 ml, 1¼ cups) dry white wine
1½ pints (900 ml, 1¾ pints) game or chicken stock
 (broth)
6 slices fried bread, crusts removed
12 slices Parma ham
Sauce alla Cacciatora

In a large casserole, melt the butter and brown
the birds in it over medium heat, turning them
twice. Then wrap 3 pieces of bacon around each
bird, replace them in the casserole and add the
lemon rind, bay leaves, freshly ground pepper
and salt to taste, the white wine and the stock
(broth). Cook over low heat for 30–35 minutes.
Use the liquid left in the casserole as the base for
the Sauce alla Cacciatora.

To serve, place the slices of fried bread on a
heated serving dish and put 1 bird on each.
Surround the birds with the Parma ham and
serve with the sauce.

*Preparation time: 10 minutes
Cooking time: 45 minutes*

Sauce alla Cacciatora

This 'Huntress' sauce is served in Italy hot or cold with all kinds of poultry and game birds, but not venison.

5 fl oz (150 ml, $\frac{2}{3}$ cup) dry white wine
1$\frac{1}{2}$ pints (900 ml, 1$\frac{3}{4}$ pints) game stock (broth)
juice of 1 large or 2 small lemons
2 tablespoons (30 ml) Italian parsley or coriander (Chinese parsley), chopped finely
2 tablespoons (30 ml) onion, chopped finely
1 bay leaf
$\frac{1}{2}$ teaspoon (2.5 ml) ground mace
$\frac{1}{2}$ teaspoon (2.5 ml) freshly grated nutmeg
1 oz (25 g, $\frac{1}{3}$ cup) dry breadcrumbs
salt
5 black peppercorns and 5 juniper berries, crushed together in a mortar and pestle

In a medium-sized saucepan pour the wine, the game stock (broth) and the lemon juice. Add the remaining ingredients and cook over a low heat, stirring, for approximately 10 minutes. Before serving, either hot or cold, remove the bay leaf.

Preparation time: approximately 10 minutes
Cooking time: approximately 10 minutes

Brazilian Pork Kebabs

2$\frac{1}{2}$ lb (1 kg) lean boneless pork, cut into cubes

For the marinade:
2 fl oz (50 ml, $\frac{1}{4}$ cup) good olive oil
2 fl oz (50 ml, $\frac{1}{4}$ cup) lemon juice
5 oz (150 g, 1 cup) onion, chopped finely
3 cloves garlic, chopped finely
2 tablespoons (30 ml) brown sugar
8–10 Brazil nuts, grated in a nutmeg grater
2 tablespoons (30 ml) coriander seeds, roasted and ground
$\frac{1}{4}$ teaspoon (1.5 ml) dried red chilli pepper, crushed

In a deep dish, combine all the ingredients for the marinade, then add the pork and marinate for at least 2 hours. Reserve the marinade.

Place the pork on skewers and either put them over a barbecue or preheat the oven to 450°F, 230°C, Mark 8 and bake for 25–30 minutes, until they are thoroughly cooked, basting with the marinade twice. When cooked, remove the meat from the skewers and serve together with the remaining marinade.

Marinating time: 2–3 hours
Preparation time: 20–25 minutes
Cooking time: approximately 25–30 minutes

Cavoli con Castagne

This slightly different way of cooking cabbage is delicious served with game or baked ham.

1 small cabbage, shredded finely
2 fl oz (50 ml, ¼ cup) white wine vinegar
2 tablespoons (30 ml) olive or vegetable oil
1 teaspoon (5 ml) salt
freshly ground white pepper
1 tablespoon (15 ml) sugar
2 oz (50 g) sultanas (white raisins)
8 oz (225 g, 1 cup) chestnuts, peeled and blanched
_   or 10-oz (375-g) can whole chestnuts_
1 tablespoon (15 ml) plain (all-purpose) flour

Place the shredded cabbage in a small colander over a pan. Pour over it 8 fl oz (225 ml, 1 cup) boiling water, to which vinegar has been added. Cover and allow it to steam for 10 minutes. Save the water.

In a sauté pan heat the oil and brown the cabbage, adding the salt and pepper. To the vinegar water add the sugar, sultanas (white raisins) and chestnuts. Cook, covered, until the chestnuts are tender. Sprinkle the flour over the cabbage, add it to the chestnut mixture and cook for a few minutes more. Serve hot.

Preparation time: approximately 20 minutes if
using canned chestnuts
40 minutes if using fresh chestnuts
Cooking time: approximately 30 minutes

*Ksheer Annam

This delicious rice pudding dish is like no other you have tasted. I am not a fan of the English or American rice pudding, but this one from the Tamil Nadu region of south-eastern India is very special.

7 oz (200 g, 1 cup) short or long grain rice,
_   washed and drained (if using enriched American_
_   rice, do not wash)_
3½ pints (2 litres, 8 cups) milk
4 cardamom pods
14 oz (400 g, 1¾ cups) granulated sugar
pinch of saffron strands
2 tablespoons (30 ml) slivered blanched almonds,
_   optional_
ground cardamom to taste

In a medium-sized saucepan, boil the rice in water to cover for 5 minutes. Drain. In a large saucepan bring the milk to the boil with the cardamom pods in it. Pour in the rice and simmer for 1 hour or until the rice is soft and the milk thick. You will find that while the milk is thickening you will need to stir it to prevent it sticking to the bottom and sides of the pan. In another large saucepan, make a sugar syrup with the sugar and 8 fl oz (225 ml, 1 cup) water, but do not allow it to brown.

When the rice and milk mixture is cooked, add it to the thickened sugar syrup together with the saffron strands and continue cooking until it reaches the consistency of porridge. Remove from the heat and pick out the cardamom pods. Serve hot or cold, with powdered cardamom and slivered almonds sprinkled on top, either in individual glass dessert dishes or in a large glass bowl.

Preparation time: approximately 15 minutes
Cooking time: approximately 1½ hours

DINNER

SERVES 6

Caracoles
(Spanish Snails in Tomato and Chorizo)

---

*Lamb Baked in Phylo Pastry

*Baked Aubergines (Eggplants) (see page 52)

---

*Maple Walnut Mousse with Maple Walnut Sauce (see page 99)

The first course is snails with a difference, _not_ like the French snails in butter. The lamb may be prepared up to the moment of cooking, then it should go in the oven just before you sit down to dinner, as should the aubergine (eggplant). The dessert can be prepared totally ahead of time, as it is chilled and removed from the refrigerator only just before serving.

94

Caracoles

2 4½-oz (140-g) cans of snails (24 snails)
4 fl oz (125 ml, ½ cup) olive oil
1-lb (450-g) can plum tomatoes in their juice
2 tablespoons (30 ml) plain (all-purpose) flour
12 ½-inch (1.2-cm) thick slices jamon serrano,
    prosciutto or Parma ham, chopped coarsely
4 oz (125 g, ⅔ cup) walnuts, chopped
1 chorizo or garlic sausage, chopped
6 tablespoons (90 ml) parsley or fresh coriander
    (Chinese parsley), chopped finely
freshly ground black pepper
1 dried red chilli pepper
6 fl oz (175 ml, ¾ cup) dry white wine

Drain the snails in a colander, rinse and pat dry.
Put the oil into a deep frying-pan, heat slowly,
then add the tomatoes and stir. Mix the flour with
3 tablespoons (45 ml) cold water and add to the
pan, stirring continuously over a low heat. Mix in
the ham, walnuts, chorizo, parsley or coriander
(Chinese parsley), black pepper and chilli pepper
and simmer for 5–7 minutes. Then add the white
wine and simmer for an added 5 minutes. Now
add the snails and simmer for a final 5 minutes.
Serve in small earthenware dishes which will
retain the heat and keep the sauce sizzling while
you are eating the snails.

Preparation time: 15 minutes
Cooking time: 25 minutes

Lamb Baked in Phylo Pastry

Claudia Roden, the brilliant cook and historian
of Middle Eastern food, taught me this recipe; I
find it invaluable for dinner parties. Once
again everything can be prepared ahead, ready
for cooking at the last moment. There is no
carving to be done, and it is easy to prepare. I
have slightly adapted the recipe.

24 vine leaves
3 lb (1.4 kg) boneless leg of lamb
5 tablespoons (75 ml) olive oil
freshly ground black pepper
2 cloves garlic, crushed
1–2 teaspoons (5–10 ml) dried oregano
3 sheets of phylo pastry
3 tablespoons (45 ml) melted butter
salt

If you are using fresh vine leaves, blanch them for
1 second to make them limp. If you buy them in
brine, soak the leaves in boiling water for at least
30 minutes, changing the water once, then drain
them. Remove all the fat from the lamb, then cut
the meat into 6 fat slices and place them in a
shallow dish large enough for them to lie flat in
one layer. Add the olive oil, black pepper, garlic
and oregano and leave to marinate for 1 hour, at
least.
    Divide each sheet of phylo in two lengthwise,
and brush each piece very lightly with melted
butter. Place 2 vine leaves tail to tail near one
edge. Lay one slice of lamb over them and
sprinkle with salt. Cover with 2 more vine leaves.
Fold the phylo so as to make a neat packet. Repeat
this process with all the rest and place them on a
greased baking tray. At this point you can leave
them for about 2 hours until ready to cook.
    Preheat the oven to 300°F, 150°C, Mark 3.
Place the baking tray with the lamb packets in
the preheated oven for 25 minutes, until the
phylo pastry is golden and the meat still very
tender.

Soaking time if using canned vine leaves: 30
minutes
Marinating time: 1 hour
Preparation time: 30 minutes
Cooking time: 25 minutes

Autumn or Winter

DINNER
SERVES 8

Mushrooms Stuffed with Garlic Prawns (Shrimp)

Goose alla Genovese

Roasted Jerusalem Artichokes

*Yan Kit's Chinese Pickled Cabbage, Peking-style (see page 84)

---

*Maple Walnut Mousse with Maple Walnut Sauce

The first course is just a 'gout', a taste to whet the appetite for the goose to follow. Roasted artichokes take the place of potatoes and are, I find, much more popular. The pickled cabbage has a special flavour not usually found in most cabbage dishes. The cooling Maple Walnut Mousse adds the right touch to finish, not too sweet.

Mushrooms Stuffed with Garlic Prawns (Shrimp)

8 very large button or flat mushrooms, trimmed and wiped
6 tablespoons (90 ml) corn or groundnut (peanut) oil
6 oz (175 g, ¾ cup) butter
4 cloves garlic, peeled
salt
4 tablespoons (60 ml) parsley or fresh coriander (Chinese parsley), chopped
3 tablespoons (45 ml) lemon juice
1 lb (450 g) peeled prawns (shrimp)
watercress for garnish

Preheat the oven to 325°F, 160°C, Mark 3. In a frying-pan, heat the oil and fry the mushrooms for about 1 minute each side. Remove from the heat and put aside. Crush the garlic with a little salt to make a smooth paste.

In a medium-sized saucepan melt the butter, add the garlic paste, then the parsley or coriander (Chinese parsley), the lemon juice and finally, the prawns (shrimp). Mix well and spoon the mixture into the mushrooms. Place in an ovenproof dish and bake in the preheated oven for 20 minutes. Garnish with watercress and serve immediately with French bread.

Preparation time: approximately 20 minutes
Cooking time: 25–30 minutes

* Can be prepared to this point, put in fridge, cook 20 m. before eating

Goose alla Genovese

goose liver, scalded and puréed
1 oz (25 g, ⅓ cup) fresh breadcrumbs
½ tablespoon (7.5 ml) finely chopped onion
½ tablespoon (7.5 ml) sage, chopped
1 tablespoon (15 ml) fresh coriander (Chinese
   parsley) or Italian parsley, chopped
pinch of ground mace
grated rind of 1 lemon
salt and freshly ground pepper
2 eggs, well beaten
10-lb (4.5-kg) goose, cleaned
butter
2–3 tablespoons (30–45 ml) Italian mustard (see
   page 99)
6 oz (175 g, 1 cup) dry breadcrumbs

For the sauce:
2 tablespoons (30 ml) butter
1 oz (25 g, 2 tablespoons) plain (all-purpose) flour
½ pint (300 ml, 1¼ cups) goose, game or chicken
   stock (broth)
1 tablespoon (15 ml) Italian mustard (see page
   99)
1 tablespoon (15 ml) red wine vinegar
salt and freshly ground pepper

Preheat the oven to 400°F, 200°C, Mark 6. Make the stuffing. In a bowl put the puréed liver, the breadcrumbs, onion, herbs and mace, the lemon rind, salt and pepper to taste. Mix it well and add the beaten eggs. Place the stuffing inside the cavity of the goose, leaving plenty of room for it to expand. If there is any left over put it in a ramekin or small soufflé dish and bake it separately, dotted with butter. Truss the goose, cover with butter and place in a roasting pan. Place in the pre-heated oven and cook for 15 minutes.

Reduce the heat to 350°F, 180°C, Mark 4, cook the goose on one side for 20 minutes, then turn it and cook it for 20 minutes on the other side, continually basting it. Then place it breast side up and cook it for 1½–2 hours. You may find that another 20–30 minutes is needed since a stuffed bird takes longer to cook than an unstuffed one. When it is almost cooked (test by piercing the leg and looking at the juices running out; if they are yellow or clear rather than pink, then the bird is cooked) mix some of the basting butter sauce with the Italian mustard and pour it over the goose. Cover the goose with breadcrumbs and continue cooking until the breadcrumbs have browned well.

Meanwhile make the sauce. Melt the butter in a small saucepan and stir in the flour to make a smooth white roux. Slowly add the stock (broth), cooking and stirring until the sauce thickens. Add mustard, vinegar, salt and pepper to taste and simmer for 6–7 minutes.

To serve, place the goose on a heated platter, surrounded by roasted Jerusalem artichokes and serve the sauce separately.

Preparation time: 30–40 minutes
Cooking time: 2½–3½ hours

Roasted Jerusalem Artichokes

2 lb (900 g) Jerusalem artichokes, scrubbed

Place the artichokes in a large saucepan with water to cover. Parboil them for 15 minutes, then drain them. Place the artichokes in the roasting pan around the goose, halfway through its cooking. Baste them as you baste the goose.

*Italian Mustard

This will keep for months. It is particularly delicious used in Goose alla Genovese (see page 98).

10 fl oz (300 ml, 1¼ cups) dry white wine
1 small onion, stuck with 5 or 6 cloves
salt
4 fl oz (125 ml, ½ cup) Dijon-type mustard

In a small saucepan pour the white wine. Add the onion stuck with cloves and salt to taste, and stew over a low heat for 15 minutes. Strain through a sieve and stir in the mustard, tablespoon by tablespoon, mixing well. Pour into a sterilized screw-top jar or earthenware jug and store in the refrigerator.

Cooking time: approximately 15 minutes

*Maple Walnut Mousse with Maple Walnut Sauce

8 fl oz (225 ml, 1 cup) milk
12 fl oz (350 ml, 1½ cups) maple syrup
3–4 egg yolks, beaten
16 fl oz (475 ml, 2 cups) double (heavy) cream, whipped
4 oz (125 g, ¾ cup) walnuts, chopped

In the top of a double boiler, or a bain marie on a stand, over simmering water, put the milk, 8 fl oz (225 ml, 1 cup) maple syrup and the egg yolks. Cook, stirring constantly, until the resulting custard coats the back of a wooden spoon. Remove from the heat and cool completely. When it is cool, add the whipped cream and 3 oz (75 g, ½ cup) walnuts, folding them into the mixture well. Take a kugelhupf mould or a metal mould in the shape of a half-melon, rinse it with cold water and pour in the maple-nut mixture. Place it in the freezer or the freezing compartment of a refrigerator for 4–5 hours.

When ready to serve, place a serving plate over the bottom of the mould, invert it and shake out the mousse.

Heat the remaining maple syrup, add the remaining walnuts and pour the sauce over the ice cream. Serve immediately.

Preparation time: approximately 15 minutes
Cooking time: 20–25 minutes
Freezing time: 5 hours

SUNDAY LUNCH
SERVES 8–10

Baked Ham with Redcurrant Sauce

or

Indonesian Pork Kebabs

*Riso al Sugo d'Arancia
(Spanish Orange Rice) (see page 47)

Yan Kit's Stir-fried Spinach in Bean Curd
'Cheese' Sauce

———

*Flaming Fruit with Brandy Sauce (see
page 107)

The spinach for the Chinese vegetable
may be blanched 2 hours before cooking
and stir-fried at the last moment. The
orange rice may be prepared ahead of
time, as may the dessert, and reheated.

Baked Ham

*12-lb (5.3-kg) cooked Alderton (baked Virginia)
ham*
2 tablespoons (30 ml) plain (all-purpose) flour
2 tablespoons (30 ml) stout or dark ale
6 oz (175 g, 1 cup) brown sugar
cloves
*½ pint (300 ml, 1¼ cups) stout or dark ale, for
basting*

Preheat the oven to 400°F, 200°C, Mark 6. Scrape
off any dressing from the outside of the ham.
Make diamond-shaped cuts in the fat. Mix a paste
of flour, stout and brown sugar, spread it over the
ham and stud the fat with cloves. Put the ham in
a roasting pan and bake in the preheated oven for
10 minutes. After this add some more stout,
reduce the heat to 350°F, 180°C, Mark 4, and
continue to cook for about 1 hour, basting well
with stout every 10 minutes. When ready to
serve, cut in thin slices lengthwise across the top.
Serve with redcurrant sauce. This is also delicious
cold.

Preparation and cooking time: approximately 2
hours

Redcurrant Sauce

1-lb (450-g) jar redcurrant jelly
2 tablespoons (30 ml) vinegar
pinch of dry mustard
4½ oz (125 g, 1 cup) seedless raisins
salt and pepper

Melt the redcurrant jelly in a saucepan, then add
the vinegar. When these have cooked together
for a few minutes, add the pinch of dry mustard,
the seedless raisins and salt and pepper to taste.
When the raisins are soft, the sauce is done. Serve
hot.

Cooking time: approximately 10 minutes

Yan Kit's Stir-fried Spinach in Bean Curd 'Cheese' Sauce

2½ lb (1.1 kg) fresh spinach, washed, string roots
  and hard stalks removed
2 teaspoons (10 ml) salt
8 tablespoons (120 ml) groundnut (peanut) oil
10 cloves garlic
6 cakes fermented bean curd with chilli (available
  in jars in Oriental supermarkets)
1½ teaspoons (7.5 ml) sugar
1 fresh green or red chilli (optional)
2 tablespoons (30 ml) Shaohsing wine or sherry

Bring 4 pints (2.4 litres, 5 pints) water to the boil
and add the salt and 2 tablespoons (30 ml) oil.
Blanch the spinach, cooking for 1 minute after
the water has returned to the boil. Drain the
spinach in a colander and refresh with cold water
immediately. Drain well and put aside. *This can be
done a few hours beforehand without the spinach
losing its vivid colour and texture.*

Peel the garlic and chop it finely. Then mash
the fermented bean curd in a small bowl with a
small amount of juice from the jar. Stir in the
sugar. Remove the stem and seeds from the chilli
and cut it into tiny rounds.

Just before serving, heat a wok over high heat
until wisps of smoke arise. Pour in 6 tablespoons
(90 ml) oil, swirl it around and tip in the garlic.
Add the fermented bean curd and chilli, stir and
splash the Shaohsing wine or sherry along the
rim of the wok above the ingredients. Tip in the
spinach, stir and turn continuously with the wok
scoop for 1–2 minutes to incorporate the sauce.
Lower the heat if the sauce is being absorbed too
quickly. Remove to a warm serving plate. Serve
immediately while the wok fragrance is still at its
optimum.

*Preparation time: 15–20 minutes
Cooking time: 2–3 minutes*

Indonesian Pork Kebabs

3 oz (75 g, ½ cup) pine nuts (pine kernels), crushed
3 tablespoons (45 ml) roasted and freshly ground
  coriander seeds
2 cloves garlic, crushed
1 small onion, chopped finely
½ teaspoon (2.5 ml) freshly ground black pepper
dash of cayenne pepper
1 teaspoon (5 ml) salt
5 tablespoons (75 ml) lemon juice
4 fl oz (125 ml, ½ cup) soy sauce
2 tablespoons (30 ml) brown sugar
2½ lb (1.1 kg) lean pork, cut into cubes
4 cucumbers
6 tomatoes, cut into eighths
4 oz (125 g, ½ cup) butter, melted

In a shallow glass or earthenware dish mix the
first 10 ingredients and add the pork cubes,
turning them several times to coat them
thoroughly. Leave the meat to marinate overnight, or for at least 4 hours, turning the pieces
occasionally. Peel the cucumbers, quarter them
lengthwise, remove the seeds and cut into 1-inch
(2.5-cm) pieces. Thread the meat and cucumber
alternately on skewers and cook over charcoal or
under a grill (broiler) for 30 minutes or until the
meat is thoroughly cooked, basting occasionally
with the marinade and melted butter.

*Marinating time: 4–24 hours
Preparation time: 20–30 minutes
Cooking time: approximately 30 minutes*

—— *DINNER PARTY SPECIAL* ——
SERVES 8

*Soufflé Roulé aux Epinards (see page 82)

*Veal Milanese with Mushroom Sauce

*Carrots in Orange Liqueur

French Beans with Paprika and Pine Nut
(Pine Kernel) Butter

*Hazelnut Crêpes Pralinées with Liqueur
Sauce

Although you would think so, there is no
duplication in the two liqueur dishes.
Once more, almost everything for this
menu may be prepared in advance, with
some things needing only reheating.
Both the first and last courses may be
prepared the day before, the crêpes may
be prepared weeks ahead and frozen if
you wish.

*Veal Milanese with Mushroom Sauce

Marcella Hazan, the brilliant Italian cookery
writer, introduced me to the papillote method
of cooking veal escalopes. Cooked this way
they need not be left to the last minute. I
devised the following recipe, using her
technique, which has been a tremendous
success at many dinner parties. It can all be
prepared 2–3 hours ahead and reheated while
you eat the first course.

8 veal escalopes, pounded thinly
1 egg yolk, beaten
6 oz (175 g, 1 cup) dry breadcrumbs
4 oz (125 g, $\frac{1}{2}$ cup) unsalted butter
4 tablespoons (60 ml) fresh tarragon, or 2
  tablespoons (30 ml) dried tarragon
juice of 1 lemon
2 fl oz (50 ml, $\frac{1}{4}$ cup) marsala or port
chopped fresh coriander (Chinese parsley) or
  parsley to garnish

For the sauce:
1$\frac{1}{2}$ lb (700 g) button mushrooms, sliced thinly
2 oz (50 g, $\frac{1}{4}$ cup) unsalted butter
juice of 1 lemon
4 tablespoons (60 ml) chopped fresh tarragon, or 2
  tablespoons (30 ml) dried tarragon
2 fl oz (50 ml, $\frac{1}{4}$ cup) marsala or port
freshly ground pepper
2 egg yolks, beaten

Dip the escalopes into the egg yolk and then the
breadcrumbs, both sides. Leave aside on kitchen
paper towels for 10 minutes. Take a large roasting pan, two if necessary, and line it with enough
aluminium foil so that it reaches up over the side.
In a large frying-pan melt 2 oz (50 g, $\frac{1}{4}$ cup) butter
and add a few sprigs of tarragon. When the butter
sizzles put in 3–4 escalopes, depending upon the
size of your pan and of the veal. Brown on one
side for 1 minute, turn over the escalopes and
brown the other side for 1 minute. Pour a little
lemon juice and half the marsala or port into the
pan, tilting the pan so that all the veal cooks in
the juices. Then remove the meat to the lined
roasting pan, with one escalope overlapping
another. Repeat the same process with the remaining escalopes.

After finishing the last piece of veal, add 2 oz
(50 g, $\frac{1}{4}$ cup) butter to the frying-pan, then the
sliced mushrooms and the lemon juice, lower the
heat and cover tightly. Sweat the mushrooms
over low heat for 5–7 minutes. Then add the
tarragon and the marsala or port and freshly
ground pepper to taste. Simmer for a further 5
minutes. Finally add the beaten egg yolks, whisk
thoroughly and simmer over low heat until the
sauce thickens. When cooked, take a teaspoon
(5 ml) of the sauce and place it in the middle of
each veal escalope. Put the rest of the sauce aside,
covered, to reheat later. Take a large enough
piece of aluminium foil to cover the roasting pan,
and crush the edges together with the foil lining.
This makes a tight seal. You may then put the
meat dish on one side. *Do not refrigerate.* This
whole process may be done 2–3 hours before
serving.

When ready to serve, preheat the oven to
400°F, 200°C, Mark 6. Place the roasting pan or
pans in the oven for 15 minutes. The meat will be
heated up by the steam within the papillote but
will not over-cook. Sprinkle fresh coriander
(Chinese parsley) or parsley over the meat and
serve with the reheated mushroom sauce.

Preparation time: 30 minutes
Cooking time: approximately 1 hour

*Carrots in Orange Liqueur

Every summer I make my own orange liqueur, but you can use Curaço, which is useful for adding a special delicate taste to anything from soups to desserts. Here it makes a particular difference to carrots. This dish can be prepared an hour or two ahead of time, then reheated when needed.

1½ lb (700 g) whole young carrots, or older ones, sliced
4 fl oz (125 ml, ½ cup) chicken or game stock (broth)
4 oz (125 g, ½ cup) unsalted butter, melted
1 tablespoon (15 ml) granulated sugar
freshly grated nutmeg
2 fl oz (50 ml, ¼ cup) orange liqueur or Curaço
salt and pepper

In a saucepan, cook the carrots in the stock (broth) until they are just tender but still crunchy. Then drain them, reserving the liquid, and purée them together with 2 fl oz (50 ml, ¼ cup) of the cooking liquid, in a food processor or blender. Return the purée to the saucepan, heat it and add the butter, sugar and freshly grated nutmeg to taste. Add the orange liqueur and season to taste with salt and pepper.

Preparation time: 15 minutes
Cooking time: 20 minutes

French Beans with Paprika and Pine Nut (Pine Kernel) Butter

1½ lb (700 g) French (string) beans, topped and tailed
2 tablespoons (30 ml) butter
2 oz (50 g, ⅓ cup) pine nuts (pine kernels)
2 teaspoons (10 ml) paprika

Tie the beans in small, neat bundles and place them in a colander or in a covered Chinese steamer basket. Steam over boiling water for 7 minutes or until they are just tender but still bright green. Meanwhile in a frying-pan, melt 1 tablespoon (15 ml) butter over low heat and toast the pine nuts (pine kernels) in this, continually stirring, until they have turned a light brown. Add the remaining butter and the paprika and toss the nuts around in the mixture until they are well coated.

Remove the strings, and place each bundle of beans around the edge of the serving dish, leaving a space for the carrot purée between each bundle. Pour paprika and pine nut (pine kernel) butter over each bundle.

Preparation time: approximately 25 minutes
Cooking time: 12–15 minutes

Hazelnut Crêpes Pralinées with Liqueur Sauce

A light, but special, dessert to finish off a dinner. The crêpes and praline can be prepared in advance, only the sauce need be made at the last minute. The crêpes may be frozen and the praline kept in a jar with a tight cover.

2 eggs
6 fl oz (175 ml, ¾ cup) milk
1 oz (25 g, ¼ cup) plain (all-purpose) flour
pinch of salt
3 tablespoons (45 ml) lightly toasted ground hazelnuts
clarified butter
3 oz (75 g, ⅓ cup) unsalted butter
3 tablespoons (45 ml) caster (superfine granulated) sugar

For the praline:
4 oz (125 g, ½ cup) caster (superfine granulated) sugar
4 oz (125 g, ¾ cup) shelled, skinned, lightly toasted hazelnuts
6 oz (175 g) plain (semi-sweet) chocolate, melted

For the liqueur sauce:
8 oz (225 g, 1 cup) caster (superfine granulated) sugar
½ pint (300 ml, 1¼ cups) Espresso or very strong black coffee
juice of 1 orange
2 tablespoons (30 ml) Cognac
2 tablespoons (30 ml) Tia Maria or rum
rind of 2 oranges, chopped finely

To make the crêpes, put the eggs in a food processor or blender with the milk, flour, salt and ground hazelnuts and blend the mixture at high speed for a few seconds. With a rubber spatula push down any flour clinging to the sides of the container. Blend the batter for a few seconds more, then pour it into a bowl and allow it to stand, covered, for 1 hour. Heat a 6-inch (15-cm) crêpe pan until it is hot, otherwise the crêpe will not set properly. Brush the pan with clarified butter and pour in 2 tablespoons (30 ml) batter. Quickly tilt and rotate the pan so that the batter covers the bottom in a thin layer, and return any excess to the bowl. Cook the crêpe until it is lightly browned on the bottom, and the top liquid has set. With a spatula or small fish slice turn over the crêpe and cook it until the other side is browned. Slip the crêpe on to a plate. Continue

making crêpes in this manner until all the batter is used. Keep the crêpes warm, lightly covered with foil in a 300°F, 150°C, Mark 2 oven.

If, however, you are making the crêpes well in advance and freezing them, pile them on a sheet of aluminium foil, with each crêpe separated from the other by small squares (4 inches/10 cm) of foil or freezer tissue. Then wrap up in the foil, label and freeze.

To make the praline, in a medium-sized saucepan slowly dissolve the sugar in 6 table-spoons (90 ml) water over low heat then bring to the boil and boil until the mixture turns to a light caramel colour. Add the nuts and turn the mixture on to lightly oiled greaseproof paper or waxed paper on a wooden board, and leave to cool. Chop the nut mixture into small but coarse bits and blend with the melted chocolate. Again, pour the chocolate-nut mixture on to greaseproof or waxed paper and allow to cool. Mince either in a food processor or blender. Put in a jar with a tight-fitting top. This will keep for weeks.

To make the sauce, in a medium-sized saucepan slowly dissolve the sugar in 6 fl oz (175 ml, ¾ cup) water over low heat, then bring it to the boil and boil until it reaches a pale caramel colour. Lower the heat and add the remaining ingredients (except the orange rind) and simmer for 1 minute more.

To serve, take each crêpe and spread the praline filling over one half of it. Fold the crêpes in half, then in half again, making a fan shape. Place the crêpes in an attractive pattern on a shallow fireproof serving dish, pour the sauce over them, and reheat them over a low heat or in a low oven for a few minutes. Sprinkle with finely chopped orange rind.

Total cooking and preparation time:
approximately 2 hours
(Crêpes: 1 hour 40 minutes
Praline: 30–40 minutes
Sauce and finishing: approximately 30 minutes)

Opposite: Mushrooms Stuffed with Garlic Prawns (Shrimp), p. 97 Overleaf: (left to right) Barbecued Devilled Pheasants with Jerusalem Artichoke Chips, pp. 83–4; Yan Kit's Chinese Pickled Cabbage, Peking-style, p. 84; Soufflé Roulé aux Épinards with Fresh Coriander Cream Sauce, pp. 82–3

*Stuffed Seafood Profiteroles with
Coriander Yoghurt Sauce

———

Veal Scallopini with Foie Gras and
*Spinach Fritters

———

Stir-fried Mangetout (Snow Peas) with
Toasted Sesame Seeds (see page 66)

———

*Flaming Fruit with Brandy Sauce

Everything can be prepared in advance
up to a point. The first course may be
prepared the day before, then the stuffing
put in an hour or two before the dinner.
The coriander sauce may be prepared the
day before. The veal scallopini may be
prepared a few hours before, then
reheated. The spinach fritters can be
halfway prepared then finished off, and
the dessert, 1 hour before. Only the
mangetout (snow peas) must be fried at
the last moment while the meat is
reheating and the spinach fritters are
cooking.

*Stuffed Seafood Profiteroles with Coriander Yoghurt Sauce

This very special first course is light, delicious
and decidedly different. The combination of
tastes is unique. The choux puffs can be baked
2 hours before the meal, or even the day
before and refrigerated, then filled and heated
just before serving.

For the profiteroles:
4 tablespoons (60 ml) unsalted butter
1 tablespoon (15 ml) granulated sugar
½ teaspoon (2.5 ml) salt
5 oz (150 g, 1 cup) unbleached flour, sifted
4 eggs

Opposite: Flaming Fruit with Brandy Sauce, p. 107

For the filling:
8 oz (225 g, 1 cup) cream cheese
2 tablespoons (30 ml) milk
1 teaspoon (5 ml) grated horseradish
¼ teaspoon (1.5 ml) salt
dash of pepper
7 oz (200 g) smoked prawns (shrimp), smoked
   trout or mackerel
2 tablespoons (30 ml) onion, chopped
2 oz (50 g) red caviar
2 oz (50 g, ⅓ cup) almonds, chopped finely

For the coriander yoghurt sauce:
1 bunch coriander (Chinese parsley)
3 fl oz (75 ml, ⅓ cup) plain yoghurt
6 oz (175 g, ¾ cup) cream cheese
3 tablespoons (45 ml) strong horseradish cream
salt and freshly ground white pepper

Preheat the oven to 425°F, 220°C, Mark 7. In a
large heavy saucepan bring 6 fl oz (175 ml, ¾ cup)
water to the boil over moderate heat, then add
the butter, sugar and salt. When the butter has
melted, remove the pan from the heat and pour in
the flour, all at once. Beat the dough until the
mixture pulls away from the sides of the pan and
forms a ball. Add 3 eggs, one by one, beating each
into the dough until well blended before adding
the next. When the eggs have been absorbed, the
mixture should be thick and glossy.

Grease 2 baking sheets and flour them. Drop
rounded teaspoons of dough on the baking sheets
– the puffs will expand quite a bit during baking,
so allow plenty of space between each mound.
Beat the remaining egg and lightly brush the top
of each choux puff with it. Bake in the centre of
the preheated oven for 10 minutes.

Reduce the temperature to 350°F, 180°C, Mark
4 and continue to bake for a further 15–20
minutes. By the end of the cooking time the puffs
will have doubled in size and should be light
brown in colour. Remove the pastries from the
oven, turn off the heat and cool them on a wire
rack for 10 minutes.

To make the filling, combine the cream cheese,
milk, horseradish, salt and pepper and mix until
smooth. If using smoked prawns (shrimp), place
the shelled prawns (shrimp) in a food processor or
blender and make into a paste. If using smoked
trout or mackerel, skin, bone and flake the fish.
Add the smoked fish to the cream cheese mixture
together with the onion, red caviar and almonds.

To make the sauce, in a food processor, mince
the coriander leaves and add the remaining
ingredients. Chill.

To fill the puffs, gently split them, fill with the

smoked fish mixture and heat at 350°F, 180°C, Mark 4 for 10 minutes. Serve the chilled sauce over the hot profiteroles.

Preparation time: 35 minutes
Cooking time: 35–40 minutes

Veal Scallopini with Foie Gras and *Spinach Fritters

The spinach fritters can be prepared up to the last minute, frying a few hours in advance. Then they can be refried at the last minute while the meat is cooking.

2 lb (900 g), fillet of veal, cut into 8 thin slices
· and beaten
salt
6 tablespoons (90 ml) olive oil
8 thin slices of white bread
4 oz (125 g, ½ cup) unsalted butter
½-lb (225-g) can foie gras, duck or goose

For the spinach fritters:
2 lb (900 g) fresh spinach, stems removed, leaves
washed, or 1½ lb (700 g) frozen leaf spinach
8 fl oz (225 ml, 1 cup) olive oil
6 oz (175 g, ¾ cup) unsalted butter
1 large onion, chopped finely
1 teaspoon (5 ml) salt
freshly ground black pepper
freshly ground nutmeg
2 teaspoons (10 ml) ground mace
10 eggs
4 oz (125 g, ½ cup) dry breadcrumbs

Prepare the fritters first. If you are using fresh spinach, blanch the leaves in boiling salted water for 2 minutes, drain and chop. If you are using frozen spinach, defrost it and drain it, squeezing out all the moisture. In a large frying-pan, melt 2 oz (50 g) butter together with 3 tablespoons (45 ml) olive oil and sauté the onion until it softens. Add the spinach, season it with ½ teaspoon (2.5 ml) salt, pepper, nutmeg and mace to taste, and cook it for 2–3 minutes, until the spinach has completely wilted. Mix well with the onion and put aside.

Put 8 eggs, ½ teaspoon (2.5 ml) salt and some freshly ground black pepper in a bowl and beat well with a fork until the eggs are well blended. Add the spinach and mix well. Heat a seasoned omelet pan and melt 2 oz (50 g) butter, tilting it quickly around the pan so that it coats the bottom and sides. As soon as the foam from the butter subsides, pour in the spinach and egg mixture, stirring briskly in a circular motion, while shaking the pan back and forth, until the mixture begins to set. Allow it to cook for 1 minute. Shake the pan again, making sure that the omelet moves freely. Turn the omelet over with a wide spatula and cook for another minute, then turn it on to a plate to cool. When cool, cut into triangles. *Up to this point, the preparation may be done a few hours in advance.*

Season each veal fillet with salt. In a frying-pan, heat 2 tablespoons (30 ml) olive oil and fry each slice of bread, turning once, so they are golden. Remove them from the pan, spread some butter on each slice, then some foie gras and place on a hot serving dish. In the same olive oil, adding more if necessary, sauté the veal fillets, 1–2 minutes on each side, no longer, as you want them underdone on the inside. When cooked, place 1 veal fillet on each piece of bread, top with a few dots of butter and place in a warm oven while you finish the spinach fritters.

Dip each spinach triangle in the remaining beaten eggs and then into the breadcrumbs and fry in the olive oil mixed with the remaining butter, until they are golden brown and crisp. Drain on kitchen paper towels. Garnish around the veal and serve at once.

Preparation time: approximately 25 minutes
Cooking time: 15–20 minutes

*Flaming Fruit with Brandy Sauce

My mother gave me this recipe. It is perfect for a cold winter evening. One of the joys of it is that most of the work can be done hours ahead, including the sauce. It has always been a tremendous success in our house.

1.82-lb (825-g) can pear halves
1.82-lb (825-g) can peach halves (white, if possible)
1.82-lb (825-g) can apricot halves
1.82-lb (825-g) can pitted black Bing cherries
5–6 whole cloves
5 oz (150 g, 1 cup) seedless raisins, or seeded muscat raisins
rind of 1 lemon, shredded finely
4–6 tablespoons (60–90 ml) dry sherry or port
Brandy Sauce

Preheat the oven to 350°F, 180°C, Mark 4. Pour all the fruit into a colander standing in a medium-sized bowl which will catch all the juices. Then pour half the amount of fruit juice into a small saucepan and add the cloves. Boil down this mixture until it thickens. Remove the cloves and discard.

Arrange the fruit in a shallow ovenproof serving dish. Place the pears, peaches and apricots alternately around the edge of the dish and the cherries in a mound in the centre. Sprinkle the raisins over all the fruit, then the lemon rind and finally 2–3 tablespoons (30–45 ml) sherry or port.

Place a lid or some aluminium foil tightly over the dish and place it in the preheated oven for 15–20 minutes. Remove the cover and sprinkle some of the thickened juice over the fruit, then put it back into the oven. Continue adding the juice from time to time, cooking for 1–1½ hours. The fruit can be kept warm in a very low oven, 250°F, 130°C, Mark ½, until just before serving. Then heat through, pour on the remaining sherry or port, flame it and serve with Brandy Sauce.

Preparation time: approximately 25 minutes
Cooking time: 1½–2 hours

*Brandy Sauce

4 egg yolks
1 tablespoon (15 ml) caster (superfine granulated) sugar
8 fl oz (225 ml, 1 cup) single (light) cream
2–3 tablespoons (30–45 ml) brandy

In a small mixing bowl beat the egg yolks with a wire whisk, then add the sugar, beating the mixture until it turns light and creamy. In a small saucepan, heat the cream but do not allow it to boil. In the top of a double boiler or a bain marie set on a stand over simmering water, combine the egg yolk mixture and cream. Heat, continually stirring, until the custard coats the back of a wooden spoon. Remove and cool it. Add the brandy. Serve separately with the baked fruit.

Preparation time: 10 minutes
Cooking time: 15–20 minutes

Kerala Fried Liver Masala

1-inch (2.5-cm) cinnamon stick
2 cardamom pods
4 cloves
1 teaspoon (5 ml) anise seeds
1 teaspoon (5 ml) coriander seeds
1 teaspoon (5 ml) cumin seeds
1½ oz (37 g, ½ cup) unsweetened desiccated coconut
4 dried red chillies
1-inch (2.5-cm) piece fresh ginger, peeled
4 slivers garlic
½ teaspoon (2.5 ml) turmeric powder
1 lb (450 g) lamb's or calf's liver, cut into 1-inch (2.5-cm) cubes
2 tablespoons (30 ml) vegetable oil
1 teaspoon (5 ml) black mustard seeds
1 large onion, sliced thinly
2–3 fresh curry leaves
1 tablespoon (15 ml) lime juice

In an electric coffee grinder, used only for spices, grind the cinnamon, cardamom, cloves and anise seeds. Reserve them for garnish. Then in the same, but cleaned, coffee grinder grind the coriander, cumin, coconut, chillies, ginger, garlic and turmeric powder until they form a smooth paste. In a bowl mix this paste with the liver cubes, so that each piece of meat is well coated with the spicy mixture. *Up to here everything may be prepared a few hours beforehand.*

Put the liver in a sauté pan, add 8 fl oz (225 ml, 1 cup) water and cook, stirring constantly, for 5 minutes until the liver is tender and dry. In a large frying-pan heat the oil, add the mustard seeds and fry until the mustard starts popping. Add the sliced onion and curry leaves and cook until the onion turns light golden. Put in the liver and sauté over high heat until it turns a light golden colour. Sprinkle it with lime juice and the reserved ground spices and serve at once.

Preparation time: 20 minutes
Cooking time: 15 minutes

---

*Zuppa Gruesa di Verdura

4 fl oz (125 ml, ½ cup) olive oil
2 lb (900 g) leeks, cleaned and cut into ½-inch (1.2-cm) pieces
1 tablespoon (15 ml) chopped celery
salt and pepper
juice of 1 lemon
½ lb (225 g) spinach, washed, stems removed and chopped
2 lb (900 g) fresh peas, shelled, or 1 lb (450 g) frozen
¼ lettuce, cleaned and shredded
1 tablespoon (15 ml) chopped mint leaves
2 pints (1.2 litres, 2½ pints) chicken stock (broth)
milk, if necessary

In a large saucepan, heat the olive oil, then sauté the leeks, celery, salt, pepper and lemon juice. Simmer slowly, over low heat, for 20 minutes. Add the spinach, peas, lettuce and mint. Cook, stirring, for 2 minutes then add the stock (broth) and cook for 10 minutes. Pour the soup into a food processor or blender, when smooth and thick pour it back into the saucepan. If the soup is too thick, add a little milk before serving.

Preparation time: 20–30 minutes
Cooking time: approximately 45 minutes

Fernanda's Portuguese Baked Marinated Pork Loin

1 medium-sized onion, sliced thinly
3 garlic cloves, crushed
1 tablespoon (15 ml) salt
1 tablespoon (15 ml) freshly ground black pepper
6 dashes Tabasco sauce
pinch of turmeric powder
¼ teaspoon (1.25 ml) ground cumin
½ teaspoon (2.5 ml) chili powder
1 bay leaf
8 fl oz (125 ml, 1 cup) red wine
4 fl oz (125 ml, ½ cup) red wine vinegar
3 lb (1.4 kg) pork loin on the bone, scored

In a medium-sized ovenproof casserole, earthenware or enamel, mix all the ingredients and add the pork loin. Do not use an aluminium dish as it will make the wine and vinegar turn acid, which will make you ill. Marinate for 4 days, turning the pork twice a day. Left in a cool place, the wine and vinegar will preserve the pork for a long time.

Preheat the oven to 350°F, 180°C, Mark 4. Place the pork in its marinade in the preheated oven, cover and bake for 2 hours. Uncover and bake for an additional 30 minutes to make the crackling crisp. Lamb and chicken are also delicious marinated and cooked in this manner.

Marinating time: 4 days
Cooking time: 2½ hours

DINNER
SERVES 6

*Zuppa d'Ostrice
(Oyster Soup)

Garlic Chicken

or

*Veal Goulash

*Pasta Verde
(Fresh Green Tagliatelli)

Mixed Green Salad of your choice

Cheese and Biscuits

*Zuppa d'Ostrice

1 dozen raw oysters
16 fl oz (475 ml, 2 cups) fish stock (broth) or clam juice
2 oz (50 g, ¾ cup) fresh soft breadcrumbs
1 sprig parsley
1 bay leaf
1 tablespoon (15 ml) olive oil
1 medium-sized onion, chopped finely
2 stalks celery, cleaned and chopped finely
1 tablespoon (15 ml) plain (all-purpose) flour
16 fl oz (475 ml, 2 cups) milk, scalded
salt and pepper

Clean and pick over the oysters, *reserving their liquid.* Cut the firm muscle off the soft part of the oyster and chop each separately. In a large saucepan heat the fish stock (broth) or clam juice, add the breadcrumbs, parsley, bay leaf and the chopped firm muscles of the oysters. Simmer over a low heat for 3 minutes. In a frying-pan, heat the olive oil, add the onion and celery and cook until the vegetables are softened. Sprinkle in the flour, stir until the flour becomes incorporated in the vegetables, then pour in the reserved oyster liquid. Simmer and stir until it becomes thick and creamy. Add this to the stock (broth). Mix well, then pour into a food processor or blender and mix until it becomes thick and smooth. Up to this point the soup may be prepared in advance, then reheated. To reheat return soup to the saucepan, bring to the boil, add the milk and the chopped soft part of the oysters. Season. Serve hot, with salted biscuits.

Preparation time: 15–20 minutes
Cooking time: approximately 20 minutes

Garlic Chicken

2½–3-lb (1.1–1.4-kg) chicken, cut into serving
  pieces
salt and pepper
12 cloves garlic, peeled
1 medium-sized onion, sliced thinly
5 oz (150 g, 1 cup) celery, chopped
2 carrots, sliced thinly
1 oz (25 g, ¼ cup) fresh coriander (Chinese
  parsley) or parsley, chopped finely
3 fl oz (75 ml, ⅓ cup) medium dry sherry
3 fl oz (75 ml, ⅓ cup) sour cream or plain yoghurt

Preheat the oven to 350°F, 180°C, Mark 4. Place
the chicken pieces in a casserole and sprinkle
them with salt and pepper, garlic, onion, celery,
carrots and coriander (Chinese parsley) or parsley. Pour the sherry over the chicken and
vegetables. Cover tightly and bake in the preheated oven for 1½ hours. Remove from the oven
and stir in the sour cream or yoghurt. You will
find that this dish has a subtle taste particularly
suited to serving with pasta or kasha.

Preparation time: approximately 30 minutes
Cooking time: 1½ hours

*Pasta Verde

Makes approximately 1½ lb (700 g)

¼ lb (125 g) spinach, washed and trimmed
4 eggs, lightly beaten
1 lb (450 g) flour, preferably unbleached or durum
  wheat, sifted with a pinch of salt
salt
1 teaspoon (5 ml) olive oil

Blanch the spinach for 2 minutes in boiling
water. Drain thoroughly, squeezing out all the
liquid by putting it in a tea towel (dish towel) and
squeezing dry. Then chop it finely or put it in a
food processor or vegetable mill. Mix the spinach
and eggs. If the spinach is not totally dry, you
may need to add a little flour.

On a pastry board put the flour in a mound and
make a well, then pour the spinach and egg
mixture into the centre. With a fork, work the
flour from the outside of the mound into the
middle and over the eggs; work this into a smooth
dough, kneading until it is smooth, firm and has
an elastic consistency. This should take about 10
minutes. Roll into a ball and place in a plastic bag
to rest in a cool place for 30 minutes.

If you are using a pasta machine, divide the
dough into 2 pieces, dust with flour and, starting
with the widest opening, run the piece through
the machine. Then fold the piece into 3, like an
envelope, and run it through again, always
turning it around so that it never goes through
the same way twice in succession. Each opening,
usually 3, should be used 4 times, until the dough
is thin enough to be cut into narrow strips.
Sprinkle it with flour. Then run it through the
tagliatelle or fettucine cutter. The flour will keep
the strips from sticking to one another. Or, roll
the dough by hand as thinly as possible, and cut it
with a knife to the desired width.

Put the pasta on a platter lightly sprinkled with
flour and allow it to dry for at least 10 minutes
before using. If you have made more than you
need at the moment, either make nests of the
strips, allow to dry completely and keep sealed in
a tin, or dry on a pasta rack and place the extra in
a plastic bag and freeze. Some experts maintain
that pasta should not be frozen, but I have always
had excellent results doing so. However, when it
is placed in boiling water you must stir it with a
fork so that the strips do not stick together
forming a lump.

To cook, fill a large pot with water – the pasta
must have plenty of room in which to cook,
otherwise it will stick. Add 1 tablespoon (15 ml)
salt and 1 teaspoon (5 ml) olive oil. Bring the
water to a rapid boil and add the pasta. Cook for
2–3 minutes, until it is *al dente*, and empty it into a
colander to drain.

Preparation time: approximately 45 minutes
Resting time: 30 minutes
Drying time: 10 minutes
Cooking time: 2–3 minutes

Veal Goulash

3 lb (1.4 kg) shoulder of veal, cut into 1½-inch
  (3.8-cm) cubes
2 oz (50 g, ¼ cup) commercial shredded beef suet
1 bay leaf
1 tablespoon (15 ml) caraway seeds
1 tablespoon (15 ml) dill seeds
1 tablespoon (15 ml) salt
½ tablespoon (7.5 ml) black peppercorns
1 pint (600 ml, 2½ cups) veal or beef stock (broth)
15 oz (425 g) onion rings
3 tablespoons (45 ml) butter
2 tablespoons (30 ml) plain (all-purpose) flour
4 tablespoons (60 ml) paprika, or more
11 fl oz (325 ml, 1⅓ cups) sour cream

In a deep saucepan render the beef suet. Add the
veal cubes and brown. Add the bay leaf, caraway
seeds, dill seeds and salt. Tie the peppercorns in a
cheesecloth bag and add, together with the stock
(broth). Cover and cook slowly for 1–1½ hours, or
until the meat is tender. Meanwhile, cook the
onion rings in the butter until they are soft. Add
them to the meat 20 minutes before the end of the
cooking time. Blend the flour with 3 fl oz (75 ml, ⅓
cup) cold water and stir it into the cooking liquid.
Stir until thickened. Discard the bag of peppercorns and remove the pot from the heat. Stir in
paprika to taste, add the sour cream and heat
thoroughly, but do not boil. Serve with pasta or
kasha.

Preparation and cooking time: approximately 2
hours

—————— DINNER ——————
SERVES 4

Baked Halibut Mousse with *Mustard
Hollandaise Sauce

———

Sesame Chicken

or

Kamargah
(Kashmiri Spare Ribs)

*Bhindi-do-Piaza
(Indian Okra with Onions)

———

*Greek Yoghurt Cake

Baked Halibut Mousse with Mustard Hollandaise Sauce

I had this delicious dish at luncheon many
years ago and was given the recipe by my
host, to whom I am extremely grateful.

1 lb (450 g) halibut, cleaned, skin removed,
  chopped
3 egg whites
8 fl oz (225 ml, 1 cup) double (heavy) cream
salt, white pepper and cayenne pepper
1 tablespoon (15 ml) freshly grated nutmeg

Preheat the oven to 350°F, 180°C, Mark 4. Place
the halibut in a food processor and mix until the
fish has made a completely smooth paste. Then
place in the freezer for a few minutes so that it
cools down. Pour the fish paste into a medium-
sized bowl, then place this bowl in a larger bowl
filled with ice cubes.

In another bowl beat the egg whites until they
hold stiff peaks. In yet another bowl, beat the
cream until it becomes stiff. Gradually fold the
egg whites into the fish paste, then gradually beat
in the cream. Season generously with salt and
freshly ground white pepper and then cayenne to
taste. Add the nutmeg.

Butter 4 individual dariole moulds and pour in
the well-stirred mixture. Cover the moulds with
aluminium foil and place in a baking pan with
about 1 inch (2.5 cm) boiling water in it. Place the
baking pan in the preheated oven and bake for 25
minutes. When cooked, remove from the oven,
remove the aluminium foil and slide a knife
around the inside edge of each mould. Place a
heated plate upside down over the top of the
mould, and turn it over so that the mousse is
released on to the plate. Spoon some Mustard
Hollandaise (see page 112) over each serving of
mousse and serve the rest in a sauceboat.

Preparation time: approximately 30 minutes
Cooking time: 25 minutes

Mustard Hollandaise Sauce

Makes approximately 16 fl oz (475 ml, 2 cups)

2 tablespoons (30 ml) white wine vinegar
salt and freshly ground white pepper
4 egg yolks, beaten
8 oz (225 g, 1 cup) unsalted butter, softened and
    divided into 12 parts
1 teaspoon (5 ml) lemon juice
1–2 tablespoons (15–30 ml) Dijon-type mustard

In a small heavy saucepan combine the vinegar
with 2 teaspoons (10 ml) water, salt and pepper,
and cook the mixture over high heat until it has
reduced to 1 tablespoon (15 ml). Remove the pan
from the heat and add 1 tablespoon (15 ml) cold
water. Pour the mixture into the top of a double
boiler placed over warm water on low heat. Add
the egg yolks and stir briskly with a wire whisk
until they become thick and creamy. Start beating in the butter, one part at a time, lifting the pan
off the heat occasionally to cool the mixture.
Make sure that each part of the butter has
completely melted before adding more. Continue
to beat the sauce until it is thick and firm. When
all the butter has been used, add the lemon juice
and the mustard. Mix well. Keep it hot, off the
heat but sitting over the warm water, covered.

Cooking time: 15 minutes

Sesame Chicken

juice of 2 oranges
2 fl oz (50 ml, $\frac{1}{4}$ cup) olive oil
$\frac{1}{4}$ teaspoon (1.25 ml) Tabasco sauce
$\frac{1}{4}$ teaspoon (1.25 ml) dried dillweed
2 cloves garlic, minced finely
salt and pepper
4-lb (1.8-kg) chicken, cut into 8 pieces
3 oz (75 g, $\frac{1}{2}$ cup) sesame seeds

To make the marinade, in an earthenware or
glass dish combine the orange juice, olive oil,
Tabasco sauce, dillweed, garlic, salt and pepper.
Mix well, then place the chicken pieces in the
marinade, making sure to coat all sides of each
piece. Cover and marinate in the refrigerator for
at least 2 hours, or even overnight, turning over
the chicken pieces from time to time.

Preheat the grill (broiler). Place the pieces of
chicken, skin side down, on a baking tray. Spoon
half the marinade over them and sprinkle half the
sesame seeds over them as well. Grill (broil) the
meat about 4 inches (10 cm) below the heat for
about 15 minutes, or until the meat begins to
char. Turn the chicken skin side up and pour over
the remaining marinade. Sprinkle with the remaining sesame seeds. Grill (broil) for about
15–20 minutes more, or until the skin is crisp.

Preparation and marinating time: 2–3 hours
Cooking time: 30–40 minutes

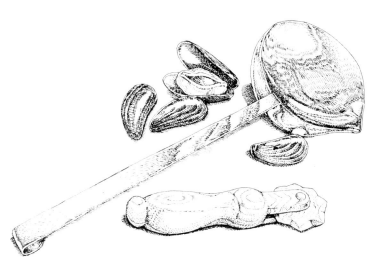

Kamargah

These are what you might call 'Kashmiri spare ribs', except they are not baked or barbecued, but deep-fried. These served with Raita (see page 51) and Kashmiri Divani Handia, a mixed vegetable dish (see page 154), make another interesting combination.

12 pieces of lamb breast, with 2 ribs in each
19 fl oz (550 ml, 1⅓ cups) milk
4 small cardamom pods
1 teaspoon (5 ml) anise seeds
4 cloves
1-inch (2.5-cm) cinnamon stick
4 oz (125 g, 1 cup) besan (chickpea or gram) flour
2 oz (50 g, ½ cup) rice flour
salt
½ teaspoon (2.5 ml) cayenne pepper
pinch of asafoetida
4 fl oz (125 ml, ½ cup) ghee or vegetable oil

Place the ribs in a large saucepan with the milk and 19 fl oz (550 ml, 1⅓ cups) water. Tie the cardamom pods, anise seeds, cloves and cinnamon stick in a piece of muslin (cheesecloth) and add it to the lamb. Boil for 30 minutes or until the lamb becomes tender. While the meat is cooking prepare the batter. Mix the besan (chickpea or gram) and rice flour with a little water. Mix well until it reaches a light consistency. To test it, drop 1 teaspoon (5 ml) of the batter into a cup of water. If the batter floats, the consistency is right. If not, beat again. Add the salt, cayenne pepper and asafoetida and mix well.

Drain the meat. Heat the oil in a deep frying-pan until it reaches 360°F (184°C). Dip the pieces of meat into the batter and fry in a single layer until they are golden brown. Drain on kitchen paper towels. Serve hot.

Preparation time: 20 minutes
Cooking time: 45 minutes

*Bhindi-do-Piaza

To prepare okra (ladies' fingers), wash them and pat dry. Then cut off the tops and snip off the tails. Do not scoop the okra when it is cooked because it will become mashed. Toss it instead with a flat spatula.

1 lb (450 g) okra (ladies' fingers) topped and tailed and cut into ½-inch (1.2-cm) pieces
3 tablespoons (45 ml) vegetable oil or ghee
1 teaspoon (5 ml) cumin seeds
1 medium-sized onion, chopped finely
1-inch (2.5-cm) piece fresh ginger, peeled and chopped
½ fresh green chilli, stem and seeds removed, chopped
½ lb (225 g) tomatoes, skinned and chopped
1 teaspoon (5 ml) turmeric powder
1 teaspoon (5 ml) cayenne pepper
1 medium-sized onion, quartered and quartered again
2 tomatoes, quartered and quartered again
1 teaspoon (5 ml) roasted or grilled cumin seeds, ground in a mortar (see p. 12)
fresh coriander (Chinese parsley), chopped finely for garnish
1 teaspoon (5 ml) fresh ginger, peeled and julienned
3 fresh green chillies, slit and stems and seeds removed

In a frying-pan heat 2 tablespoons (30 ml) oil and cook the okra (ladies' fingers) until three-quarters done. In a sauté pan, heat the remaining oil, then add the cumin seeds and cook over low heat. When they start to brown, add the chopped onion and cook until it turns a golden brown. Now add the chopped ginger and green chilli, stir, cook for 2 minutes, then add the chopped tomatoes, turmeric powder and cayenne. Mix well and cook this masala until the oil separates out. Then add the quartered onion and cook until it turns translucent. To this add the fried okra and quartered tomatoes and cook for 5 minutes. Sprinkle in the roast cumin seed powder and toss the mixture. Serve hot, garnished with chopped fresh coriander (Chinese parsley), ginger julienne and slit green chillies.

Preparation time: 30–40 minutes
Cooking time: approximately 50 minutes

*Greek Yoghurt Cake

I ate this cake at a Greek friend's house one day and begged for the recipe. Like all good cooks her measures were not always accurate but between the two of us we worked them out and this is the delicious result.

8 oz (225 g, 1 cup) unsalted butter
12 oz (350 g, 1½ cups) granulated sugar
5 eggs, beaten
1 teaspoon (5 ml) vanilla essence (extract)
10 oz (275 g, 2 cups) plain (cake) flour
1 teaspoon (5 ml) bicarbonate of soda (baking soda)
1 teaspoon (5 ml) baking powder
1 teaspoon (5 ml) ground cloves
2 teaspoons (10 ml) ground cinnamon
rind of ½ lemon, grated
8 fl oz (225 ml, 1 cup) plain yoghurt
11 oz (300 g, 2 cups) chopped walnuts or blanched almonds, if preferred

For the syrup:
12 oz (350 g, 1½ cups) granulated sugar
4 fl oz (125 ml, ½ cup) clear honey
½ teaspoon (2.5 ml) lemon juice
1 teaspoon (5 ml) vanilla essence (extract)

Preheat the oven to 325°F, 170°C, Mark 3. In a food processor or using an electric hand mixer, cream the butter and sugar together until it becomes light and creamy. Start adding the eggs one at a time, mixing well before adding the next one, and finally add the vanilla; again mix well.

In a large bowl, sift the flour together with the next 5 ingredients and mix well. Then add the egg batter to this, alternating with the yoghurt. Mix well and pour into a 13 × 9-inch (32.5 × 23-cm) greased baking pan and bake in the preheated oven for 1 hour.

Meanwhile make the syrup by boiling 16 fl oz (475 ml, 2 cups) water with the sugar, honey and lemon juice for 20–25 minutes, then add the vanilla. Pour the hot syrup over the cake and allow it to cool. Sprinkle chopped walnuts on top before serving.

Preparation time: approximately 45 minutes
Cooking time: approximately 1 hour

—————— *DINNER* ——————
Serves 4

*Chicken Rouxinol
(Portuguese Chicken and Chorizo Casserole)

or

Turkey alla Cittadina

*Kasha (see page 131)

Radicchio, Belgian Endive and Watercress Salad

———

Oo'whamat Pastry (Lebanese Pastry) with *Attar Syrup

The dough for this sweet pastry may be made in advance, as can the attar syrup, and the dough balls deep-fried at the last minute. The Chicken Rouxinol is always at its best the day *after* it has been made, so make it before you need it.

*Chicken Rouxinol

2 cloves garlic
12 fl oz (350 ml, 1½ cups) dry white wine
9 oz (250 g, 1½ cups) crushed (not ground) almonds
4 oz (125 g, ½ cup) lard
1 medium-sized onion, chopped
1 teaspoon (5 ml) cayenne pepper
1½ dried chilli peppers or 1 teaspoon (5 ml) chili powder
2 oz (50 g) Spanish chorizo sausage or any spicy sausage
3-lb (1.4-kg) chicken, quartered
salt and pepper
2 bay leaves

This dish improves with reheating and can be made the night before serving. This makes it particularly suitable for buffets. Crush the cloves of garlic and mix them with the white wine and crushed almonds. Allow the mixture to stand for about 1 hour so that the almonds and garlic soak up the wine. In a fireproof casserole melt the lard, add the onion and brown slightly. Add the cayenne, chilli peppers or chili powder and the chorizo (important: make a slit lengthwise in the sausage to keep it tender while cooking). Cover the casserole and allow it to simmer on low heat for 3–4 minutes, or until the chorizo is tender. Add the chicken to the mixture in the casserole and continue to cook on low heat for 25 minutes. (If the chicken is not young and tender, cook it longer but not quicker, otherwise it will fall apart.) Add the wine mixture to the casserole and season with salt and pepper to taste. Remove the lid and continue cooking until the sauce thickens (about 30 minutes). Add the bay leaves and allow to cool. Reheat the following day.

Preparation time: 1½ hours
Cooking time: approximately 1½ hours

Turkey alla Cittadina

What do you do with all that leftover turkey after Christmas? This Italian dish, with the delicate herbs, gives turkey a new dimension.

1 lb (450 g) cooked turkey
½ lb (225 g) cooked ham, sliced thinly
1 onion, sliced thinly
1 bay leaf
1½ tablespoons (22.5 ml) lemon thyme, chopped
1½ tablespoons (22.5 ml) fresh basil, chopped or 1 tablespoon (15 ml) dried basil
4 fl oz (125 ml, ½ cup) dry white wine
3 oz (75 ml, ⅓ cup) tomato purée (paste)
2 pints (1.2 litres, 2½ pints) turkey or chicken stock (broth)
salt
10 oz (300 g) whole black olives, pitted

In a fireproof casserole, place the ham slices on the bottom then the turkey pieces on top of them. Add the sliced onion, bay leaf, lemon thyme, basil and white wine. Dissolve the tomato purée (paste) in the stock (broth) and pour over the meat, adding salt to taste. Cook over low heat for 30 minutes, then strain the liquid and return it to the casserole, together with 4 oz (125 g) whole black olives and 6 oz (175 g) black olives pounded in a mortar and pestle to a purée. Continue cooking for an added 15 minutes, then serve.

Preparation time: 15 minutes
Cooking time: approximately 45 minutes

Oo'whamat Pastry

$\frac{1}{4}$ oz (7.5 g) dried yeast, or $\frac{1}{2}$ oz (15 g) fresh yeast
1 lb (450 g, 3$\frac{1}{2}$ cups) plain (cake) flour
1 teaspoon (5 ml) caster (superfine granulated)
  sugar
16 fl oz (475 ml, 1 pint) Attar Syrup
corn or groundnut (peanut) oil for frying
ground cinnamon

In a large mixing bowl dissolve the yeast in 2 fl oz (5 ml, $\frac{1}{4}$ cup) lukewarm water. Add the sugar and set it aside until the mixture rises and foams. Sift the flour into another mixing bowl. Then beat 18 fl oz (550 ml, 2$\frac{1}{4}$ cups) lukewarm water into the yeast and gradually add the flour, beating it constantly until you get a sticky batter. This may also be done very quickly in a food processor. Cover the batter with a damp cloth and put in a warm place for approximately 1$\frac{1}{4}$ hours, until it has risen, beating every 15 minutes.

In a deep-fat frying-pan pour approximately 3 inches (7.6 cm) oil and heat it to 360°F (184°C). Dip a teaspoon into cold water, then into the batter and drop balls of batter into the oil. Do not put too many in at one time because each ball will swell. When the balls have floated to the top, lower the heat and fry them until they turn a golden brown and are crisp. Drain on kitchen paper towels and dip while still hot into *cold* Attar Syrup. In this way the syrup will penetrate the pastry.

Bring the oil up to the very hot temperature again and fry the next batch. While they are frying, sprinkle the first batch with cinnamon. They may be served hot or cold.

Preparation time: approximately 25 minutes
Rising time: 1$\frac{1}{4}$ hours
Cooking time: 30–40 minutes

*Attar Syrup

Makes 1$\frac{1}{2}$ pints (900 ml, 2 pints)
As this can be used for other sweet dishes, I make up a batch and store it in an airtight jar in the refrigerator.

2 lb (900 g) granulated sugar
1$\frac{1}{2}$ tablespoons (22.5 ml) lemon juice
1$\frac{1}{2}$ teaspoons (7.5 ml) rosewater or orange
  blossom water

In a saucepan, preferably unlined copper, dissolve the sugar in 16 fl oz (475 ml, 2 cups) water, add the lemon juice and bring to the boil. Remove any foam rising to the surface and simmer for approximately 10 minutes, until the syrup thickens slightly. Then add the rosewater or orange blossom water and allow to cool.

Preparation and cooking time: 10 minutes

DINNER
SERVES 6

Kadhi (Gujarati Soup) with *Pakodas

Barbecued Butterflied Leg of Lamb

or

*Osso Buco

*Baked Aubergines (Eggplants) (see page 52)

Mixed Green Salad and Cheese

Ginger Ice Cream (see page 66)

The Pakodas (Indian fritters) may be prepared in advance to put in the hot soup. The baked aubergine, prepared in advance, may be finished off by putting it in the oven as you begin the first course.

Kadhi with *Pakodas

This is a delicately spiced Gujarati soup from the North Western part of India, a vegetarian region where asafoetida (a pungent resin), fenugreek, coriander, ginger, turmeric and garlic are used a great deal. In India, they eat this with the pakodas (fritters) in the soup as part of a meal. If you find this too rich, the soup is extremely good on its own.

For the pakodas:
8 oz (225 g, 2 cups) chickpea flour (besan or gram)
½ teaspoon (2.5 ml) baking powder
2 teaspoons (10 ml) salt
2 teaspoons (10 ml) cumin seeds
1 teaspoon (5 ml) cayenne pepper
1 teaspoon (5 ml) turmeric powder
1½ teaspoons (7.5 ml) ground coriander
½ teaspoon (2.5 ml) asafoetida
1 tablespoon (15 ml) plain yoghurt
9 fl oz (250 ml, 1⅛ cups) vegetable oil, or ghee, for frying

For the soup:
½ bunch fresh coriander (Chinese parsley) leaves
1½-inch (3.8-cm) piece of fresh ginger
3 green chillies, stems removed and seeded
4 cloves garlic, peeled
¾ pint (450 ml, 2 cups) plain yoghurt
1½ tablespoons (22.5 ml) chickpea flour (besan or gram)
1 tablespoon (15 ml) salt
1½ teaspoons (7.5 ml) turmeric powder
¾ teaspoon (3.75 ml) cayenne pepper
1 tablespoon (15 ml) vegetable oil or ghee
1 teaspoon (5 ml) asafoetida
4 sticks cinnamon
6 cloves
10 peppercorns
½ teaspoon (2.5 ml) ground fenugreek
3 curry leaves
3 dried red chillies
chopped green coriander (Chinese parsley) leaves

To make the pakodas, sift the flour, baking powder and salt into a bowl. Add remaining ingredients, except for the oil, beating continuously. Gradually add enough water to make a thickish batter. Cover. Put aside for 15 minutes.

Heat the oil in a deep-fat frying-pan to 360°F (184°C), or until a piece of bread turns golden. With a teaspoon, drop the batter into the hot oil (making approximately 12 at a time), keeping the fritters separate. Fry until golden brown, then remove and drain on kitchen towels. Repeat with the remaining batter. (Makes about 24 fritters.)

To make the soup, in a food processor, herb grinder or mortar and pestle, grind the coriander (Chinese parsley) leaves, ginger, green chillies and garlic. Beat the yoghurt until it turns smooth and of a buttermilk consistency. Add 1 pint (600 ml, 2½ cups) water and beat again. Then add the ground mixture of spices and herbs along with the flour, salt, turmeric and cayenne.

In a small frying-pan heat the oil and when it begins to smoke, make a *bhagar*, by frying the asafoetida, cinnamon, cloves, black peppercorns and fenugreek in it. Add the curry leaves and red chillies for a second or two. Add this to the yoghurt mixture, turn into a large saucepan and simmer for 2 minutes, covered. Remove the lid and simmer over low heat for 15 minutes. Drop the pakodas in the mixture and simmer for 15 minutes over moderate heat. Pour into a dish and sprinkle with coriander (Chinese parsley) leaves. Serve hot.

Preparation time: 25–30 minutes
Cooking time: 1 hour

Barbecued Butterflied Leg of Lamb

4½-lb (2-kg) leg of lamb, boned and butterflied

For the marinade:
1 teaspoon (5 ml) rosemary, crushed
1 teaspoon (5 ml) thyme, crushed
1 teaspoon (5 ml) marjoram, crushed
½ teaspoon (2.5 ml) oregano, crushed
2 tablespoons (30 ml) spring onions, chopped
2 cloves garlic, minced
¼ teaspoon (1.25 ml) ground black pepper
½ teaspoon (2.5 ml) Worcestershire sauce
1 teaspoon (5 ml) salt
4 fl oz (125 ml, ½ cup) olive oil
8 fl oz (225 ml, 1 cup) red wine

Mix the marinade ingredients thoroughly and pour over the lamb in a shallow pan. Cover and allow to stand for 24 hours, basting it occasionally. Preheat the grill (broiler) and grill (broil) or cook on a barbecue for 45 minutes, turning frequently and basting with the marinade, using a branch of rosemary as a brush if possible. *Do not cook to well done.* The lamb should be crusty on the outside and pink in the centre.

Marinating time: 24 hours
Preparation time: approximately 25 minutes
Cooking time: approximately 45 minutes

*Osso Buco

The idea of using gooseberries instead of tomatoes was given to me by Jane Grigson. It gives a delicious tart taste to the stew.

6 2-inch (5-cm) thick slices of veal shin
salt and pepper
flour for dredging
3 fl oz (75 ml, ⅓ cup) olive oil
2 cloves garlic
1 large onion, chopped finely
1 large carrot, chopped finely
1 large stalk celery, chopped finely
4 fl oz (125 ml, ½ cup) dry white wine
1 lb (450 g) cooking gooseberries, topped and tailed
bouquet garni (parsley sprigs, 1 small bay leaf, 6 peppercorns, all tied in muslin/cheesecloth)
8 fl oz (225 ml, 1 cup) beef stock (broth)
rind of 1 lemon, chopped finely
3 tablespoons (45 ml) fresh coriander (Chinese parsley) or parsley, chopped finely

Preheat the oven to 350°F, 180°C, Mark 4. Sprinkle the meat with salt and pepper. Dredge with flour and shake off the excess. Heat half the olive oil in a large ovenproof, lidded casserole. Add 1 clove of garlic and brown until golden. Remove, chop it very finely and set aside. To the same oil add the veal shin pieces and brown carefully on all sides without losing the marrow. Add the onion, carrot and celery and more oil if needed, and cook for about 4 minutes, stirring constantly so as not to burn the vegetables. Add the white wine and boil the mixture for a minute or so to reduce it a little. Add the gooseberries, bouquet garni and chopped cooked garlic. Boil briskly. Pour in the stock (broth), stir well and bring to the boil. Cover and place in the preheated oven for 1 hour. Uncover and correct the seasoning. *Up to this point the dish may be prepared in advance and reheated.* Continue cooking, uncovered, for 10–15 minutes longer.

Meanwhile, make the gremolata. Mince the remaining clove of garlic, lemon rind and fresh coriander (Chinese parsley) or parsley. The quick way is to put them into an electric coffee grinder or food processor. Transfer the osso buco to a heated serving dish, spoon the gooseberries and sauce around them and sprinkle the gremolata over the meat.

Preparation and cooking time: approximately 2 hours

─────────── DINNER ───────────
SERVES 6

*Walnut Soup
───────

Hyderabad Barbecued Chicken

or

Eels alla Milanese

Pilaf à la Grecque with Vegetables
───────

*Biscottini
(Macaroons in Wine)

*Walnut Soup

2 tablespoons (30 ml) unsalted butter
2 tablespoons (30 ml) plain (all-purpose) flour
2½ pints (1.5 litres, 3¼ pints) rich beef stock
  (broth) or canned bouillon, heated
8 oz (225 g, 1⅓ cups) walnuts, chopped finely
½ teaspoon (2.5 ml) salt
freshly ground black pepper
½ teaspoon (2.5 ml) Worcestershire sauce
a dash or two of Tabasco sauce
walnut halves for garnish

In a large saucepan over low heat, melt the butter, then stir in the flour and whisk until it turns into a smooth roux. Continue to stir while slowly adding the hot beef stock (broth) or bouillon. Allow the mixture to become thick and creamy in texture. Then add the walnuts, salt and pepper to taste. Worcestershire and Tabasco sauces. Simmer the soup over low heat for 30 minutes. Pour into heated soup bowls, garnish with walnut halves and serve hot with hot French bread.

*Preparation time: approximately 15 minutes
Cooking time: approximately 40 minutes*

Hyderabad Barbecued Chicken

4-1 lb (1.8-kg) chicken
3 small onions, chopped finely
1-inch (2.5-cm) piece fresh ginger, peeled
4 slices garlic
4 red chillies, stems and seeds removed, chopped
2 teaspoons (10 ml) garam masala (see page 181)
2 teaspoons (10 ml) roasted and ground cumin seeds (see page 12)
10 fl oz (300 ml, 1¼ cups) plain yoghurt, beaten
3 tablespoons (45 ml) ghee or clarified butter
red food colouring (optional)

Cut deep slits all over the body of the chicken. In a food processor grind the onions, ginger, garlic and chillies to a smooth paste. In a medium-sized bowl mix the paste, together with the garam masala and ground cumin, into the beaten yoghurt and ghee. Mix well so that it becomes smooth. Rub the mixture thoroughly into the chicken, making sure that it goes into all the slits. Allow it to marinate for 2–3 hours.

Preheat the oven to 375°F, 190°C, Mark 5, or start the charcoal fire. Bake the chicken in the preheated oven for 1 hour, or on a charcoal grill (time depends on the specific barbecue) until the juice in the thigh runs clear when pricked.

*Preparation time: 20 minutes
Marinating time: 2–3 hours
Cooking time: approximately 1 hour*

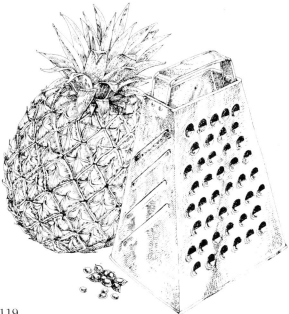

Eels alla Milanese

2 tablespoons (30 ml) unsalted butter
1 oz (25 g, 2 tablespoons) plain (all-purpose) flour
10 fl oz (300 ml, 1¼ cups) red wine
3 1-lb (450-g) or 2 1½-lb (700-g) eels, skinned, cleaned and cut into 2½-inch (6.3-cm) pieces
1 large onion, chopped finely
3 large cloves garlic, chopped finely
2 tablespoons (30 ml) fresh coriander (Chinese parsley) or parsley, chopped finely
2 tablespoons (30 ml) dried rosemary
2 teaspoons (10 ml) freshly grated nutmeg
1 teaspoon (5 ml) ground mace
2 bay leaves
salt
5 cloves
slices of lemon for garnish

In a fireproof casserole melt the butter, then add the flour and stir to make a smooth white roux. Slowly pour in the red wine, cooking until the sauce becomes thicker. Add the eels and the remaining ingredients except for the lemon slices. Cook over low heat for 30–40 minutes, or until the eel is tender. Place the fish on a heated dish, strain the sauce, pour it over the fish and garnish with lemon slices.

Preparation time: approximately 15 minutes, if fishmonger skins and cleans eels, 30–40 minutes if you do
Cooking time: 40–50 minutes

Pilaf à la Grecque with Vegetables

3 tablespoons (45 ml) unsalted butter
1 onion, chopped finely
1 small clove garlic, crushed
3–4 leaves of green lettuce, shredded
2 fresh pork sausages, sliced
3 large flat mushrooms, sliced
3 tomatoes, peeled, seeded and diced
7 oz (200 g, 1 cup) long grain rice, washed 3 times
16 fl oz (475 ml, 2 cups) chicken stock (broth)
1 teaspoon (5 ml) salt
dash of freshly ground black pepper
2 tablespoons (30 ml) seedless raisins
½ lb (225 g) cooked peas
1 sweet red pepper, chopped finely

In a large saucepan melt 2 tablespoons (30 ml) butter and brown the onion in it. Add the garlic, lettuce, sausages, mushrooms and tomatoes. To this mixture add the rice and mix it well. Pour in the chicken stock or broth and season with salt and pepper. Cover tightly and cook over low heat for 20 minutes. In the remaining tablespoon (15 ml) butter, sauté the raisins for 5 minutes in a small frying-pan, stirring continuously.

When the pilaf is cooked, mix it well with a fork and add the peas, the sweet pepper and sautéd raisins. Serve with lamb or poultry as a side dish, or use as a stuffing for poultry or veal.

Preparation time: 30–40 minutes
Cooking time: 25–30 minutes

*Biscottini

1 dozen almond macaroons (see recipe below)
8 fl oz (225 ml, 1 cup) red wine
8 fl oz (225 ml, 1 cup) double (heavy) cream,
    whipped
2 tablespoons (30 ml) icing (confectioners') sugar

Dip each macaroon into the red wine, but do not allow it to become too soft. Combine the whipped cream with the sugar. Sandwich the biscuits together with the cream and stand them in rows at the base of a shallow dish. Cover with the whipped cream, and make sure all the spaces between the piles of biscuits are filled. Chill in the refrigerator for 24 hours before serving.

Preparation time: approximately 15 minutes
Chilling time: 24 hours

*Almond Macaroons

Makes 3 dozen

6 egg yolks
8 oz (225 g, 2 cups) icing (confectioners') sugar
$\frac{1}{4}$ teaspoon (1.25 ml) salt
1 teaspoon (5 ml) grated orange rind
$7\frac{1}{2}$ oz (212 g, 1$\frac{1}{2}$ cups) plain (all-purpose) flour,
    sifted 3 times
6 egg whites, beaten stiffly
9 oz (250 g, 1$\frac{1}{2}$ cups) almonds, blanched and
    ground

Preheat the oven to 350°F, 180°C, Mark 4. In a large saucepan, over low heat, cook the egg yolks, sugar, salt and orange rind until they become thick and creamy. Then stir in half the flour and fold in half the egg whites. When blended, stir in the remaining flour and then the remaining egg white. Fill a pastry bag with the mixture, and squeeze out rounds about 3 inches (7.6 cm) in diameter on to a buttered and floured baking sheet. Sprinkle some of the ground almonds on top and bake in the preheated oven for 15 minutes or until they turn a pale brown.

Preparation time: approximately 20 minutes
Cooking time: approximately 30 minutes

─── DINNER ───
SERVES 8

*Caldo Verde

───

Selvaggina
(Italian Venison)

Curried Corn Pudding

───

*Flaming Fruit with Brandy Sauce (see
page 107)

───

The purée for the soup may be prepared in advance, only the cabbage and chorizo to be added when it is reheated. The curried corn pudding should go into the oven 30 minutes before dinner, to be ready with the venison.

---

*Caldo Verde

In Portugal this famous soup is made from the dark green cabbage, *couve*. The best substitute is ordinary cabbage, finely shredded and cooked for only 1–2 minutes otherwise it will be flabby rather than crisp.

$2\frac{1}{2}$ pints (1.5 litres, 3 pints) chicken stock (broth)
1$\frac{1}{2}$ large onions, chopped
1$\frac{1}{2}$ lb (700 g) potatoes, peeled and sliced
4 fl oz (125 ml, $\frac{1}{2}$ cup) single (light) cream
2 teaspoons (10 ml) ground cumin
salt and freshly ground pepper
1 lb (450 g) cabbage, shredded finely
$\frac{1}{2}$ lb (225 g) chorizo, chopped

In a large saucepan, heat the chicken stock (broth) over low heat, add the onions and potatoes and cook for 20 minutes, or until the potatoes become soft. Pour the mixture into a food processor or blender and mix until the purée is smooth. Return the purée to the saucepan, add the cream and season with the cumin, and salt and freshly ground black pepper to taste. *Up to this point the soup may be prepared in advance.*
Blanch the cabbage in salted water for 2 minutes, drain and refresh it under cold water. Drain again and stir into the hot soup. Pour the soup into heated bowls and top with the chorizo.

Preparation time: approximately 20 minutes
Cooking time: approximately 25 minutes

Selvaggina

16 fl oz (475 ml, 2 cups) red wine vinegar
3 cloves garlic, smashed flat
4 tablespoons (60 ml) chopped parsley
1 clove
2 large onions, sliced thinly
1 tablespoon (15 ml) dried oregano
4½ lb (2 kg) loin of venison
6 strips salt pork
1½ lb (200 g) canned peas and diced carrots
10 fl oz (300 ml, 1¼ cups) medium dry sherry

In an enamel saucepan (not aluminium or stainless steel because of the vinegar), combine the vinegar with 2 pints (1.2 litres, 2½ pints) water and bring to the boil. Add the garlic, parsley, clove, 1 sliced onion and the oregano. Remove from the heat and cool. Place the venison in this mixture and leave it to marinate, covered, overnight. Turn it once or twice so that all the meat is well marinated.

Preheat the oven to 350°F, 180°C, Mark 4. Remove the venison from the marinade and dry it on kitchen paper towels. Place it in a casserole together with the salt pork. Brown the meat on one side for 15 minutes, turn and brown on the other side for 15 minutes. Cover with the second sliced onion and marinade, then add the peas and carrots, and bake in the preheated oven for 1½ hours, basting occasionally. Finally add the sherry and simmer for 10 minutes. To serve, slice the meat thinly and place in a warm dish surrounded by the vegetables.

Preparation time: approximately 25 minutes
Marinating time: 24 hours
Cooking time: approximately 2¼ hours

Curried Corn Pudding

2 oz (50 g, ¼ cup) unsalted butter
3 oz (75 g, ¾ cup) onion, chopped finely
3 oz (75 g, ¾ cup) green pepper, chopped finely
1 tablespoon (15 ml) curry powder
11-oz (300-g) can corn kernels, drained
16 fl oz (475 ml, 2 cups) single (light) cream
3 eggs, beaten lightly
1 teaspoon (5 ml) salt
½ teaspoon (2.5 ml) granulated sugar
fresh parsley, chopped finely

Preheat the oven to 350°F, 180°C, Mark 4. In a medium-sized frying-pan melt the butter and sauté the onion and green pepper in it until they soften. Stir in the curry powder, mix well and transfer the mixture to a mixing bowl. Add the corn kernels, cream, eggs, salt and sugar. Mix thoroughly and pour into an 8-inch (20.3-cm) soufflé dish. Bake in the preheated oven for 45 minutes, until it has puffed up and turned golden. Sprinkle parsley on top. Serve with baked ham, roast chicken or game.

Preparation time: approximately 20 minutes
Cooking time: approximately 1 hour

Winter

Uova con Salsa di Funghi e Capperi

The sauce which accompanies this dish is delicious over any type of eggs.

1 dozen eggs, separated
2 teaspoons (10 ml) salt
freshly ground white pepper
6 oz (175 g, 2 cups) parsley, chopped finely
3 tablespoons (45 ml) olive oil

For the sauce:
3 tablespoons (45 ml) olive oil
1 medium-sized onion, chopped finely
8 ripe olives, green or black, chopped finely
$1\frac{1}{2}$ green peppers, chopped finely
14-oz (400-g) can plum tomatoes, chopped
2 7-oz (200-g) can mushrooms, drained and sliced
3 tablespoons (45 ml) capers
$\frac{1}{2}$ teaspoon (2.5 ml) cayenne pepper

First make the sauce. In a saucepan heat the olive oil, then cook the onions, olives and green peppers for a few minutes until the onions and green peppers become soft. Add the tomatoes and cook until the liquid evaporates. Then add the mushrooms, capers and cayenne pepper.

Preheat the oven to 425°F, 220°C, Mark 7. In a large bowl, beat the egg yolks until they are thick and creamy, then add the salt, pepper, parsley and 6 tablespoons (90 ml) hot water. Mix well. In a copper bowl beat the egg whites until stiff, then fold them into the yolk mixture. Take a fireproof dish and heat the olive oil in it. Cook the egg mixture in the oil over medium heat until the eggs set and are browned on the bottom. Then put into the preheated oven for 3–4 minutes or until the top of the eggs are browned.

Serve immediately with the mushroom and caper sauce.

Preparation time: approximately 20 minutes
Cooking time: approximately 25 minutes

Scallops Florentine

6 scallop shells
3 lb (1.4 kg) scallops, cleaned, tough muscle removed
$\frac{1}{2}$ lb (225 g) raw spinach, cleaned, stems removed, shredded
4 oz (125 g, $\frac{1}{2}$ cup) butter
2 tablespoons (30 ml) onion, chopped finely
3 tablespoons (45 ml) lettuce, chopped finely
2 tablespoons (30 ml) celery, chopped finely
3 tablespoons (45 ml) dry breadcrumbs
$\frac{1}{2}$ teaspoon (2.5 ml) anchovy paste
$\frac{1}{2}$ teaspoon (2.5 ml) dried dillweed
$\frac{1}{4}$ teaspoon (1.25 ml) dried tarragon, or $\frac{1}{2}$ teaspoon (2.5 ml) fresh tarragon, chopped
freshly ground white pepper

In a medium-sized saucepan, scald the spinach in boiling water, drain and set aside. Melt one-third of the butter in a small frying-pan, add all the remaining ingredients, except the scallops, mix well and heat thoroughly.

Preheat the grill (broiler). Place the scallops on a foil-lined baking pan, dot each with butter and place under the grill (broiler) until lightly browned. Divide the vegetable mixture equally between the 6 scallop shells, then divide the scallops equally and place them on top of the vegetable mixture. Sprinkle the spinach on top, return to grill (broiler) for 1–2 minutes until it has heated through. Serve immediately.

Preparation time: approximately 30 minutes
Cooking time: approximately 7 minutes

Cream di Granchi

3 tablespoons (45 ml) olive oil
1 teaspoon (5 ml) grated onion
1 oz (25 g, ¼ cup) celery, chopped finely
1 oz (25 g, ¼ cup) green pepper, chopped finely
4 tablespoons (60 ml) plain (all-purpose) flour
1 pint (600 ml, 2½ cups) milk
salt, pepper, paprika
1 lb (450 g) crab meat
4 tablespoons (60 ml) fresh coriander (Chinese
    parsley) leaves or parsley, chopped finely
6 pieces toast

In a large saucepan heat the oil, then sauté the
onion, celery and green pepper for 3 minutes
until they are softened. Stir in the flour, mixing
well, then add the milk, stirring constantly, and
cook until thickened. Add the seasonings to taste
and cook for a further 4 minutes. Finally, stir in
the crab and cook until the mixture is heated
thoroughly. *Do not allow it to boil.* Serve on toast,
surrounded by noodles.

Preparation time: approximately 20 minutes
Cooking time: 10–15 minutes

*Lemon Bread

4 oz (125 g, ½ cup) unsalted butter
8 oz (225 g, 1 cup) granulated sugar
2 eggs, slightly beaten
6½ oz (190 g, 1¼ cups) plain (all-purpose) flour
1 teaspoon (5 ml) baking powder
¼ teaspoon (1.5 ml) salt
4 fl oz (125 ml, ½ cup) milk
grated rind and juice of 1 lemon
3 oz (75 g, ½ cup) walnuts or pecans, chopped
    finely (optional)
2 oz (50 g, ¼ cup) granulated sugar

Preheat the oven to 350°F, 180°C, Mark 4. Cream
together the butter and sugar, then stir in the
eggs. Sift together the flour, baking powder and
salt and stir it into the creamed mixture alternately with the milk. Add the lemon rind and
nuts, if you wish, at this point. Pour into a 9 × 5-
inch (22.8 × 12.7-cm) loaf pan, and bake in the
preheated oven for 1 hour.

Remove the bread from the oven and pierce the
surface with a small skewer or toothpick to make
small holes all over the top. Combine the sugar
and lemon juice, heat until the sugar has dissolved, then pour very slowly over the hot bread,
so that it penetrates the bread through the holes.
Allow to cool.

Preparation time: approximately 15 minutes
Cooking time: approximately 1 hour

─ LIGHT VEGETARIAN LUNCHEON ─
SERVES 4

Polish Baked Mushrooms

Belgian Endive, Watercress and
Radicchio Salad

Cheese and Biscuits

─────── DINNER ───────
SERVES 8

*Thai Lemongrass Soup

Pigeons alla Sorrentina
(Italian Squabs)

or

Kashmiri Gustaba
(Meatballs in Yoghurt)

*Lebanese Spiced Rice (see page 86)

Tao Gugi
(Kashmiri Turnips)

Cheese and Biscuits

*Meloma Karona
(Greek Honey-dipped Sweet Biscuits)

Coffee

Polish Baked Mushrooms

½ lb (225 g) mushrooms
2 teaspoons (10 ml) lemon juice
1 tablespoon (15 ml) finely minced onion
3 tablespoons (45 ml) butter
¼ teaspoon (1.5 ml) salt
pinch of freshly ground black pepper
1 tablespoon (15 ml) flour
2 tablespoons (30 ml) freshly grated Parmesan
  cheese
8 fl oz (225 ml, 1 cup) double (heavy) cream
2 egg yolks, lightly beaten
2 tablespoons (30 ml) fine white breadcrumbs

Preheat the oven to 425°F, 220°C, Mark 7. Butter 4 individual ramekins. Wash the mushrooms and cut off their stems. Slice thinly and sprinkle with the lemon juice to prevent discoloration. In a saucepan with a tightly fitting lid, simmer the mushrooms and onion in 1 tablespoon (15 ml) butter until soft. Season with salt and pepper. Stir in the flour and grated Parmesan cheese and cook for about 3 minutes.

Spoon the mushroom mixture into the prepared ramekins. Mix the cream and egg yolks together and pour over the mushrooms. Sprinkle with the breadcrumbs and dot with the remaining butter. Place the ramekins in a shallow baking dish half-filled with hot water and bake in the preheated oven for about 10 minutes, or until golden brown. Serve immediately.

Preparation and cooking time: approximately 30 minutes

*Thai Lemongrass Soup

3¼ pints (2 litres, 2 quarts) clear chicken stock
  (broth)
6 tablespoons (90 ml) Thai fish sauce, from
  Oriental grocery stores
4 spring onions (scallions), sliced thinly
2–4 dashes chilli pepper sauce to taste (optional, if
  you like it very hot)
6 cloves garlic, minced
4 teaspoons (20 ml) ground coriander
2 large handfuls lemongrass
24 prawns (shrimp), smoked if possible, leaving
  tails on
fresh coriander (Chinese parsley) or parsley,
  chopped finely for garnish

Combine the first 7 ingredients in a saucepan and simmer for 1 hour. Up to this point the soup may be prepared in advance, then reheated. Then add the prawns (shrimp) and simmer for another 5 minutes. Garnish each serving with chopped coriander (Chinese parsley) or parsley.

Preparation time: 15 minutes
Cooking time: 65 minutes

Pigeons alla Sorrentina

8 whole pigeons (squabs), cleaned, trussed and
   oven-ready
8 fl oz (225 ml, 1 cup) groundnut (peanut) oil
6 pieces celery, chopped coarsely
1 large onion, stuck with 6–8 cloves
6 tablespoons (90 ml) chopped fresh basil, or 5
   tablespoons (75 ml) dried basil
salt
2½ pints (1.5 litres, 3 pints) game or chicken stock
   (broth)
1½ tablespoons (22.5 ml) plain (all-purpose) flour
juice and grated rind of 3 lemons
6 tablespoons (90 ml) Cognac or port
8 slices fried bread, crusts removed, cut into strips
Italian parsley, chopped finely

In a large casserole, place the pigeons (squabs)
together with the oil, celery, clove-stuck onion,
basil, salt to taste and stock (broth). Cook over
low heat for 1 hour. Remove the birds to a heated
dish and place in a low oven (275°F, 140°C, Mark
1) to keep warm. Strain the cooking liquid
through a sieve into a small saucepan and place
over low heat. Whisk in the flour until it becomes
thoroughly amalgamated, with no lumps visible,
then add the lemon juice, lemon rind and Cognac
or port. Simmer until the liquid has reduced to a
thick sauce. Arrange the fried bread strips around
the pigeons (squabs) and pour the sauce over.
Garnish with parsley.

Preparation time: 20 minutes
Cooking time: 1¼ hours

Kashmiri Gustaba

2 lb (1 kg) tender boned leg of lamb, trimmed of
   fat
2 teaspoons (10 ml) coriander seeds
1 teaspoon (5 ml) cumin seeds
1 teaspoon (5 ml) cayenne pepper
5 tablespoons (75 ml) arrowroot
salt
8 fl oz (225 ml, 1 cup) ghee or vegetable oil
1 egg
4 fl oz (125 ml, ½ cup) plain yoghurt, beaten
   lightly
1 teaspoon (5 ml) granulated sugar
1 inch (2.5 cm) fresh ginger, peeled and grated
bunch of coriander (Chinese parsley) leaves

It is very important to pound the meat well in
order to break down the fibres. You can do this
either with a wooden mallet made for the purpose
or put it twice through a food processor. In a dry
frying-pan, roast the coriander seeds and cumin
seeds until they start jumping in the pan and turn
pale brown. Remove and grind in a mortar and
pestle. Add these spices, the cayenne, arrowroot
and a pinch of salt to the minced meat. Then roll
the meat into balls 2 inches (5 cm) in diameter.

In a wok or karhai, as it is known in India, heat
about 2–3 tablespoons (30–45 ml) ghee until it
starts to smoke, then fry the meatballs until they
are golden brown. Remove them from the pan.
Beat the egg into the yoghurt to prevent it
curdling. Take a casserole (I use a *degchi* which is
the traditional heavy-bottomed brass vessel with
lid), pour in the yoghurt and over a low heat cook
it until the oil is absorbed and the liquid becomes
creamy. Stir frequently in one direction only to
avoid curdling.

Add the remaining ghee and stir until the
yoghurt completely absorbs it. Then add the
sugar and ginger and stir continuously until the
oil floats to the top. Pour in 1¼ pints (725 ml, 3
cups) water. When the liquid begins to boil put
the fried meat balls in and cook for 15–20
minutes. Then lower the heat to the barest
simmer, cover the casserole, and cook for another
15–20 minutes. Remove and sprinkle with fresh
coriander (Chinese parsley) leaves.

Preparation time: 40 minutes
Cooking time: approximately 1 hour

Tao Gugi

2 lb (1 kg) small turnips, peeled and quartered
4 fl oz (125 ml, ½ cup) ghee or vegetable oil
1 teaspoon (5 ml) cumin seeds
pinch of asafoetida
4 cloves
1 fresh green chilli, stem and seeds removed and
    chopped finely
1 inch (2.5 cm) fresh ginger, peeled and crushed
1 teaspoon (5 ml) ground ginger
salt and cayenne pepper
1 teaspoon (5 ml) turmeric powder
1 teaspoon (5 ml) sugar
2 teaspoons (10 ml) ground coriander
1 teaspoon (5 ml) garam masala (see page 181)
fresh coriander (Chinese parsley) leaves, chopped
    finely, for garnish

In a large frying-pan, heat 2 fl oz (50 ml, ¼ cup) ghee or vegetable oil, and sauté the turnips lightly until they turn golden. Put aside. In a medium-sized saucepan, heat the remaining ghee and fry the cumin seeds, asafoetida, cloves, green chilli, ginger and ground ginger for a few seconds. Add the turnips, salt and cayenne to taste, turmeric powder and sugar and 12 fl oz (350 ml, 1½ cups) water. Simmer over low heat for about 10 minutes, then add the ground coriander and the garam masala, and simmer until all the liquid has been absorbed. Garnish with fresh coriander (Chinese parsley) leaves.

Preparation time: approximately 30 minutes
Cooking time: approximately 20 minutes

*Meloma Karona

Makes about 50 biscuits (cookies)

4 oz (125 g, ½ cup) unsalted butter, at room
    temperature
8 fl oz (225 ml, 1 cup) olive or vegetable oil
2 oz (50 g, ½ cup) icing (confectioners') sugar
2 tablespoons (30 ml) clear honey
juice of 1 orange
juice of ½ lemon
2 tablespoons (30 ml) Cognac or whisky
1 teaspoon (5 ml) vanilla essence (extract)
2 egg yolks
1 lb (450 g) plain (cake) flour
2 teaspoons (10 ml) baking powder
½ teaspoon (2.5 ml) bicarbonate of soda (baking
    soda)
1 teaspoon (5 ml) ground cinnamon

For the syrup:
1 lb (450 g, 1 cup) clear honey
6 oz (175 g) almonds or pecans, chopped

Preheat the oven to 350°F, 180°C, Mark 4. In a medium-sized bowl, with an electric mixer, cream the butter, oil and sugar together until it becomes light and fluffy. Then add the orange and lemon juice, Cognac or whisky, vanilla and egg yolks. In another bowl, sift the dry ingredients together and gradually add them to the creamed mixture, mixing well after each addition, until it turns into a soft dough. (This can all be done in no time in a food processor.) Taking 2 tablespoons, make oval shapes from the dough and place on a greased and floured baking sheet and bake in the preheated oven for 15 minutes, until the biscuits (cookies) have turned golden.

Meanwhile make the syrup. In a saucepan put the honey and 2 fl oz (50 ml, ¼ cup) water and boil for 5 minutes. Turn down the heat. While the syrup is still warm, dip each baked biscuit (cookie) into the syrup and then sprinkle with the chopped nuts. Cool and store in an airtight container.

Preparation time: 35 minutes
Cooking time: 15 minutes

───────── DINNER ─────────
SERVES 4

Mussel Soup
────────

Chinese Casserole of Mushroom Pigeons
(Squabs)

or

Chinese Pork Chops

Sweet and Sour Green Beans

*Kasha
────────

*Fichi Speziati con Crema
(Spiced Figs with Cream)

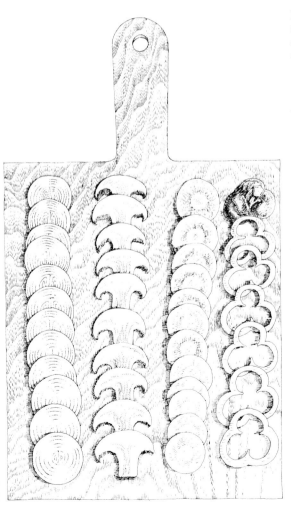

Mussel Soup

24 mussels, cleaned and beards removed
2 tablespoons (30 ml) olive or vegetable oil
1 large onion, chopped finely
1 large tomato, peeled, seeds removed and chopped
  finely
½ teaspoon (2.5 ml) salt
freshly ground pink peppercorns
1 teaspoon (5 ml) ground cumin
1 teaspoon (5 ml) ground ginger
6 oz (175 g) sliced and toasted white bread, crusts
  removed (6–8 slices)
2 oz (50 g, ⅓ cup) almonds, roasted
2 cloves garlic
2 sprigs fresh coriander (Chinese parsley) or
  parsley
1 egg, hard-boiled

In a dry frying-pan place the mussels and cook
over high heat, shaking gently, until the shells
open. Discard any mussels whose shells have not
opened. Remove the mussels from their shells but
reserve the liquid.

In a large saucepan, heat the oil and sauté the
onion and tomato until the onion has softened.
Add the salt, pepper, cumin, ginger and mussels
and the reserved juice and sauté them together
for 2–3 minutes over low heat. Add 2 pints (1.1
litres, 2½ pints) hot water, bring to the boil, then
add the bread. In a mortar and pestle or a food
processor, mix the almonds, garlic and coriander
(Chinese parsley) or parsley until it becomes a
paste. Chop up the hard-boiled egg and add it,
together with the almond paste, to the soup. Test
for seasoning and simmer over low heat for 45
minutes.

Preparation time: 45 minutes
Cooking time: 55 minutes

Chinese Casserole of Mushroom Pigeons (Squabs)

4 fat pigeons (squabs), split in half
7 teaspoons (35 ml) soy sauce
3 tablespoons (45 ml) groundnut (peanut) or corn
    oil
4 slices prosciutto or Parma ham, cut in half
1½ teaspoons (7.5 ml) salt
1 teaspoon (5 ml) sugar
1 teaspoon (5 ml) 'five-spice' powder
2 tablespoons (30 ml) Shaohsing wine or dry
    sherry
about 8 fl oz (225 ml, 1 cup) chicken or game
    stock (broth)
16 fresh white mushrooms or 1 7-oz (200-g) can
    mushrooms, drained
½ lb (225 g) mangetout (snow peas)
pinch of bicarbonate of soda (baking soda)
1 teaspoon (5 ml) cornflour (cornstarch)

Rub 1 teaspoon (5 ml) soy sauce into *each* pigeon (squab) (both halves). In a casserole, heat 2 tablespoons (30 ml) oil and sauté the pigeon (squab) halves, skin side down, to a dark golden-brown colour. Then turn over the birds and place a piece of ham between each two halves, so that the birds are sitting in the pan as 4 whole pigeons (squabs).

In a bowl, mix ½ teaspoon (2.5 ml) salt, the sugar, the 'five-spice' powder, 2 teaspoons (10 ml) soy sauce, 1 tablespoon (15 ml) Shaohsing wine or dry sherry and pour it over the pigeons (squabs). To this add chicken or game stock (broth) to cover. Bring to the boil, cover, turn down the heat and simmer for approximately 1 hour. Add the mushrooms and continue to simmer for 30 minutes, or until the pigeons (squabs) are tender.

Just before the pigeons (squabs) are cooked, in a wok, heat 1 tablespoon (15 ml) oil, and add the mangetout (snow peas) with 1 teaspoon (5 ml) salt, a pinch of bicarbonate of soda (baking soda) and 2 tablespoons (30 ml) chicken stock (broth). Cover and braise for 2–4 minutes, until the vegetables are just tender but still crunchy. Drain and reserve in a warm oven for use as a garnish.

When cooked, place the pigeons (squabs) on a warm serving dish and garnish them with the ham slices, mushrooms and mangetout (snow peas). Keep warm while you reheat the sauce and add a mixture of the cornflour (cornstarch), 1 teaspoon (5 ml) chicken stock (broth) and 1 tablespoon (15 ml) Shaohsing wine or sherry.

Allow the sauce to thicken, then pour it over the pigeons (squabs).

Preparation time: approximately 20 minutes
Cooking time: approximately 2 hours

Chinese Pork Chops

1 teaspoon (5 ml) Dijon-type mustard
2½ fl oz (62 ml, ⅓ cup) thick Chinese soy sauce
juice of ½ lemon
4 fl oz (125 ml, ½ cup) Madeira, port or Shaohsing
    wine
4 pork chops
8 fl oz (225 ml, 1 cup) chicken stock (broth)
1 large onion, cut in ½-in (1.2-cm) slices
1 tablespoon (15 ml) cornflour (cornstarch)
2 tablespoons (30 ml) fresh coriander (Chinese
    parsley) or parsley, chopped finely

In a fireproof dish large enough to hold the meat flat, combine the first 4 ingredients and place the pork chops in it to marinate for 2 hours, turning them occasionally.

Then preheat the grill (broiler) and grill (broil) the chops for 20 minutes, basting often with the marinade. If the marinade evaporates too quickly add some chicken stock (broth). Turn over the chops and add the sliced onion and cook for 20 minutes. When the chops are well-cooked (important: pork must *never* be pink), remove them to a heated dish and keep warm.

Stir the cornflour (cornstarch) into the chicken stock (broth) and simmer until it thickens a bit and then add it to the marinade. Cook over low heat until the gravy thickens and becomes smooth. Add the fresh coriander (Chinese parsley) or parsley, stir and pour over the pork chops. Serve immediately.

Marinating time: 2 hours
Preparation time: approximately 20 minutes
Cooking time: approximately 50 minutes

Sweet and Sour Green Beans

1 lb (450 g) French or runner (string or stick)
   beans, cleaned and sliced
salt
4 slices lean bacon
1 tablespoon (15 ml) white wine vinegar
1 tablespoon (15 ml) soft brown sugar

Place the prepared beans in a pan of lightly salted boiling water; cover and simmer for about 7 minutes. Meanwhile, slice the bacon crosswise into narrow strips. *Fry without any extra fat* until the bacon bits are crisp. Lift them out with a slotted spoon and keep warm. Stir the vinegar and sugar into the bacon fat, add the drained beans and stir to coat them evenly with the sweet and sour mixture. Spoon the beans and liquid into a heated dish, and sprinkle with the bacon bits.

Preparation time: approximately 25 minutes
Cooking time: approximately 15 minutes

*Kasha

4 tablespoons (60 ml) butter, or 2 tablespoons
   (30 ml) each butter and goose fat
7 oz (200 g, 1 cup) kasha or buckwheat
1 egg
16 fl oz (475 ml, 2 cups) chicken stock (broth)
salt

In a heavy frying-pan sauté the kasha in 2 tablespoons (30 ml) butter for 1 minute. Stir in the egg and cook the mixture, stirring continuously over low heat, until it is dry and the grains are well coated with egg. Add the chicken stock (broth) and salt to taste. Cook the kasha over low heat, covered, for about 30 minutes or until all the grains are tender and all the liquid is absorbed. Add the remaining butter or goose fat and toss the mixture with a fork to separate the grains.

Cooking time: approximately 40 minutes

*Fichi Speziati con Crema

15-oz (425-g) can figs
3 tablespoons (45 ml) brown sugar
½ teaspoon (2.5 ml) ground ginger
2 sticks cinnamon
whipped cream
rum

In a sauté pan, pour the figs and their juice together with the brown sugar, ginger and cinnamon. Cook over low heat, uncovered, for approximately 15 minutes or until the liquid thickens. Pour the figs and sauce into a bowl, cover and chill for 2 hours. Serve with rum-flavoured whipped cream.

Cooking time: 15 minutes
Chilling time: 2 hours

SPECIAL OCCASION OR CHRISTMAS DINNER
SERVES 6–8

Goose alla Marchesa with Sauce alla Genovese

*Wild Rice and Mushrooms (see page 91)

Cavoli con Castagne
(Cabbage with Chestnuts) (see page 94)

*Black Fruit Cake with Brandy Butter
(Hard Sauce)

The Black Fruit Cake is like no other cake you have eaten. It remains moist. Like Christmas pudding, it must be made weeks in advance and 'fed' brandy once or twice a week until you serve it.

Goose alla Marchesa

This recipe takes some time and is quite expensive, but if you want something really special for Christmas or for a dinner party, it is well worth it. If you wish you can prepare the stuffing ahead, even the night before, but keep it separately in the refrigerator. Do not stuff the bird until you are ready to cook it, otherwise it may go bad.

10–11-lb (4.5–4.9-kg) goose, boned

For the stuffing:
6 oz (175 g) raw veal, ground
6 oz (175 g) lean pork, ground
3 oz (75 g) beef marrow, ideally, or use butter
4 oz (125 g, 1⅓ cups) fresh breadcrumbs
8 fl oz (225 ml, 1 cup) goose, game or chicken stock (broth)
3 oz (75 g, 1 cup) grated hard cheese (Cheddar, Parmesan, Pecorino)
salt
2 teaspoons (10 ml) ground mixed spice
5 mushrooms, salted and chopped finely
3 oz (75 g) cooked ham, diced
grated rind of 1 lemon
3 egg yolks
¾ pint (450 ml, 2 cups) dry white wine
bunch each fresh marjoram, basil, thyme
Sauce alla Genovese

In a bowl combine the raw veal and pork, add the beef marrow or butter and mix. Soak the breadcrumbs in the stock (broth) for 5 minutes, then strain them and add to the stuffing, along with the grated cheese, a pinch of salt, the mixed spice, chopped mushrooms, diced meat and ham and grated lemon rind. Beat the egg yolks, pour them on to the stuffing and mix thoroughly. Finally mix in ¼ pint (150 ml, ⅔ cup) white wine.

Stuff the bird so that it resumes its shape and sew the cavity openings tightly. Take a casserole and place the goose in it, together with the bunch of sweet herbs and salt to taste. Pour the rest of the white wine over it, then add warm water to cover. Cover with the lid and simmer for approximately 2 hours, over low heat, until thoroughly cooked. As with all poultry, there must be no pink meat. Remove the bird from the casserole, leaving the herbs behind. Serve on a heated serving dish.

Preparation time: approximately 30 minutes, if butcher has boned goose
Cooking time: approximately 2 hours

Sauce alla Genovese

This is a kind of Italian hollandaise sauce which is light but piquant, served with steak or lamb cutlets/chops, or with Goose alla Marchesa.

3 oz (75 g, ⅓ cup) butter
juice of 1 lemon
2 egg yolks, beaten well
grated rind of ½ lemon
salt
pinch of cayenne pepper
1 clove garlic, chopped finely (optional)

In a bain marie or the top of a double boiler, melt the butter. Then over a low heat, add the lemon juice, the beaten egg yolks, lemon rind, salt to taste and cayenne pepper and cook, stirring constantly, until the sauce thickens. If you like it, add the chopped garlic.

Cooking time: approximately 15 minutes

*Black Fruit Cake

16 fl oz (475 ml, 1 pint) hot, strong black coffee
1¼ lb (575 g, 2½ cups) granulated sugar
8 oz (225 g, 1 cup) unsalted butter
2 lb (900 g) seeded, not seedless, raisins (puffed, seeded Muscat raisins are the best)
2½ teaspoons (12.5 ml) ground cinnamon
1 teaspoon (5 ml) ground cloves
2 pinches salt
1¼ lb (575 g, 4 cups) plain (all-purpose) flour
2 teaspoons (10 ml) bicarbonate of soda (baking soda)
8 oz (225 g, 1½ cups) walnuts, chopped roughly
brandy or rum

Preheat the oven to 325°F, 170°C, Mark 3. Make the coffee and allow it to cool. Then cream the sugar with the butter, add the raisins, spices and salt. When the coffee has cooled, add it to the mixture. Sift together the flour and soda and add to the mixture with the nuts. Mix well.

Grease an 8-inch (20-cm) cake pan and line it with greaseproof or waxed paper. Pour the mixture into it and bake in the preheated oven for 20 minutes. Then turn the oven down to 250°F, 130°C, Mark ½ and bake it for a further 2–3 hours.

When cooked cool the cake on a wire rack, then wrap in cling film (Saran Wrap) *not aluminium foil* and store it in a tin. Pour on brandy or rum and leave it in the tin in a cool larder, not in the refrigerator. Keep adding brandy or rum from time to time to keep it moist. It will keep for a long time. To serve, heat the cake and serve with brandy butter (hard sauce) or just eat cold as a fruit cake.

Preparation time: 30 minutes
Cooking time: 2–3 hours

Brandy Butter (Hard Sauce)

6 oz (175 g, 2/3 cups) unsalted butter
6½ oz (185 g, 1½ cups) icing (confectioners') sugar
2 fl oz (50 ml, ¼ cup) Cognac, or to taste
pinch of salt

Cream the butter well with an electric beater and gradually add the sugar, then the Cognac. Beat until the mixture is well mixed and light and fluffy. Add the salt. Mix and spoon into a dish. Chill for 2 hours.

Preparation time: 10 minutes
Chilling time: 2 hours

Curried Pheasant

*1 lb (450 g) leftover pheasant or poultry, all skin
and fat removed, chopped coarsely*
2 tablespoons (30 ml) vegetable oil
2 oz (50 g, ¼ cup) butter
1½ tablespoons (22.5 ml) curry powder
1 tablespoon (15 ml) plain (all-purpose) flour
1 medium-sized onion, chopped
1 small apple, peeled and chopped
6 prunes, stones removed, cut in half
24 sultanas (white raisins) or raisins
1 tablespoon (15 ml) mango chutney

In a large deep saucepan or casserole fry the meat
in the oil for 3 minutes. In another saucepan melt
the butter, add the curry powder, mix well, then
add the flour and mix well. Add the onion and
apple and cook, stirring constantly, until they
turn a golden brown. Add the meat, stir in the
prunes, sultanas (white raisins) and chutney and
simmer over the heat until the sauce has thickened. The pheasant should be hot and tender.
Serve with brown rice or Kasha.

Preparation time: approximately 20 minutes
Cooking time: approximately 20 minutes

=========== DINNER ===========
SERVES 4

*Smoked Fish Soup (see page 92)
———
Rabbit with Sweet and Sour Sauce

or

Curried Pheasant

or

Minced Pheasant in Baked Potatoes

Braised Cabbage à la Grecque (see page
86)

*Kasha (see page 131)
———
Fritelle alla Fiorentina

Rabbit with Sweet and Sour Sauce

This inexpensive and incredibly easy recipe
derives from Sicily, where it is a basic peasant
dish.

8 fl oz (225 ml, 1 cup) red wine vinegar
4 fl oz (125 ml, ½ cup) tomato pulp
3 stalks celery, cleaned and chopped
10 black olives, pits removed, chopped
1 tablespoon (15 ml) capers
4 tablespoons (60 ml) granulated sugar
½ teaspoon (2.5 ml) salt
1 rabbit, cut up into 8 pieces

In a casserole large enough to contain all the
rabbit pieces, mix the first 7 ingredients. Add the
rabbit, cover and stew in the sauce, over medium
heat, for about 1½ hours or until the meat is quite
tender. Serve in the casserole.

Preparation time: 15 minutes
Cooking time: approximately 1½ hours

Minced Pheasant in Baked Potatoes

This also makes a good luncheon or light
supper dish, and is equally delicious made with
chicken or turkey.

4 baking potatoes, cooked
1 lb (450 g) leftover pheasant
2 shallots, chopped
2 oz (50 g) parsley, chopped finely
salt and pepper
1 pheasant or chicken liver, minced
2 oz (50 g) cooked ham or tongue, minced
1 egg, well beaten
butter

Preheat the oven to 350°F, 180°C, Mark 4. Cut off
the tops of the potatoes lengthwise and scoop out
most of the flesh, leaving a good lining of potato
inside. (Reserve the rest of the potato for another
use.) Place the empty potato skins on a buttered
baking tray. In a bowl mix the minced pheasant,
shallots, parsley, salt and pepper together with
the liver and ham or tongue. Bind the mixture
with the beaten egg and fill the hollow potatoes.

Bake in the preheated oven until the tops turn brown. Just before serving place a small piece of butter on each potato.

Preparation time: approximately 15 minutes
Cooking time: approximately 15 minutes, if potatoes are already cooked
1½ hours if you must cook the potatoes

Fritelle alla Fiorentina

8 oz (225 g, 1¾ cups) plain (all-purpose) flour
pinch of salt
4 egg yolks
grated rind of 1 lemon
3 oz (75 g, ½ cup) hazelnuts, chopped
3 oz (75 ml, ½ cup) seedless raisins, or seeded Muscat raisins
vegetable oil
icing (confectioners') sugar

In a large bowl mix the flour with warm water until it forms a stiff batter; add the salt, egg yolks, lemon rind, nuts and raisins. Mix well until the dough leaves the side of the bowl. Heat plenty of oil in a deep-fat frying-pan to 360°F (184°C) and drop teaspoonfuls of the batter into it, frying them on all sides until they turn golden. Pile them on to a heated serving dish and sprinkle with sugar. Serve warm.

Preparation time: approximately 20 minutes
Cooking time: approximately 20 minutes

— DINNER —
SERVES 2

*Seviche (Marinated Fish with Ginger and Coriander Sauce) (see page 136)

Guinea Hen in Boursin
*Yan Kit's Chinese Pickled Cabbage, Peking-style (see page 84)

Buñuelitos de San José (St. Joseph's Day Fritters)

Guinea Hen in Boursin

1 guinea hen, cleaned and plucked
2 tablespoons (30 ml) unsalted butter or oil
1 6-oz (175-g) packet Boursin cream cheese, with garlic and herbs
5 fl oz (150 ml, ⅔ cup) sour cream
1 large clove garlic, crushed
2 teaspoons (10 ml) arrowroot
6 fl oz (175 ml, ¾ cup) red wine
10 fl oz (300 ml, 1¼ cups) chicken stock (broth)
salt and freshly ground pepper

Preheat the oven to 375°F, 190°C, Mark 5. In a large fireproof casserole, heat the butter or oil and brown the guinea hen on all sides. In a medium-sized mixing bowl blend the cheese and the sour cream. Add the crushed garlic. Mix the arrowroot in a little of the red wine until it becomes smooth. Pour the mixture, and the rest of the red wine, into the cheese mixture; blend well and pour over the guinea hen. Add enough chicken stock (broth) to cover. Place in the preheated oven for 45 minutes–1 hour. Remove and season. Cut the guinea hen in half and serve with the sauce.

Preparation time: 15 minutes
Cooking time: approximately 1 hour 10 minutes

Buñuelitos de San José

4 oz (125 g, ½ cup) short grain rice
1 pint (600 ml, 1¼ pints) milk
2 oz (50 g, ¼ cup) granulated sugar
1 vanilla pod or 2 teaspoons (10 ml) vanilla
    essence (extract)
grated rind of 1 lemon
3 eggs
juice of 1 lemon
2 oz (50 g, ⅓ cup) plain (all-purpose) flour
4 fl oz (125 ml, ½ cup) sweet sherry
3 oz (75 g, ½ cup) dry breadcrumbs
vegetable oil for frying
icing (confectioners') sugar

In a medium-sized saucepan, boil the rice in the
milk, with the sugar and vanilla pod or essence
(extract) for about 15–20 minutes or until it is
tender and has absorbed all the milk. Add the
lemon rind. Remove from the heat and leave to
cool. Then beat in 2 whole eggs, the lemon juice,
flour and sherry. Mix well and leave in the
refrigerator for 2 hours. Roll the rice mixture into
little balls or croquettes. Dip them in the remaining egg, beaten, then the breadcrumbs. In a deep
saucepan, heat the oil to 360°F (184°C) and fry
them. Drain well on kitchen paper towels, pile on
to a plate and sprinkle with icing (confectioners')
sugar. Serve immediately.

Chilling time: 2 hours
Preparation time: 15–20 minutes
Cooking time: 30–40 minutes

DINNER
SERVES 4

*Seviche (Marinated Fish with Ginger
and Coriander Sauce)

---

*Kadai Gosht (Curried Lamb)

or

Iscas a Lisbôa
(Liver and Smoked Ham, Lisbon-style)

*Mushroom Pullao (see page 167)

Palak Paneer (Spinach with Indian
Cream Cheese) (see page 54)

---

*Lemon Squares (see page 58)

*Seviche

This is a particularly delicious light first course
which is eaten in South America and Italy.
The citrus fruits 'cook' the fish as their acid
liquid penetrates the flesh. Any firm white fish
may be used.

6 fl oz (175 ml, ¾ cup) fresh lemon juice
6 fl oz (175 ml, ¾ cup) fresh lime juice
2 fl oz (50 ml, ¼ cup) fresh orange juice
4 teaspoons (20 ml) fresh coriander (Chinese
    parsley) leaves, chopped finely
1½ lb (700 g) fresh scallops, cut into bite-sized
    pieces (in Britain and Europe, use the corals as
    well)
1 teaspoon (5 ml) peeled and grated fresh ginger
1 teaspoon (5 ml) cayenne pepper
salt and freshly ground black pepper
1 clove garlic, crushed
2 tablespoons (30 ml) good olive oil
1 large red onion, sliced thinly
1 crisp lettuce

In a china or glass bowl, mix the fruit juices and 2
teaspoons (10 ml) chopped coriander (Chinese
parsley) leaves. Place the pieces of fish in it. Put
the bowl in the refrigerator, covered, for 3–4
hours, and turn the fish from time to time so that
it becomes completely marinated. The fish will
turn opaque from the effect of the acid juices.

One hour before serving, combine the remaining coriander (Chinese parsley) leaves and all the
other ingredients, except for the onion, in another bowl. Drain the scallops, discarding the
fruit juices, and toss them in the oil and spices.
Place some crisp lettuce around the edges of a
serving dish, pile the fish into the centre, pour on
the oil mixture and top with the onion rings.

Preparation time: 20 minutes
Marinating time: 3–4 hours

Opposite: *Austrian Eggs Czernin with Fried Parsley,
pp. 78–9 Overleaf: (left to right) Hot and Sour Soup, p.
165; Large Mixed Green Salad; Chicken Tikka Makhani
(Indian Chicken in Yoghurt and Tomato Sauce), p. 166
and Mushroom Pullao, p. 167*

*Kadai Gosht

2½ lb (1.1 kg) boneless lean lamb, cubed
4 oz (125 g, ½ cup) ghee or clarified butter
7 oz (200 g, 1½ cups) onions, chopped
7 oz (200 g, 1½ cups) tomatoes, chopped
1 teaspoon (5 ml) black peppercorns
1 teaspoon (5 ml) cayenne pepper
1 teaspoon (5 ml) coriander seeds, roasted
1 teaspoon (5 ml) cumin seeds, roasted
salt
1 teaspoon (5 ml) peeled and chopped fresh ginger
3 fresh green chillies, stems and seeds removed
1 pinch garam masala (see page 181 or buy it in
   an Indian or Oriental shop)
1 bunch fresh coriander (Chinese parsley) leaves,
   chopped

In a fireproof casserole brown the lamb cubes in
the hot ghee or clarified butter, then add the
onions and tomatoes and simmer for 10 minutes,
stirring continuously. Place the black peppercorns, cayenne pepper, roasted coriander and
cumin seeds in a mortar and pestle and pound
them together to a masala powder. Add the
masala to the casserole and toss the mixture
briskly over high heat. Then add salt to taste, the
ginger, green chillies, garam masala and chopped
fresh coriander (Chinese parsley) leaves. Mix well
and simmer for 7–8 minutes so that you get a rich
brown gravy.

*Preparation time: 20–30 minutes
Cooking time: approximately 20 minutes*

Iscas a Lisbõa

It is terribly important to have the liver sliced
extremely thinly. If you can find the
Portuguese smoked ham *presunto*, well and
good. If not substitute Parma ham, proscuitto
or even smoked bacon.

1 lb (450 g) calves' or lambs' liver, sliced thinly
2 tablespoons (30 ml) unsalted butter
3 oz (75 g) smoked ham or bacon, sliced thinly
½ lb (225 g) potatoes, peeled, boiled and sliced
   thinly
1 teaspoon (5 ml) white wine vinegar

For the marinade:
4 fl oz (125 ml, ½ cup) dry white wine
1 bay leaf
1 clove garlic, chopped
freshly ground black pepper
1 teaspoon (5 ml) salt
1 tablespoon (15 ml) finely chopped parsley

In a bowl, place the liver slices in the marinade for
1 hour. Then remove the meat, reserving the
liquid. In a large frying-pan, melt the butter over
high heat and brown the liver quickly on both
sides. Lower the heat and add the smoked ham or
bacon, and the sliced potatoes. Cook for 5
minutes, then pour in the marinade and the
white wine vinegar. Cook for an extra 2 minutes
and serve.

*Preparation time: 15 minutes
Marinating time: 1 hour
Cooking time: 8–10 minutes*

Opposite:
*Buñuelitos de
San José (St Joseph's
Day Fritters)*, p. 136

DINNER
SERVES 2

Carciofi con Funghi
(Artichokes with Mushrooms)

———

Portuguese Marinated Mackerel and
Onions

or

Baked Mackerel with Sauce alla
Napolitana

Fried Semolina

Spinacci con Limone (see page 91)

———

Cheese and Biscuits

Carciofi con Funghi

2 artichokes, stems and pointed ends of leaves
*   removed*
3 tablespoons (45 ml) olive oil, or vegetable oil
1 small onion, chopped finely
4 large mushrooms, chopped finely
2 tablespoons (30 ml) tomato purée (paste)
salt and freshly ground black pepper
pinch of dried oregano
1½ oz (42 g, ¼ cup) dry breadcrumbs
4 strips bacon
3 tablespoons (45 ml) white wine

Preheat the oven to 350°F, 180°C, Mark 4. Boil
the artichokes in salted water for 20–40 minutes,
depending upon their size, or until the leaves pull
out easily. Drain.

In a small frying-pan, heat the oil and cook the
onion and mushrooms for 5 minutes, then add
the tomato purée (paste), salt and freshly ground
black pepper and oregano. Cook over low heat for
3–5 minutes. Spread the leaves of the artichokes,
remove the chokes and fill with the mushroom
mixture. Top with breadcrumbs. Place the artichokes close together in a baking dish, put one
strip of bacon over each artichoke, and add the
wine and 3 tablespoons (45 ml) water. Bake in the
preheated oven for 10 minutes, basting twice.
When cooked, remove the bacon strips and serve.

Preparation time: 15–20 minutes
Cooking time: 40–60 minutes

Portuguese Marinated Mackerel and Onions

2 mackerel, cleaned, heads removed, and cut into 2
*   or 3 2-inch (5-cm) pieces*
3 large onions, sliced thinly
seasoned flour for dredging
4 tablespoons (60 ml) vegetable oil

For the marinade:
4 fl oz (125 ml, ½ cup) dry white wine
4 fl oz (125 ml, ½ cup) white wine vinegar
6 cloves garlic, crushed
1 bay leaf
1 tablespoon (15 ml) dried oregano
1 teaspoon (5 ml) ground mace
2 teaspoons (10 ml) ground dried thyme,
preferably lemon thyme
1 teaspoon (5 ml) chili powder
2 teaspoons (10 ml) salt
4 teaspoons (20 ml) freshly ground black pepper

Make the marinade by mixing the wine, vinegar,
garlic, bay leaf, herbs, chili powder, salt and
pepper. Place it in a glass dish or earthenware
casserole with a cover. Place the mackerel and
onions in the marinade, cover and leave for 2–3
days in the refrigerator.

Remove the mackerel from the marinade,
drain and reserve the marinade to use in the
sauce. Dredge the fish in the seasoned flour,
shaking off the excess. Heat the oil in a frying-pan
large enough to hold 2 mackerel lying flat. Fry the
mackerel over a moderate heat for about 10
minutes. Then dredge the onions in seasoned
flour and add them to the frying-pan. When the
fish and onions are brown and crisp, remove
them to a heated earthenware dish and keep hot.
Pour the reserved marinade into the frying-pan
and boil it up until it turns brown, approximately
4–5 minutes. Remove from the heat, pour the
marinade sauce over the fish and onions, and
serve with squares of Fried Semolina.

Marinating time: 2–3 days
Cooking time: approximately 30 minutes

Fried Semolina

2 tablespoons (30 ml) vegetable or olive oil
1 clove garlic, crushed
$\frac{1}{4}$ lb (125 g) semolina
oil for frying

Heat 2 pints (1.1 litres, 2$\frac{1}{2}$ pints) water, the oil and garlic until the water is just warm with tiny bubbles; if the water is too cold or too hot the semolina will form lumps. Then pour the semolina gradually into the water, stirring constantly, until you have a creamy mixture. Lower the heat and cook for 30 minutes, stirring occasionally. When it is cooked, pour the semolina on to a flat dish so that it forms a cake approximately 1 inch (2.5 cm) thick.

Leave the semolina to cool until it becomes hard. This is best when made either the night before, if serving it for lunch, or in the morning, if serving it for dinner. When you are ready to serve it, cut it into 2-inch (5-cm) squares and fry in oil until it becomes light brown. Serve hot.

Cooking time: 35 minutes plus frying time

Baked Mackerel

2 large mackerel, cleaned, heads removed and roes reserved
2 oz (50 g, $\frac{1}{2}$ cup) fresh coriander (Chinese parsley) or Italian parsley, chopped finely
1 teaspoon (5 ml) rosemary
grated rind of 1 lemon
2 tablespoons (30 ml) fresh breadcrumbs
2 fl oz (50 ml, $\frac{1}{4}$ cup) tarragon vinegar
salt
1 egg, beaten
butter
6 oz (175 g, 1 cup) dry breadcrumbs
Sauce alla Napolitana

Preheat the oven to 350°F, 180°C, Mark 4. In some water, boil the mackerel roes for 3 minutes, drain and chop them. Place in a medium-sized bowl. Add the coriander (Chinese parsley) or parsley, rosemary and lemon rind. Soak the fresh breadcrumbs in the vinegar, then strain (use the vinegar for the Sauce alla Napolitana) and add the crumbs to the roe mixture with salt to taste. Bind the stuffing with the beaten egg and fill the fish with it. Spread butter over the fish, coat them in the dry breadcrumbs and place them in a well greased baking dish in the preheated oven for 20

minutes, or until cooked. Serve with Sauce alla Napolitana separately.

Preparation time: approximately 30 minutes
Cooking time: approximately 20 minutes

Sauce alla Napolitana

4 fresh anchovies, boned or 2-oz (50-g) can anchovy fillets, drained
$\frac{1}{4}$ lb (125 g) black olives, pits removed, chopped
2 tablespoons (30 ml) good olive oil
1 tablespoon (15 ml) white wine or tarragon vinegar
2 small onions, peeled
whole cloves, to taste
1 tablespoon (15 ml) plain (all-purpose) flour
4 fl oz (125 ml, $\frac{1}{4}$ cup) tarragon vinegar

In a medium-sized enamel or copper, not aluminium, saucepan place the anchovies, olives, olive oil, 1 tablespoon (15 ml) vinegar and onions stuck with the cloves. Dissolve the flour in the tarragon vinegar and add to the mixture. Cook over low heat, mashing down the anchovies with a fork to mix with the rest of the ingredients. Stir in 1 pint (600 ml, 2$\frac{1}{2}$ cups) water little by little and cook until the sauce has reduced to a thick purée. Remove the onions and cloves before serving.

Preparation and cooking time: approximately 25 minutes

All Year
Round

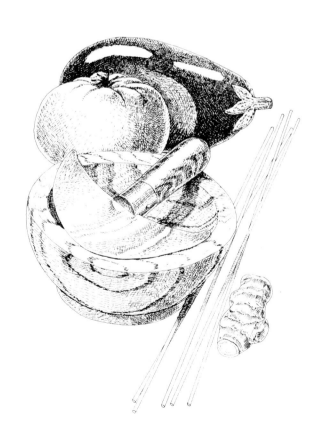

```
_____ BRUNCH _____
         SERVES 4

      Uova alla Cacciatora
    (Italian Eggs Hunter-style)

              or

       Uova e Salsicca
   (Italian Eggs and Sausages)

     *Philadelphia Scrapple

       Paxemedia Toast

    *Greek Apricot Marmalade
```

Uova alla Cacciatora

4 chicken livers, white muscle removed, chopped
salt and freshly ground black pepper
garlic salt
2 tablespoons (30 ml) olive oil
2 fl oz (50 ml, $\frac{1}{4}$ cup) dry white wine
3 tablespoons (45 ml) onion, chopped
4 tablespoons (60 ml) tomato purée (paste)
4 eggs
toast

Season the chicken livers with salt, pepper and garlic salt and brown lightly in the hot oil in a sauté pan. Remove the livers and put aside on a plate. Add the wine and the onion to the oil and cook over low heat until the onion softens.

Pour in the tomato purée (paste) and cook for another 10 minutes. Return the livers to the sauce, break the eggs over them, cover and cook for about 4 minutes. Serve hot on toast.

Preparation time: approximately 10 minutes
Cooking time: approximately 20 minutes

Uova e Salsicca

1 lb (450 g) Italian sausages, split in half
2 fl oz (50 ml, $\frac{1}{4}$ cup) dry white wine
6 eggs, beaten
salt and freshly ground black pepper

In a sauté pan fry the split sausages slowly in the wine, so the juices run out of the sausages. When the sausages are cooked, drain off all but 3–4 tablespoons (45–60 ml) of the juice, then pour the eggs over the sausages, season to taste and cook until the eggs are done. Serve hot.

Preparation time: 10 minutes
Cooking time: approximately 15 minutes

*Philadelphia Scrapple

$\frac{3}{4}$ lb (350 g) lean pork, diced
1 bunch spring onions (scallions), diced
$1\frac{1}{2}$ teaspoons (7.5 ml) salt
$\frac{1}{2}$ teaspoon (2.5 ml) dried sage
$\frac{1}{2}$ teaspoon (2.5 ml) dried marjoram
10 oz (275 g, 2 cups) cornmeal
10 oz (275 g, 2 cups) whole wheat flour

Boil the pork in $6\frac{1}{4}$ pints (3.1 litres, 4 quarts) water for 2 hours. Drain, reserving 5 pints (2.5 litres, 3 quarts) of the liquid. Grind the meat finely.

Bring the reserved broth to the boil and add the onions (scallions) and seasonings. Gradually stir the cornmeal and flour into the boiling broth. Add the meat, cooking slowly for 30 minutes and stirring frequently. Pour into 2 loaf pans and chill. To serve, slice and fry until brown.

Preparation time: approximately 25 minutes
Cooking time: approximately 3 hours

Paxemedia Toast

This 'toast' was given to me with morning coffee – unbelievably delicious.

4 oz (125 g, ½ cup) butter
8 fl oz (225 ml, 1 cup) corn oil
12 ôz (350 g, 1½ cups) granulated sugar
3 eggs
2 fl oz (50 ml, ¼ cup) whisky
juice and grated rind of 1 orange
1 teaspoon (5 ml) ground cinnamon
½ teaspoon (2.5 ml) ground cloves
1 teaspoon (5 ml) bicarbonate of soda (baking soda)
1 tablespoon (15 ml) baking powder
2 lb (900 g, 7 cups) plain (cake) flour
3 oz (75 g, ½ cup) walnuts, ground
2 tablespoons (30 ml) milk

Preheat the oven to 300°F, 150°C, Mark 2.

In a saucepan heat the butter and oil. Pour into a large mixing bowl and, with an electric mixer, beat in the sugar until it becomes light and fluffy. Add the eggs, one at a time, beating well after each addition. Then pour in the whisky and orange juice. In another bowl sift the orange rind, cinnamon, cloves, soda and baking powder with the flour. Then add this mixture to the creamed fat and eggs and beat well. Finally add the nuts. Mix well and knead into a soft dough. Take a piece of dough and roll it into a strip 1 inch (2.5 cm) thick, long enough to fit on a baking sheet. Continue making these strips until you use up the dough. Place them wide enough apart to allow for expansion, and mark out diagonal cuts (do not cut through) at approximately 1-inch (2.5-cm) intervals. Bake in the preheated oven for about 1 hour, or until well browned. Remove from the oven and separate each 'toast' with a knife at the marked cuts. Return the 'toasts' to the baking sheet, with the cut side up, and brown.

Preparation time: approximately 30 minutes
Cooking time: approximately 1 hour

*Greek Apricot Marmalade

This delicious concoction can be used as a filling for very thin crêpes, as well as on toast or muffins. It keeps for several days.

1 lb (450 g) dried apricots
8 fl oz (225 ml, 1 cup) clear honey
1½ oz (37 g, ½ cup) pistachio nuts, shelled and chopped
¼ teaspoon (1.25 ml) dried mint
1 tablespoon (15 ml) pine nuts (pine kernels)

Soak the apricots in water to cover for a few hours, then drain and cut them into pieces. In a medium-sized saucepan, combine the honey and 4 fl oz (125 ml, ½ cup) water and bring to the boil. Add the chopped apricots and cook until the mixture becomes thick and syrupy, then add the mint and nuts. Cook for 3–4 minutes longer. Keep for a day or two before using.

Soaking time: 2–3 hours
Preparation time: approximately 25 minutes
Cooking time: 15–18 minutes

Cilbir

This dish takes no time to make and is extremely healthy.

½ pint (300 ml, 1¼ cups) plain yoghurt
fresh or dried mint or tarragon to taste
1–2 cloves garlic, crushed (optional)
6 eggs
1 tablespoon (15 ml) vinegar
salt
3 tablespoons (45 ml) butter
1 tablespoon (15 ml) paprika
2 tablespoons (30 ml) pine nuts (pine kernels)

If you are using commercial yogurt, you can thicken it by allowing it to drain through a muslin (cheesecloth) lined strainer. When drained add the mint or tarragon and garlic. Set aside.

To poach the eggs, dip them, still in their shells, into boiling water for a few seconds so as to set the thin layer of white nearest to the shell. This will prevent the egg white from spreading too much. Then break each egg into a cup and slide it into another saucepan of simmering water to which the vinegar and salt have been added. Remove the pan from the heat and leave it, covered, for 4 minutes. Then remove the eggs with a perforated spoon to some paper kitchen towels to drain.

Take a warm serving dish, spread half the yoghurt on the bottom, place the eggs on top and cover the eggs with the remaining yoghurt. In a small frying-pan, melt the butter, stir in the paprika and pine nuts (pine kernels). Stir over low heat until the nuts turn golden. (This may be done while the eggs are poaching.) Dribble the paprika butter and nuts over the yoghurt and serve.

Preparation time: 10 minutes
Cooking time: approximately 10 minutes

*Tabbouleh

This salad may be used with many dishes, and not just those of Middle Eastern origin.
It is more substantial than most simple green salads because of the burghul, which is quite filling. Do not use ordinary cracked wheat – only the Lebanese crushed wheat, known as burghul.

½ lb (225 g, 1½ cups) burghul
8–10 spring onions (scallions)
salt and freshly ground black pepper
¼ teaspoon (1.5 ml) ground allspice
7 oz (200 g, 2 cups) fresh coriander (Chinese parsley) or parsley, chopped finely
3 generous tablespoons (50 ml) fresh mint, chopped or 2 tablespoons (30 ml) dried mint
3–4 tablespoons (45–60 ml) good olive oil
fresh lettuce leaves such as Romaine or Cos
3–4 tomatoes, diced

Soak the burghul in water to cover for 30 minutes so that it expands. Drain it by squeezing out the excess water with your hands. Trim the spring onions (scallions) so that the coarse green end bits and the root end are removed. Chop up the white bulb and stalk separately from the green of the onion, keeping the green to combine with the tomatoes. Mix the white part with the burghul, the salt, black pepper and allspice, and place in the refrigerator for 30 minutes so that the taste is infused into the crushed wheat.

When ready to serve, mix in the coriander (Chinese parsley) or parsley and the mint. Then pour in the lemon juice and oil and toss the salad well. Line a bowl with Romaine or Cos lettuce, pile the salad in the middle and top with tomatoes and the green parts of the spring onions (scallions). Note: some people like to add sweet green or red peppers.

Preparation time: 1 hour 20 minutes, including soaking and marinating

Onion Bread

10 oz (275 g, 2 cups) plain (all-purpose) flour
1 tablespoon (15 ml) baking powder
salt
1 oz (25 g) butter
1 oz (25 g) lard
6 fl oz (175 ml, ¾ cup) cold milk
9 oz (250 g, 2 cups) onion, chopped
2 fl oz (50 ml, ¼ cup) vegetable oil
freshly ground black pepper
8 fl oz (225 ml, 1 cup) sour cream
3 egg yolks

Preheat the oven to 450°F, 230°C, Mark 8.

Sift the flour with the baking powder and ½ teaspoon (2.5 ml) salt into a large bowl, then sift once more and cut in the butter and lard. Stir in the milk to make a soft dough. Knead the dough on a lightly floured board, then roll it out to ¼-inch (0.6-cm) thickness.

In a frying-pan, sauté the onions in the oil until they turn soft and transparent. Season with salt and pepper to taste, then remove the onions to a shallow baking dish. Place the rolled out dough over the onions. In a small bowl beat the sour cream and egg yolks so that they are well blended, then spread the mixture over the dough and bake the bread in the preheated oven for 12–15 minutes. To serve, cut the bread into individual servings.

Preparation time: approximately 20 minutes
Cooking time: 12–15 minutes

VEGETARIAN LUNCHEON
SERVES 6

*Sorrel Soup, Hot or Cold (see page 67)

Stufato de Funghi
(Italian Mushroom Stew)

Large Mixed Green Salad

Farfallette and Coffee

For a vegetarian luncheon, make the Sorrel Soup with vegetable stock in place of the chicken stock in the original recipe.

Stufato di Funghi

1 lb (450 g) mushrooms
4 large potatoes, peeled and chopped finely
2 medium-sized onions, sliced
2 oz (50 g, ½ cup) celery, chopped finely
2 tomatoes, peeled and quartered
1 green pepper, chopped finely
2 carrots, chopped finely
2 fl oz (50 ml, ¼ cup) olive or vegetable oil
2 teaspoons (10 ml) finely chopped fresh basil or 1
   teaspoon (5 ml) dried basil
3 tablespoons (45 ml) fresh coriander (Chinese
   parsley) or Italian parsley, chopped finely
1 teaspoon (5 ml) dried oregano
salt and pepper

In a frying-pan brown each vegetable separately but in the same oil, then place all, except the mushrooms, in a large saucepan with 4 fl oz (125 ml, ½ cup) water, and all the seasonings. Simmer until the vegetables are tender, then add the mushrooms and cook for a further 5–10 minutes. Serve hot with French or Italian bread.

Preparation time: approximately 45 minutes
Cooking time: approximately 1 hour

Farfallette

Makes 3 dozen

6 eggs
3 tablespoons (45 ml) caster (superfine granulated) sugar
$\frac{1}{4}$ teaspoon (1.25 ml) salt
6 drops almond essence (extract)
$\frac{1}{2}$ teaspoon (2.5 ml) vanilla essence (extract)
1 lb (450 g, 3$\frac{1}{2}$ cups) plain (cake) flour
2 tablespoons (30 ml) unsalted butter
1$\frac{1}{4}$ pints (725 ml, 1$\frac{1}{2}$ pints) groundnut (peanut) oil
2 oz (50 g, $\frac{1}{2}$ cup) icing (confectioners') sugar
oil for deep frying

In a medium-sized bowl, beat the eggs lightly, then add the sugar, salt and almond and vanilla essences (extracts). Blend well. In a large bowl, pour in the flour, then cut in the butter and blend in the egg mixture. Knead for 10 minutes, until the dough is smooth and fairly stiff, adding more flour if needed. Cover and put aside to rest for 30 minutes.

Divide the dough in 4, and roll out each section on a well-floured board until the dough is very thin. Cut the dough into strips, 6 inches long × $\frac{3}{4}$ inch wide (15 × 1.9 cm). Tie the strips into bow-knots, and fry them in deep oil at 360°F (184°C) for about 3 minutes, until they turn golden brown. Drain on kitchen paper towels and sprinkle with icing (confectioners') sugar.

Preparation time: approximately 45 minutes
Dough resting time: 30 minutes
Cooking time: 15–20 minutes

—— VEGETARIAN LUNCHEON ——
SERVES 4

Feijao Verde a Provinciana
(Portuguese French (String) Beans and Eggs)

Risotto

Mixed Green Salad

Feijao Verde a Provinciana

1 oz (25 g) lard or 2 tablespoons (30 ml) olive oil
1 large onion, chopped finely
1 large clove garlic, chopped finely
2 tomatoes, chopped coarsely
1 lb (450 g) French (string) beans, topped and tailed and cut in half
2 fl oz (50 ml, $\frac{1}{4}$ cup) water or chicken stock (broth)
$\frac{1}{4}$ lb (125 g) smoked ham or bacon
$\frac{1}{4}$ lb (125 g) chorizo or other peppery soft sausage, sliced
salt and freshly ground pepper
1 teaspoon (5 ml) ground ginger
4 eggs

In a deep sauté pan melt the lard or heat the oil and cook the onion and garlic for a few minutes until they have softened. Add the tomatoes, the beans, water or stock (broth), smoked ham and chorizo. Cook over low heat, covered, for about 20 minutes or until the beans are tender. Season with salt, freshly ground pepper and ginger. Make 4 hollows in the vegetable mixture, and break the eggs into them. Continue cooking until the eggs are lightly set, and serve hot.

Preparation time: approximately 30 minutes
Cooking time: 30–35 minutes

Risotto

7 oz (200 g, 1 cup) long grain rice
2 oz (50 g, ¼ cup) butter
1 onion, chopped finely
1¾ pints (1 litre, 2 pints) beef stock (broth)
salt and freshly ground pepper
3 oz (75 g, 1 cup) Parmesan cheese, grated
8 fl oz (225 ml, 1 cup) dry white wine, heated
½ teaspoon (2.5 ml) saffron
1 lb (450 g) fresh mushrooms, quartered
3 tablespoons (45 ml) olive or corn oil

In a medium-sized saucepan, brown the rice in
the butter, then add the onion and sauté for a few
minutes, until the onion is soft and transparent.
Pour in 16 fl oz (475 ml, 1 pint) stock (broth) and
bring to a rapid boil. While the rice is cooking,
gently shake the pan so that the rice doesn't stick
to the bottom as the liquid evaporates. Add the
remaining stock (broth) and the salt and freshly
ground pepper to taste. As the liquid is gradually
absorbed, lower the heat to a simmer and cook for
15 minutes. Add the cheese, wine and saffron
mixed with a very little water, and mix very
gently with a fork. Pour the rice into a colander,
cover with a cloth and place over a pan of hot
water over low heat until the rice becomes dry
and fluffy, approximately 10 minutes. *Up to this
point the risotto may be prepared in advance*; reheat
over hot water in the same colander.
   In a frying-pan sauté the mushrooms in oil and
season them. Pile the rice in the centre of a warm
serving dish and place the mushrooms around it.
Serve with a bowl of grated cheese on the side.

Preparation time: approximately 20 minutes
Cooking time: approximately 30 minutes

– SUNDAY LUNCH OR SUPPER –
SERVES 4

Fegatini di Pollo con Riso
(Chicken Livers with Rice)

or

Quick Curried Prawns (Shrimp) with
Basmati Rice

Bocconcini di Pane all'Aglio
(Garlic Bread Chunks)

Spinach, Bacon and Mushroom Salad

———

Cheese and Biscuits

By Sunday evening, no one wants to
cook very much. This makes an easy but
interesting supper.

Fegatini di Pollo con Riso

12 fl oz (350 ml, 1½ cups) chicken stock (broth)
7 oz (200 g, 1 cup) long grain rice
pinch of saffron
1½ oz (37 g, ½ cup) grated Parmesan cheese
thyme, or fresh basil
salt and pepper
3 tablespoons (45 ml) olive or vegetable oil
1 lb (450 g) chicken livers, cleaned, white muscle
   removed
fresh Italian parsley, chopped finely
paprika

In a medium-sized saucepan heat the chicken
stock (broth) to boiling, add the rice and a pinch
of saffron. Cover, bring back to the boil, then
lower the heat and simmer for 15–25 minutes,
until the rice is soft and fluffy. When the rice is
nearly done, add the grated cheese, herbs and
seasonings. Cover tightly and put aside.
   In a frying-pan heat the oil and sauté the
chicken livers for approximately 3–5 minutes
until they are brown on the outside but still pink
on the inside. Arrange the rice in a ring, pour the
chicken livers and gravy in the centre. Sprinkle
parsley and paprika over the rice and chicken
livers.

Preparation time: approximately 25 minutes
Cooking time: 20–30 minutes

Bocconcini di Pane all'Aglio

Slice a loaf of Italian or French bread into 2-inch (5-cm) slices, brush generously with garlic oil (see page 12), and toast on both sides. Sprinkle generously with grated Parmesan cheese. Serve warm.

Quick Curried Prawns (Shrimp)

2 oz (50 g, ¼ cup) butter
1 tablespoon (15 ml) garam masala (see page 181)
1 teaspoon (5 ml) turmeric powder
1 medium-sized onion, chopped finely
3–4 tablespoons (45–60 ml) plain (all-purpose) flour
12 fl oz (350 ml, 1½ cups) milk
1 teaspoon (5 ml) salt
½ teaspoon (2.5 ml) ground ginger
1 lb (450 g) cooked prawns (shrimp)
1 avocado, poached, peeled and diced (see page 88)
1¼ lb (600 g, 3 cups) cooked rice, preferably Basmati

In a large saucepan melt the butter and stir in the garam masala, turmeric and onion. Mix and simmer for 1 minute, then add the flour and mix until the roux becomes smooth. Slowly add the milk, mix well and cook over low heat, stirring continually until the sauce is thick and smooth. Add the salt and ginger, then the prawns (shrimp) and heat through. At the last minute fold in the diced avocado and serve over the hot fluffy rice.

Preparation time: approximately 15 minutes
Cooking time (including cooking the rice): approximately 25 minutes

---

—— *LUNCHEON OR SUPPER* ——
SERVES 6–8

Konafa with Spinach

Tomato, Onion and Cucumber Salad

———

*Torta di Nicciole Ciocolata (see page 69)

Konafa with Spinach

Konafa is very thin vermicelli-like pasta from the Middle East. This dish is easy to make, and particularly good for lunch or Sunday night supper. The recipe is from Claudia Roden.

½ lb (225 g, 1 cup) butter
1 lb (450 g) konafa (bought at Greek grocery shops)
2 lb (900 g) frozen chopped spinach or 3 lb (1.4 kg) fresh spinach, stems removed and leaves washed
1 lb (450 g) cottage cheese or a mixture of cottage and Cheddar cheese
3–4 eggs
salt and freshly ground black pepper
a good pinch of grated nutmeg

Preheat the oven to 375°F, 190°C, Mark 5. In a saucepan, melt the butter then allow it to cool a little. In a large bowl place the konafa, and pull it apart. Work the butter into the konafa so that it is well mixed. Spread half the konafa and butter on the bottom of a large ovenproof dish 1½–2 inches (3.8–5 cm) deep. In a bowl mix the remaining ingredients. Spread the spinach mixture over the konafa, then cover it with the second half of the konafa. Bake in the preheated oven for 45 minutes–1 hour until the top is golden. Serve hot.

Preparation time: 20 minutes
Cooking time: 45–60 minutes

DINNER

SERVES 4

Yan Kit's Chinese Sautéd Chicken Livers

*Fresh Pasta Verde (see page 110)

Mixed Green Salad

Cheese and Biscuits

*Chocolate Biscuits (Cookies) and Coffee

The Chinese chicken livers must be cooked at the last minute, but you may, and must, prepare all the ingredients in advance and line them up in the order that they enter the pot. The green tagliatelli can be cooking while you are stir-frying the livers.

Yan Kit's Chinese Sautéd Chicken Livers

1½ lb (700 g) chicken livers, trimmed
1½ level teaspoons (7.5 ml) cornflour (cornstarch)
6–7 tablespoons (90–105 ml) groundnut (peanut) or corn oil
2½–3 inches (6–7.5 cm) fresh ginger, peeled and roughly chopped
9–10 large spring onions (scallions), sliced diagonally into ½-inch (1-cm) sections, white and green parts separated
1½ tablespoons (22.5 ml) Shaohsing wine or medium dry sherry

For the marinade:
¾ teaspoon (4 ml) salt
¾ teaspoon (4 ml) brown sugar
1 tablespoon (15 ml) thick soy sauce
freshly ground black pepper
2 teaspoons (10 ml) Worcestershire sauce
2 teaspoons (10 ml) Shaohsing wine or medium dry sherry

For the sauce:
1½ teaspoons (7.5 ml) cornflour (cornstarch)
6 tablespoons (90 ml) clear chicken stock (broth) or water
2 teaspoons (10 ml) thick soy sauce
1 teaspoon (5 ml) Worcestershire sauce

Slice each liver into 2–3 pieces. Place in a colander to wash and drain well. Put into a large bowl. Add the salt, sugar, soy sauce, about 10 turns from the pepper mill, the Worcestershire sauce and wine or sherry. Stir to mix well and leave to marinate for 1–2 hours, stirring occasionally.

Prepare the sauce. Put the cornflour (cornstarch) in a small bowl and stir in 2 tablespoons (30 ml) of the stock or water to blend until smooth. Add the soy and Worcestershire sauces, and sprinkle in the remaining stock or water. Set aside.

Sprinkle the liver with the cornflour (cornstarch) and stir to coat well. Heat a wok over high heat until smoke rises. Add the oil and swirl it around. Add the ginger and white spring onions (scallions) and let them sizzle. As soon as the spring onions (scallions) take on colour, add the livers and brown for about 2 minutes, turning once or twice with a wok scoop or metal spatula to prevent sticking. Sprinkle with the wine or sherry and, when the sizzling has died down, lower the heat, cover and cook for about 2 minutes. Turn the livers over, add the green spring onions (scallions), cover and continue to cook for about 2 more minutes.

Pour the well-stirred sauce over the livers. When it thickens, mix well and remove to a warm serving plate. Serve immediately with the pasta verde. Note: If pressed for time, instead of marinating the livers, pierce them with a fork to let the marinade permeate the flesh.

Marinating time: 1–2 hours
Preparation time: approximately 45 minutes
Cooking time: 6–8 minutes

Chocolate Biscuits (Cookies)

10 oz (275 g, 1¼ cups) granulated sugar
12 oz (350 g, 1½ cups) unsalted butter
4 eggs
2 oz (50 g, ⅓ cup) unsweetened cocoa
2 oz (50 g, 2 squares) bitter chocolate, melted
1 lb (450 g, 3½ cups) plain (all-purpose) flour
1 tablespoon (15 ml) baking powder
1 tablespoon (15 ml) anise flavouring
9 oz (250 g, 1½ cups) roasted peanuts, chopped coarsely
approximately 4 fl oz (125 ml, ½ cup) milk

Preheat the oven to 375°F, 190°C, Mark 5. In a large mixing bowl, cream the sugar and butter until they become light and fluffy, then add the eggs. Mix well and add the cocoa and melted chocolate; mix well. Sift the flour and baking powder in another bowl then add them to the chocolate mixture. Mix and add the anise flavouring and the nuts. Gradually pour in the milk, mixing thoroughly. Roll the dough into small round balls the size of walnuts. Bake in batches on a baking sheet in the preheated oven for approximately 20 minutes.

Icing (Frosting)

This icing (frosting) will keep fresh for 2 weeks if kept in a tightly topped jar in the refrigerator.

1 lb (450 g, 3½ cups) icing (confectioners') sugar
2 oz (50 g, 2 squares) bitter chocolate, melted
juice of 1 lemon

In a bowl, mix all the ingredients and add just enough water to make the mixture fairly soft. Dip the baked biscuits (cookies) in the chocolate and allow them to dry on greaseproof (waxed) paper.

Preparation time: approximately 30 minutes
Cooking time: approximately 20 minutes

DINNER

SERVES 8

*Yan Kit's Deep-fried Crabmeat

Braised Satin Chicken

Pilaf à la Grecque with Vegetables (see page 120)

*Ginger Ice Cream (see page 66)

---

*Yan Kit's Deep-fried Crabmeat

4 oz (125 g) solid creamed coconut
4 oz (125 g) cooked crabmeat
1¼ teaspoons (6.25 ml) salt
freshly ground white pepper
5 tablespoons (75 ml) cornflour (cornstarch)
1 pint (568 ml, 2½ cups) milk
groundnut (peanut) or corn oil for frying

For the batter:
4 oz (125 g, ⅘ cup) plain (all-purpose) flour
5 tablespoons (75 ml) cornflour (cornstarch)
1½ teaspoons (7.5 ml) baking powder
2 tablespoons (30 ml) oil

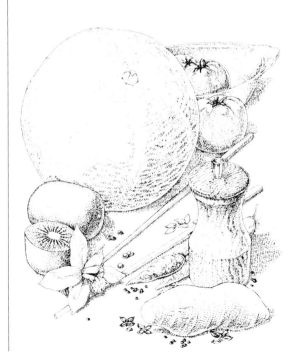

Grate the creamed coconut and put the shavings into a saucepan. Add the crabmeat, if using, and salt and about 6 turns of the pepper mill to the creamed coconut. Stir in the cornflour (cornstarch) and some of the milk and blend to a smooth paste. Then, over gentle heat, gradually add the remaining milk, stirring in the same direction all the time until the mixture has become well amalgamated and thickened. Pour it into a well-oiled shallow container 8 inches (20 cm) square and leave to set in the refrigerator for 2 hours. It can be left overnight covered with cling film (Saran Wrap).

Prepare the batter. Sift the flour and cornflour (cornstarch) into a large bowl and add the baking powder. Gradually stir in 8 fl oz (225 ml, 1 cup) water and blend to a smooth runny consistency. Leave to stand at room temperature for a minimum of 30 minutes. Blend in the oil.

Loosen the well-set mixture from the tin with an oiled palette knife. Use an oiled knife to cut it into about 32 diamond-shaped pieces. Half-fill a wok or deep-fat frying-pan with oil. Heat to a temperature of 375°F (190°C) or until a cube of stale bread browns in 50 seconds. Dip several diamond-shaped pieces into the batter and, using either a pair of chopsticks or tongs, put the pieces one by one into the oil. Deep-fry about 12 at a time, or however many will float freely, for about 3 minutes or until pale golden. Remove with a strainer and drain on kitchen paper towels. Repeat until all are done. Remove the 'bearded' excess batter from each fritter with a pair of scissors.

To crisp the fritters just before serving, reheat the oil to 375°F (190°C) and deep fry the pieces again briefly in 2 batches, each for about 1 minute. Remove and drain on kitchen paper towels. Serve immediately.

Note: Left-over pieces can be revived by deep frying for about 1 minute in oil heated to 350°F (180°C), or under the grill.

Setting time for crabmeat mixture: minimum 2 hours
Resting time for batter: 30 minutes
Cooking time: 3–9 minutes

Braised Satin Chicken

3 tablespoons (45 ml) soy sauce
3 tablespoons (45 ml) Shaohsing wine or sherry
1½ teaspoons (7.5 ml) sugar
½ teaspoon (2.5 ml) salt
½ teaspoon (2.5 ml) white pepper
2 slices fresh ginger, minced
8 breasts of chicken, skin on
8 Chinese mushrooms, soaked and cleaned
16 golden lilies (gum jum, see page 182), soaked
    and cleaned
4 tablespoons (60 ml) groundnut (peanut) or corn
    oil
3 oz (75 g, ¾ cup) cloud ears (wun yee), soaked in
    2 fl oz (50 ml, ¼ cup) warm water for 30
    minutes
8 fl oz (225 ml, 1 cup) chicken stock (broth)
1 tablespoon (15 ml) cornflour (cornstarch)

In a flat dish mix 2 tablespoons (30 ml) soy sauce,
2 tablespoons (30 ml) Shaohsing wine or sherry,
1 teaspoon (5 ml) sugar, the salt, pepper and
ginger, then rub the mixture well into the
chicken and leave for 15 minutes.

Slice the soaked mushrooms and cut the
soaked golden needles in half. In a medium-sized
fireproof casserole, heat the oil and brown the
chicken in it. Then add the remaining marinade,
the mushrooms, golden needles, cloud ears and
chicken stock (broth). Bring the contents to the
boil, cover, turn down the heat and simmer for
30–40 minutes, or until the chicken is tender.
Remove the chicken from the casserole and slice
into pieces approximately 1 inch (2.5 cm) wide.
Remove the mushrooms, golden needles and
cloud ears and heap them on a warm serving
dish. Arrange the slices of chicken over them and
keep in a warm oven.

Mix the cornflour (cornstarch) and remaining
sugar with 1 tablespoon (15 ml) water and the
remaining soy sauce and Shaohsing or sherry in
a bowl, then add to the sauce in the casserole.
Reheat and stir until the sauce thickens, then
pour it over the chicken and serve immediately.

Soaking time: 30 minutes
Preparation time: 30 minutes
Cooking time: approximately 45 minutes

QUICK DINNER
SERVES 2

Gambas al'Ajillo
(Prawns (Shrimp) in Hot Garlic Oil)

Tomato, Onion and Cucumber Salad

Cheese and Biscuits

This menu is our standard dinner on
Friday nights when we go to the
country. The canned prawns (shrimp)
and other ingredients are always in the
house. It is tasty, quick and we never tire
of it.

Gambas al' Ajillo

good olive oil
4 large cloves garlic, peeled and chopped finely
4 dried chilli peppers, chopped, or 1 tablespoon
    (15 ml) cayenne pepper
1 tablespoon (15 ml) dillweed
1 lb (450 g) cooked and peeled prawns (shrimp) or
    use frozen or canned

Cover the bottom of a small frying-pan with 1
inch (2.5 cm) olive oil, then add the garlic,
chillies, dillweed and finally the prawns (shrimp).
Cover the pan and allow the prawns (shrimp) to
simmer for 6–7 minutes. Take 2 small heated
earthenware casseroles, the kind in which you
might serve onion soup, and with a slotted spoon
divide the mixture evenly between them. Then
pour the hot oil over it. Serve hot, and for this
reason try and find some wooden forks to eat
with, as the hot oil will make metal forks burn
your mouth.

Preparation time: 10 minutes
Cooking time: 6–7 minutes

Brains with Mushrooms and Cheese

When my husband first ate this dish, he said to me, 'Those scallops were really delicious'. When I told him that the 'scallops' were in fact brains, he couldn't believe it, having always been put off by the idea of that particular offal. If you don't tell people they will never know and think it delicious.

$2\frac{1}{2}$ lb (1.1 kg) brains
16 fl oz (475 ml, 1 pint) beef or fish stock (broth)
1 lb (450 g) mushrooms, sliced
3 oz (75 g, $\frac{1}{3}$ cup) butter
salt and freshly ground pepper
juice of 5 lemons
8 oz (225 g, $2\frac{1}{2}$ cups) Cheddar cheese, grated
4 oz (125 g) parsley, chopped
1 pint (600 ml, $1\frac{1}{4}$ pints) double (heavy) cream

Soak the brains in salted water for approximately $1\frac{1}{2}$ hours, then drain and remove the fine membrane. Preheat the oven to 475°F, 240°C, Mark 9. Rinse the brains and put into a saucepan, cover with the stock (broth) and bring to the boil. Then lower the heat and simmer for 10–15 minutes until the brains are just done. Drain and slice them thickly. In a frying-pan, sauté the mushrooms in butter, season with salt and pepper to taste and the lemon juice.

Grease an ovenproof dish and place the mushrooms in a layer on the bottom, then the sliced brains, and top with the grated cheese. In a bowl, mix the parsley with the cream, then pour it over the cheese. Place the dish in the preheated oven for 10 minutes. Preheat the grill (broiler) then place the dish under it until the top has browned. Serve with new potatoes and leaf spinach.

Soaking time: $1\frac{1}{2}$ hours
Preparation time: approximately 30 minutes
Cooking time: 35 minutes

*Mazurek Makaroni Kowy

This Polish cake is extremely easy to make and it should be made at least 1 day in advance, if not 2.

12 oz (350 g, 4 cups) ground almonds
1 lb (450 g, 2 cups) caster (superfine granulated) sugar
4 eggs, beaten
juice and grated rind of 1 lemon
5 tablespoons (75 ml) plain (all-purpose) flour
pinch of cream of tartar

Preheat the oven to 300°F, 150°C, Mark 2. In a large bowl mix all the ingredients. Take an 8-inch (20.3-cm) cake pan, butter it well, then line the bottom with rice paper. Pour the mixture into the cake pan and bake it in the preheated oven for approximately 1 hour until it is lightly browned on top. Remove from the oven, turn out on to a cake rack and cool. Put it into a cake tin and keep for at least 24 hours. Some people like to cover it with a thin lemon icing, but I think that is overdoing it.

Preparation time: approximately 20 minutes
Cooking time: approximately 1 hour

*Fish Soup alla Veneziana

3 oz (75 g, ⅓ cup) butter
4 oz (125 g, 1 cup) onion, chopped finely
2 oz (50 g, ½ cup) plain (all-purpose) flour
3 lb (1.4 kg) any firm white fish, boned and skin removed, and cut into small squares
2 oz (50 g, ½ cup) rosemary, chopped finely
4 oz (125 g, 1 cup) fresh coriander (Chinese parsley) or parsley, chopped finely
6 cloves
3 bay leaves
5 tablespoons (75 ml) tomato purée (paste)
salt and freshly ground pepper
grated Parmesan cheese

In a deep saucepan, melt the butter and sauté the onions until they are golden, but not brown. Add the flour and stir to make a white roux. Add 3 pints (1.7 litres, 3¾ pints) warm water slowly, stirring, and simmer until the mixture thickens slightly. Then add the rest of the ingredients and simmer over low heat for about 1 hour. When ready, pour into heated soup bowls and sprinkle grated Parmesan on top. Serve steaming hot.

Preparation time: approximately 30 minutes
Cooking time: approximately 1¼ hours

DINNER
SERVES 6

*Fish Soup alla Veneziana

Kashmiri Divani Handia
(Vegetable Curry)

*Bhindi-do-Piaza (see page 113)

Dahi Pakodi (Spicy Yoghurt) (see page 29)

Fresh Pineapple

Kashmiri Divani Handia

4 fl oz (125 ml, ½ cup) mustard oil or vegetable oil
pinch of asafoetida
½ teaspoon (2.5 ml) cumin seeds
¼ teaspoon (1.25 ml) fenugreek seeds
4 small aubergines (eggplants), chopped finely
¼ lb (125 g) fresh spinach, spines removed
1 white mooli radish, cleaned and chopped finely
1 onion, chopped finely
4 fl oz (125 ml, ½ cup) milk
salt
cayenne pepper
1–2 fresh green chillies, stems and seeds removed
1 teaspoon (5 ml) turmeric powder
1 teaspoon (5 ml) ground coriander
1 teaspoon (5 ml) ground ginger
1 inch (2.5 cm) fresh ginger, peeled and crushed
fresh coriander (Chinese parsley) leaves, chopped

In a sauté pan, heat the oil, then add the asafoetida, cumin seeds and fenugreek seeds and brown lightly. Immediately add the vegetables, cover and cook over low heat until the liquid from them evaporates. Stir them well, then add the milk and the remaining spices and cook, stirring constantly, until the milk is absorbed by the vegetables and oil appears on the surface. Remove from the heat, put in a heated serving dish and sprinkle with fresh coriander (Chinese parsley).

Preparation time: 30 minutes
Cooking time: 25–30 minutes

——— CHINESE DINNER ———
SERVES 4

*Spring Rolls
———
Cantonese Roast Pork with Broccoli

Braised Prawns (Shrimp) with
Beansprouts and Mangetout (Snow Peas)

Rice
———
*Mango and Kiwi Sorbet (see page 52)

---

*Spring Rolls

Happily for all of us, you can buy spring roll dough, or 'Wun Tun' skins frozen in packets in Chinese supermarkets, leaving only the filling to be made. Here is a choice of two: the preparation takes time, chopping and slicing, but the cooking is quick. Each filling makes 8 rolls, enough to serve 4.

Filling No. 1:
2 spring onions (scallions)
1 lb (450 g) beansprouts
2 teaspoons (10 ml) salt
3 oz (75 g, ½ cup) bamboo shoots
6 water chestnuts
6 Chinese mushrooms, soaked for 30 minutes in
   2 fl oz (50 ml, ¼ cup) warm water then sliced
   thinly
¼ lb (125 g) loin of pork, minced
4 slices Parma ham or proscuitto, diced finely
½ lb (225 g) uncooked prawns (shrimp), shelled,
   deveined and diced finely
4 oz (125 g, 1 cup) coriander (Chinese parsley) or
   parsley, chopped finely
½ teaspoon (2.5 ml) sugar
1 tablespoon (15 ml) soy sauce
¼ teaspoon (1.25 ml) freshly ground black pepper
2 teaspoons (10 ml) cornflour (cornstarch)
4 sheets spring roll dough
2 fl oz (50 ml, ¼ cup) vegetable oil for frying the
   finished rolls

Slice each spring onion (scallion) in half lengthwise and then chop finely and diagonally. Wash the beansprouts, simmer for 2 minutes in boiling water, add 1 teaspoon (5 ml) salt, drain and refresh in cold water and allow to cool. Slice the bamboo shoots, water chestnuts and the soaked Chinese mushrooms into thin matchsticks. Place all these in a large bowl and toss. Add the remaining ingredients and mix thoroughly.

To make the spring rolls
Take each square of spring roll dough and cut it in half diagonally. Place the apex of the resulting triangle pointing away from you. Take a large tablespoon (20 ml) of the filling and place it along the base of the triangle leaving ¾ inch (1.9 cm) of the edge free. Then fold over this flap, gather in the other 2 points on either side over the filling and roll the pastry, finally closing it with the apex of the triangle.

Heat the oil in a deep-fat fryer to 360°F (184°C) and fry the spring rolls in a single layer for 4–5 minutes, or until they turn golden brown in colour and crisp. Remove and repeat with the other rolls. *They can be prepared in advance up to this point, even frozen. To reheat, deep-fry them again for 2 minutes.*

Preparation time: approximately 1 hour, if frozen thaw first
Cooking time: approximately 30 minutes

Filling No. 2
½ lb (225 g) canned crabmeat, cleaned, picked over and shredded
½ lb (225 g) loin of pork, or shrimp, minced
1 teaspoon (5 ml) cornflour (cornstarch)
½ teaspoon (2.5 ml) salt
½ teaspoon (2.5 ml) sugar
1 tablespoon (15 ml) soy sauce
10 oz (275 g, 2 cups) beansprouts
8 oz (225 g, 2 cups) spinach leaves, cleaned and stems removed
4 tablespoons (60 ml) groundnut (peanut) oil
2 spring onions (scallions), chopped finely, green and white parts separate
4 Chinese mushrooms, soaked in 2 fl oz (50 ml, ¼ cup) warm water for 30 minutes, drained
1 slice fresh ginger, peeled and sliced thinly
4 sheets spring roll dough
2 fl oz (50 ml, ¼ cup) vegetable oil for frying the finished rolls

In a bowl place the crabmeat and the pork, or shrimp, then add the cornflour (cornstarch), salt, sugar and 1 teaspoon (5 ml) soy sauce. Break the beansprouts in half and shred the spinach leaves in half. In a frying-pan or wok, heat 2 tablespoons (30 ml) oil until smoke rises, add the white part of the spring onions (scallions), and cook for 1 minute. Add the mushrooms, beansprouts, the spinach leaves and 2 teaspoons (10 ml) soy sauce. Cook for 2 minutes, then remove to a dish with a slotted spoon. Add 2 more tablespoons (30 ml) oil. When smoke rises add the ginger, then the crabmeat mixture and cook for 1 minute. Add the cooked vegetables and fry for an additional 2 minutes. Add the green parts of the spring onions (scallions) for colour. Remove and allow the mixture to cool. Then fill and cook the spring rolls as in the previous recipe.

Preparation time: approximately 1 hour
Cooking time: approximately 30 minutes

Cantonese Roast Pork with Broccoli

Most Chinese take-aways have chaah sieu (roast pork), that you can buy or you can make your own. It freezes beautifully.

$\frac{1}{2}$ lb (225 g) tender young broccoli
2 tablespoons (30 ml) groundnut (peanut) or corn oil
1 clove garlic, chopped finely
1 slice ginger, chopped finely
1 teaspoon (5 ml) sugar
$\frac{1}{4}$ teaspoon (1.25 ml) salt
1 teaspoon (5 ml) potato flour
1 tablespoon (15 ml) Shaohsing wine or dry sherry
2 tablespoons (30 ml) soy sauce
$\frac{1}{2}$ lb (225 g) chaah sieu (roast pork), sliced
1 teaspoon (5 ml) sesame oil

Cut the tender stems of broccoli into $1\frac{1}{2}$-inch (3.8-cm) lengths. Peel tougher stems and split almost through, lengthwise. Use the flowerets as well. Heat a wok, add the oil and stir-fry the garlic, the ginger and the broccoli. Sprinkle with sugar and salt, cover and cook for 3–5 minutes, until the broccoli is just tender, but still crisp and green.

In the meantime, in a bowl mix the potato flour with 1 teaspoon (5 ml) water, the wine and soy sauce. Make a hollow in the centre of the ingredients, pour the sauce into it, heat and allow it to thicken slightly, then blend it into the broccoli. Cover and cook for an added 5 minutes, then add the sliced chaah sieu (roast pork) and stir-fry all the ingredients together. Sprinkle with sesame oil and serve.

*Preparation time: approximately 30 minutes
Cooking time: approximately 10 minutes*

*Chaah Sieu (Chinese Roast Pork)

2 lb (900 g) lean loin of pork
$\frac{3}{4}$ teaspoon (4 ml) salt
$\frac{3}{4}$ teaspoon (4 ml) 'five-spice' powder
8 tablespoons (120 ml) sugar
$1\frac{1}{2}$ tablespoons (22.5 ml) Shaohsing wine or sherry
4 tablespoons (60 ml) soy sauce
2 tablespoons (30 ml) hoisin sauce
2 tablespoons (30 ml) ground yellow bean sauce
2 tablespoons (30 ml) clear honey

Cut the pork *along the grain* into slices about 2 inches (5 cm) wide. Then make slashes diagonally across the slices to allow the marinade to get deeply into the pork. In a large bowl mix the remaining ingredients *except the honey*, then rub the marinade well into the pork and leave to marinate, turning over the pieces once or twice, for about 2 hours.

Preheat the oven to 350°F, 180°C, Mark 4. Place the strips of pork on a rack in the top part of the oven, with a tray of hot water beneath the rack to catch the dripping so that it doesn't burn. The steam will also prevent the pork from drying up. Roast it for 40 minutes, then dip the pork back in the marinade and roast the other side for about 20 minutes. When cooked, remove the pork from the oven, and paint it with the honey. Slice each strip *across the grain* into $\frac{1}{4}$-inch (0.6-cm) pieces and serve. This can also be served cold, and it freezes beautifully.

*Preparation and marinating time: $2\frac{1}{4}$ hours
Cooking time: 65 minutes*

Braised Prawns (Shrimp) with Beansprouts and Mangetout (Snow Peas)

1 tablespoon (15 ml) cornflour (cornstarch)
2 tablespoons (30 ml) soy sauce
1 teaspoon (5 ml) freshly ground black pepper
2 teaspoons (10 ml) sugar
2 tablespoons (30 ml) Shaohsing wine or sherry
4 tablespoons (60 ml) groundnut (peanut) or corn
   oil
1 Spanish onion, sliced finely
$\frac{1}{2}$ lb (225 g) mangetout (snow peas), topped and
   tailed
6 stalks celery, sliced finely
2 lb (900 g) beansprouts
4 oz (125 g) cloud ears (wun yee) soaked in 4 fl oz
   (125 ml, $\frac{1}{2}$ cup) warm water for 30 minutes
2 teaspoons (10 ml) salt
2 cloves garlic, crushed
4 slices fresh ginger, peeled and minced
2 lb (900 g) shelled raw prawns (shrimp), chopped
   roughly
3–4 drops sesame oil

In a bowl, combine the cornflour (cornstarch) with 2 tablespoons (30 ml) water and add the soy sauce, pepper, sugar and Shaohsing or sherry. Mix thoroughly. Heat the wok, then add 2 tablespoons (30 ml) oil. When smoke rises, stir-fry the onion, the mangetout (snow peas), celery and beansprouts together with the cloud ears and the salt. Cover and braise for about 3 minutes until the vegetables are tender but still crisp. Remove the vegetables to a warm dish. Add another 1 tablespoon (15 ml) of oil to the wok, toss in the garlic, then the ginger, then the prawns (shrimp). Cover and braise for 1 minute. Next, add the vegetables. Make a well in the centre of the mixture, mix the cornflour (cornstarch) liquid again and pour into the well. Cook for 30 seconds, then stir in the ingredients from the sides of the wok, cover and braise for 2–3 minutes. At the last minute, pour on the sesame oil for fragrance, and serve hot.

Preparation time: approximately 25 minutes
Cooking time: approximately 12 minutes

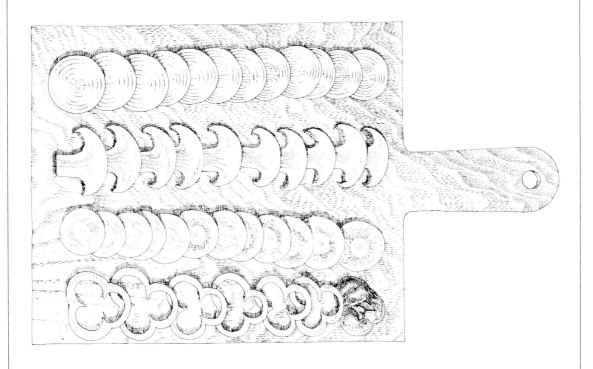

—— CHINESE DINNER ——
SERVES 4

*Fresh Corn Egg Flower Soup

Braised Beef with Turnips

Stir-fried Prawn (Shrimp) Curls in Hoisin
Sauce

Sweet and Sour Spareribs with Pickled
Cucumbers

*Rice

*Ginger Ice Cream (see page 66)

For this menu the first and last courses
may be completely prepared in advance,
the soup needing only to be reheated and
finished off. However the secret of the
whole main course is that, within each
recipe, everything must be marinated in
advance, the ingredients must be
chopped and prepared and lined up as
they will go into the wok or frying-pan.
Then they must all be cooked at the last
minute, and placed on heated dishes in a
low oven with the door open. Then serve
them all at once.

*Fresh Corn Egg Flower Soup

$\frac{1}{4}$ lb (125 g) lean pork, minced
1 tablespoon (15 ml) cornflour (cornstarch)
3 tablespoons (45 ml) groundnut (peanut) or corn
    oil
$\frac{1}{2}$ teaspoon (2.5 ml) sugar
$\frac{1}{2}$ teaspoon (2.5 ml) ground black pepper
1 tablespoon (15 ml) soy sauce
$\frac{1}{2}$ tablespoon (2.5 ml) salt
4 fresh corn-on-the-cob, or 9-oz (250-g) can corn
    kernels
1 clove garlic, minced
1 slice fresh ginger, peeled and sliced thinly
$\frac{1}{4}$ medium-sized onion, minced
1 spring onion (scallion), white and green part
    separated, minced
3 eggs, beaten

In a medium-sized bowl, place the pork, then add
the cornflour (cornstarch), 1 tablespoon (15 ml)
oil, sugar, pepper, soy sauce, salt and 2 tablespoons (30 ml) water. Using a sharp knife scrape
the fresh corn kernels into a bowl or, if using a
can, empty the corn kernels into a sieve and drain
them.

In a large saucepan heat the remaining oil.
When the smoke rises add the garlic, ginger and
onion. Cook for 1 minute, then add $2\frac{1}{3}$ pints (1.3
litres, 6 cups) boiling water and the corn kernels.
Cover, bring the soup to the boil and allow it to
simmer for 10 minutes. Add the pork mixture,
cover and simmer for another 10 minutes.
Remove the saucepan from the heat. *Up to this
point, it may be prepared in advance, then reheated.*
Stir the beaten eggs into the soup and serve.

*Preparation time: approximately 30 minutes
Cooking time: approximately 25 minutes*

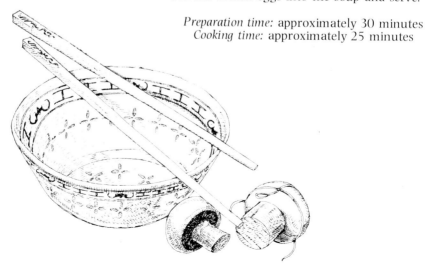

Braised Beef with Turnips

4 long turnips
½ lb (225 g) beef fillet, chuck, rump or best skirt,
  sliced thinly
2 tablespoons (30 ml) red bean sauce (saang see
  jeung)
2 teaspoons (10 ml) sugar
1 tablespoon (15 ml) soy sauce
2 teaspoons (10 ml) potato flour
freshly ground white pepper
1 tablespoon (15 ml) sesame oil
2 tablespoons (30 ml) groundnut (peanut) or corn
  oil
8 spring onions (scallions), sliced into 1-inch
  (2.5-cm) lengths, white part kept separate from
  green
salt
2 cloves garlic, chopped finely
2 slices ginger, chopped finely

Boil the turnips until they are tender, drain and peel them. Slice them into julienne strips. Slice the beef into thin strips, $1\frac{1}{2} \times 1$ inch (3.5 cm × 2.5 cm) long and ¼ inch (0.5 cm) thick. In a bowl mix the red bean sauce, 1 teaspoon (5 ml) sugar, 2 teaspoons (10 ml) soy sauce, 1 teaspoon (5 ml) potato flour, pepper to taste and the sesame oil. Add the beef and mix thoroughly so that all the meat is well coated. Leave for 30 minutes.

In another bowl mix the thickening sauce: 1 teaspoon (5 ml) potato flour, 2 tablespoons (30 ml) water, 1 teaspoon (5 ml) sugar and 1 teaspoon (5 ml) soy sauce. Heat a wok, add the oil and when hot toss in the white part of the spring onions (scallions), the turnips and salt to taste. Stir-fry for 2 minutes then, with a slotted spoon, remove the vegetables to a dish. Reheat the oil, adding to it if necessary, stir-fry the garlic and ginger, add the beef, cook for a few seconds, then stir in the vegetables. Mix well. Make a hollow in the centre of the ingredients, pour in the potato flour mixture. When it has become hot and slightly thickened, stir in the other ingredients and add the green parts of the spring onions (scallions). Mix well, cover and cook for 1–2 more minutes.

Marinating time: 30 minutes
Preparation time: 30–40 minutes
Cooking time: approximately 7 minutes

Stir-Fried Prawn (Shrimp) Curls in Hoisin Sauce

1 lb (450 g) raw prawns (shrimp) in their shells
  but with intestine removed
1 teaspoon (5 ml) salt
1 teaspoon (5 ml) bicarbonate of soda (baking
  soda)
½ teaspoon (2.5 ml) freshly ground black pepper
3 tablespoons (45 ml) hoisin sauce
2 teaspoons (10 ml) sugar
2 tablespoons (30 ml) rice vinegar
1 teaspoon (5 ml) cornflour (cornstarch)
2 teaspoons (10 ml) soy sauce
2 tablespoons (30 ml) groundnut (peanut) or corn
  oil
2 cloves garlic, chopped finely
1-inch (2.5-cm) piece fresh ginger, peeled and
  chopped finely
6 spring onions (scallions) chopped in 1-inch (2.5-
  cm) lengths, white and green parts separated
2–3 drops sesame oil

Wash the prawns (shrimp) in cold water into which you have put ½ teaspoon (2.5 ml) salt and the bicarbonate of soda (baking soda). Drain them and remove their legs, but leave on their shells. Place the prawns (shrimp) in one layer, in a flat dish and sprinkle them with freshly ground pepper.

In a bowl, make a sauce of the hoisin sauce, sugar, remaining salt and rice vinegar. In another bowl dissolve the cornflour (cornstarch) in 1 teaspoon (5 ml) water and the soy sauce, mix and put aside.

Heat the wok, add the oil and when it starts to smoke add the garlic, then the ginger, then the white parts of the spring onions (scallions). Stir-fry for 2 minutes. Add the prawns (shrimp) and stir-fry for another 2 minutes, turning them continually so that they are cooked through. Add the hoisin sauce mixture and stir-fry for 30 seconds. Make a well in the centre of the ingredients, pour in the cornflour (cornstarch) mixture and cook for another 30 seconds until the liquid thickens. Bring in the prawns (shrimp) from the side and add the green parts of the spring onions (scallions). Mix well, cover, and cook for 2 minutes. Sprinkle with sesame oil for fragrance, put on a heated dish and serve.

Preparation time: 30 minutes
Cooking time: approximately 10 minutes

Sweet and Sour Spareribs with Pickled Cucumbers

When ordering spareribs for this dish, be sure to ask for American or Chinese spareribs, which are taken from the pork belly, rather than English spareribs (country-style spareribs in America) taken from the pork shoulder.

3 lb (1.4 kg) pork spareribs (American-style)
8 tablespoons (120 ml, ½ cup) vinegar or white
   malt vinegar
8 tablespoons (120 ml, ½ cup) soy sauce
2 teaspoons (10 ml) freshly ground white pepper
4 tablespoons (60 ml) 'five-spice' powder
8 cloves garlic, crushed (4 if very large)
6 eggs, beaten
7 tablespoons (105 ml) cornflour (cornstarch)
groundnut (peanut) or corn oil for deep frying
2 cucumbers
2 carrots, sliced thinly
1 teaspoon (5 ml) salt
½ teaspoon (2.5 ml) cayenne pepper
3 tablespoons (45 ml) sugar

To finish:
1 tablespoon (15 ml) cornflour (cornstarch)
1 tablespoon (15 ml) soy sauce
4 cloves garlic, crushed

Slice the spareribs through between the bones, then chop each rib into 1-inch (2.5-cm) pieces. Boil enough water in a large saucepan to accommodate the spareribs. When the water is at a rolling boil, plunge the spareribs into it, remove the pan from the heat and allow the spareribs to stand in the water for 15 minutes. Meanwhile in a deep dish mix half the rice vinegar and the next 6 ingredients, then drain the ribs and stir them into the batter, making sure that each rib is thoroughly coated. In a deep-fat frying-pan, heat about 2 inches (5 cm) oil until it reaches 360°F (184°C). Drop in the spareribs in batches and cook for approximately 10 minutes, until they have turned a rich golden brown. Drain on kitchen paper towels. Continue in this manner until all the spareribs have been cooked.

Cut the cucumbers lengthwise, remove the seeds, rub them with salt and cut them, diagonally, into ¾-inch (1.9-cm) pieces. Rub the carrot slices with salt. In a bowl large enough to hold the vegetables, mix the remaining rice vinegar, cayenne pepper and sugar. Marinate the vegetables in this for at least 15 minutes. *Up to this point the preparation may be done ahead.* The spareribs should be piled in a heap to await final cooking.

Just before serving, remove the vegetables from the marinade with a slotted spoon and put them on a heated dish. To the marinade add a mixture of the cornflour (cornstarch), 2 fl oz (50 ml, ¼ cup) water and the soy sauce. Heat the wok, add 2 tablespoons (30 ml) of the oil in which you fried the spareribs, and stir-fry the crushed garlic cloves for 30 seconds, then stir in the vinegar-cornflour (cornstarch) mixture. Cook until the sauce thickens, then toss in the spareribs and cook for about 2 minutes, thoroughly mixing in the sauce. Arrange the spareribs and sauce on top of the marinated vegetables on the heated dish and serve.

Preparation time: approximately 45 minutes
Cooking time: approximately 45 minutes

— AFTER-THEATRE SUPPER —
SERVES 6

*Sopa de Avellanos
(Hazelnut Soup)

———

Baked Haddock with Mustard
Mayonnaise

or

Yan Kit's Stir-fried Scallops in Oyster
Sauce

Yan Kit's Stir-fried Spinach in Bean Curd
'Cheese' Sauce (see page 101)

———

Cheese and Biscuits

For this menu, all the ingredients for stir-
frying may be prepared in advance and
lined up in the order in which they will
enter the pot, so that the cooking will
only take a few minutes.

*Sopa de Avellanos

2 pints (1.2 litres, 2½ pints) chicken stock (broth)
4 oz (125 g, 1 cup) toasted breadcrumbs
a pinch of saffron
2 cloves garlic
5 oz (150 g, 1 cup) hazelnuts, skinned (see page
  69)
salt and pepper

Pour the chicken stock (broth) into a saucepan;
add the breadcrumbs and heat over a moderate
flame. Grind the saffron, garlic and nuts in a
mortar or in an electric blender until the mixture
becomes a smooth paste, then stir into the
saucepan. Season with salt and pepper to taste
and simmer slowly for 10 minutes.

Preparation time: 10 minutes
Cooking time: 10–15 minutes

Baked Haddock with Mustard Mayonnaise

½ teaspoon (2.5 ml) English mustard powder
1½ lb (700 g) fresh haddock fillets
salt
4 fl oz (125 ml, ½ cup) mayonnaise
1 teaspoon (5 ml) onion, chopped finely
½ teaspoon (2.5 ml) thyme leaves, chopped finely
1 teaspoon (5 ml) fresh lemon juice
freshly ground pepper
paprika

Preheat the oven to 350°F, 180°C, Mark 4. Soak
the mustard in 2 teaspoons (10 ml) water for 10
minutes, or until it has absorbed it. Butter a
baking dish, place the fillets in it and sprinkle
with salt. In a bowl mix the mustard, mayonnaise, onion, thyme, lemon juice and freshly
ground pepper to taste. Spread the mixture over
the fish and bake in the preheated oven for 25
minutes or until the fish is flaky and the sauce is
light golden brown. Sprinkle the paprika on top.

Preparation time: approximately 25 minutes
Cooking time: 25 minutes

Yan Kit's Stir-fried Scallops in Oyster Sauce

4 large dried Chinese mushrooms, soaked in 2 fl oz (50 ml, ¼ cup) warm water for 30 minutes
1 lb (450 g) shelled scallops, fresh or frozen
5 tablespoons (75 ml) groundnut (peanut) or corn oil
4 cloves garlic, chopped
6 thin slices fresh ginger, peeled
4 spring onions (scallions), cut into 1-inch (2.5-cm) sections, white and green parts separated
1 tablespoon (15 ml) Shaohsing wine or medium dry sherry
4–6 stalks celery, cut diagonally into thick slices
sesame oil to taste

For the marinade:
white pepper to taste
1 teaspoon (5 ml) cornflour (cornstarch)
½ egg white, lightly beaten

For the sauce:
½ teaspoon (2.5 ml) potato flour
¼ teaspoon (1.25 ml) salt
2 tablespoons (30 ml) oyster sauce
3 tablespoons (45 ml) juice from cooked scallops

Drain and squeeze out the excess water from the mushrooms but leave them damp. Quarter them. Wash the scallops and remove and discard the hard muscle. Pat dry and separate the corals or roes from the scallops. Slice each scallop cross-wise into 2–3 pieces. Pat dry again and put into a dish. Halve the corals diagonally and put into another dish.

Prepare the marinade. Add white pepper to taste, a good ½ teaspoon (2.5 ml) cornflour (corn-starch) and a little over half of the egg white to the scallops and stir to coat. Add pepper to taste, the remaining cornflour (cornstarch) and egg white to the corals. Leave to marinate for 10 minutes.

To prepare the sauce, dissolve the potato flour in 1 teaspoon (5 ml) water in a bowl. Stir in the salt and oyster sauce and put aside.

Heat a wok over high heat until smoke rises. Add 2½ tablespoons (37.5 ml) oil and swirl it around. Add half the garlic and as soon as it sizzles and takes on colour, add half the ginger, then half the white spring onion (scallion). Stir, and tip in the scallops immediately. Sliding the wok scoop or metal spatula to the bottom of the wok, turn and toss the mixture for 30–60 seconds or until the scallops are barely cooked, becoming whitish. Splash half the wine or sherry along the rim of the wok and continue to stir. As soon as the sizzling dies down, remove on a strainer over a bowl to catch the juice that will drip from the scallops.

Add another 1½ tablespoons (22.5 ml) oil to the wok and swirl it around. Stir in the rest of the garlic, ginger and white spring onion (scallion). Add the corals and stir and toss as before for about 1 minute. Splash the remaining wine or sherry along the rim of the wok, stir, cover, lower the heat and cook for about 2 more minutes or until the corals become firm to the touch. Remove on the strainer over the bowl. While the corals are being cooked, add 3 tablespoons (45 ml) of the juice from the scallops to the potato flour and oyster sauce mixture. Blend thoroughly and keep nearby. Turn up the heat again, add the remaining 1 tablespoon (15 ml) oil to the wok and swirl it around. Tip in the celery, stir, and then add the mushrooms. Stir and toss for 30–60 seconds; the celery should remain crisp and barely cooked. Push to the sides of the wok, leaving a well in the middle. Pour the well-stirred sauce into the well and when it bubbles add the scallops and corals, turning and tossing to reheat them and drawing in the celery and mushroom. Add the green spring onions (scallions) and then remove to a warm serving plate. Arrange the corals and mushrooms attractively on the plate. Sprinkle on some sesame oil to enhance the flavour and serve immediately.

Preparation time: approximately 45 minutes
Cooking time: 5–7 minutes

Clam Soufflé

*8 oz (225 g, 1 cup) shelled fresh clams, minced, or
   10-oz (275-g) can clams, drained and minced*
1 tablespoon (15 ml) lemon juice
8 fl oz (225 ml, 1 cup) clam juice
8 fl oz (225 ml, 1 cup) milk
4 tablespoons (60 ml) butter
5 tablespoons (75 ml) plain (all-purpose) flour
salt and freshly ground black pepper
2 egg whites
6 oz (175 g, 1 cup) fine dry breadcrumbs
4 oz (125 g, ½ cup) butter, melted

Preheat the oven to 425°F, 220°C, Mark 7.
Sprinkle the lemon juice over the clams and let
stand. In the top of a double boiler heat the clam
juice and milk. Melt the butter in a large
saucepan, stir in the flour and cook over low heat
until it bubbles. Slowly pour in the heated clam
juice and milk, stirring constantly to make a
smooth thick sauce. Remove the sauce from the
heat, add the clams and seasoning. *Up to this
point, the dish may be prepared in advance.*

Beat the egg whites until stiff and fold into the
clam mixture. Butter an 8-inch (20.3-cm) shallow oval dish or 4 ramekins. Fill them two-thirds
full with the mixture. Mix the dried breadcrumbs
with the melted butter and sprinkle on top of the
soufflés. Bake in the preheated oven for approximately 10 minutes.

*Preparation time: 20 minutes
Cooking time: approximately 10 minutes*

Riccini with Garlic and Anchovy Sauce

1 lb (450 g) dried riccini (corkscrew) pasta
salt
1 tablespoon (15 ml) olive oil
*fresh coriander (Chinese parsley) leaves, chopped
   finely for garnish*

For the sauce:
6–8 cloves garlic, sliced thinly
12 anchovy fillets, chopped
1 tablespoon (15 ml) butter

In a large pan bring 4 pints (2.2 litres, 2½ quarts)
water to a rapid boil, add a pinch of salt and the
oil, then add the pasta. Bring the water back to
the boil and cook the pasta for 10–12 minutes, or
until it is *al dente.*

Meanwhile make the sauce. Pound the garlic
and anchovies together in a mortar or in an
electric herb grinder. Place them in a saucepan,
add 1 tablespoon (15 ml) olive oil and the butter,
mix well and bring to the boil.

Drain the pasta in a colander, then turn it into
a heated serving dish and pour the sauce over it.
Mix well. Sprinkle fresh coriander (Chinese parsley) over the top.

*Preparation time: 20–25 minutes
Cooking time: approximately 15 minutes*

Parmesan Biscuits

Makes about 18 biscuits

This is one of Rose Sorce's most inventive and useful recipes, because not only can these rolls be eaten on their own but also the dough can be used as a crust for vegetables, meat or fowl, rolling the dough to $\frac{1}{4}$-inch (0.6-cm) thickness to cover the casserole. Press the edges of the dough to the dish, and cut an opening in the centre to allow the steam to escape.

3 oz (75 g, 1 cup) Parmesan cheese, grated
10 oz (275 g, 2 cups) plain (all-purpose) flour
4 teaspoons (20 ml) baking powder
1 teaspoon (5 ml) salt
1 oz (25 g) unsalted butter
1 oz (25 g) lard
6 oz (175 g, $\frac{3}{4}$ cup) milk

Preheat the oven to 450°F, 230°C, Mark 8. In a large bowl, mix the cheese, flour, baking powder and salt, then cut in the butter and lard and add the milk. Mix together very quickly and thoroughly, until it makes a stiff dough; knead the dough on a lightly floured board and roll it out to $\frac{1}{2}$-inch (1.2-cm) thickness. Cut into biscuit shapes 2 inches (5 cm) wide and place them on a buttered baking sheet about 2 inches (5 cm) apart so that they crust on all sides. Bake immediately in the preheated oven for 12 minutes.

Preparation time: approximately 20 minutes
Cooking time: 12 minutes

—— AFTER-THEATRE SUPPER ——
SERVES 2

*Seviche (Marinated Fish with Ginger and Coriander Sauce) (see page 136)

———

Tagliatelli with Mushroom and Anchovy Sauce

———

Rocket (Arrugula) or Watercress and Raddichio Salad

———

Cheese and Biscuits

Tagliatelli with Mushroom and Anchovy Sauce

$\frac{1}{2}$ lb (225 g) fresh tagliatelli (see page 110)
pinch of salt
fresh coriander (Chinese parsley) leaves, chopped finely for garnish

For the sauce:
2 tablespoons (30 ml) butter
4 canned anchovy fillets, chopped finely
4 mushrooms, chopped finely
8 fl oz (225 ml, 1 cup) beef stock (broth)
2 tablespoons (30 ml) red wine vinegar
2 tablespoons (30 ml) Marsala
$\frac{1}{2}$ teaspoon (2.5 ml) Dijon-type mustard
cayenne pepper
salt
1 tablespoon (15 ml) capers

Make the tagliatelli and allow it to dry for 15 minutes.

Make the sauce. Heat the butter in a medium-sized saucepan, then add the anchovies and mushrooms, and cook them until they turn golden. Pour in the stock (broth), vinegar and Marsala and cook over low heat for 20 minutes, then add the mustard, a dash of cayenne, salt to taste and the capers.

Bring 4 pints (2.2 litres, $2\frac{1}{2}$ quarts) water to a boil in a large pan, add the salt then the tagliatelli. Cook the pasta for 3 minutes after the water has returned to the boil, until the pasta is *al dente*. Drain it in a colander and turn it out into a heated serving dish. Pour the mushroom and anchovy sauce over the pasta and sprinkle fresh coriander (Chinese parsley) leaves over the top.

Preparation time: 15 minutes plus 15 minutes drying time
Cooking time: approximately 30 minutes

*Hot and Sour Soup

10 Chinese mushrooms
2½ pints (1.4 litres, 3 pints) chicken stock (broth)
5 oz (150 g) lean pork, sliced thinly
6-oz (175-g) can bamboo shoots, drained, sliced
   and cut into fine strips almost 1 inch (2.5 cm)
   long
4 dried lily flowers
6 tablespoons (90 ml) white wine vinegar
2 teaspoons (10 ml) soy sauce
½ teaspoon (2.5 ml) salt (optional)
freshly ground black pepper
2 tablespoons (30 ml) cornflour (cornstarch)
dash of Tabasco (optional)
2 eggs, beaten lightly
1 tablespoon (15 ml) sesame oil
2 spring onions (scallions), chopped finely

Soak the mushrooms in hot water for 20 minutes.
Remove the mushrooms, *reserving the water*, and
squeeze them dry. In a large saucepan, bring the
chicken stock (broth) to the boil, add the pork and
mushrooms, bring back to the boil and simmer
for 8–10 minutes. Add the bamboo shoots and lily
flowers and simmer for a further 10 minutes.
Next add the vinegar, soy sauce, salt (if desired,
but the soy sauce is quite salty) and freshly
ground black pepper to taste. Into 4 tablespoons
(60 ml) of the reserved mushroom water stir the
cornflour (cornstarch) and mix well so that it
becomes smooth and creamy. Pour this mixture
into the soup, mix well and add a dash of Tabasco
if desired. *Up to this point, the soup may be prepared
in advance, and then reheated.* Remove from the
heat, add the beaten eggs and stir. Finally, add
the sesame oil and chopped spring onions
(scallions).

Preparation time: approximately 40 minutes
Cooking time: approximately 40 minutes

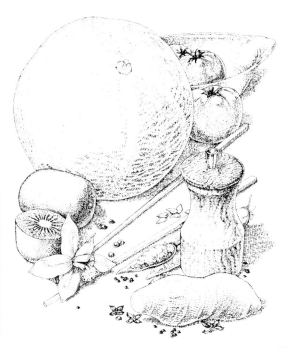

165

*Chicken Tikka Makhani

This is the most delicious dish. Do not be discouraged by the list of ingredients; it looks complicated but definitely is not. What's more it does not take a great deal of time. The result is a triumph of subtle tastes. In India we ordered this constantly – it became an addiction.

4-lb (2-kg) frying chicken, skin removed, cut into
    8 pieces (saving wings for another use)
juice of $\frac{1}{2}$ lemon
salt
fresh coriander (Chinese parsley) leaves, chopped
    finely

For the tandoori marinade:
1 teaspoon (5 ml) cumin seeds
1 onion, chopped finely
2 cloves garlic, chopped finely
$\frac{1}{2}$ nutmeg, freshly ground
1 inch (2.5 cm) fresh ginger, peeled and sliced
6 cardamom seeds
1 fresh green chilli pepper, stem and seeds
    removed, chopped finely
1 teaspoon (5 ml) red chilli paste
$\frac{1}{2}$ pint (300 ml, 1$\frac{1}{4}$ cups) plain yoghurt

For the Makhani Sauce:
8 fl oz (225 ml) tomato sauce (see page 180)
1 inch (2.5 cm) fresh ginger, peeled and grated
    finely
1$\frac{1}{2}$ teaspoons (7.5 ml) tandoori masala (available
    in Middle Eastern and Oriental shops)
1 teaspoon (5 ml) salt
$\frac{1}{4}$ teaspoon (1.5 ml) sugar
$\frac{1}{4}$ teaspoon (1.5 ml) cayenne pepper
1 teaspoon (5 ml) cumin seeds
1 fresh green chilli pepper, stem and seeds
    removed, chopped finely
2 tablespoons (30 ml) fresh coriander (Chinese
    parsley) chopped finely
5 tablespoons (75 ml) lemon juice
$\frac{1}{2}$ pint (300 ml, 1$\frac{1}{4}$ cups) double (heavy) cream
1 teaspoon (5 ml) ground white pepper
$\frac{1}{4}$ teaspoon (1.5 ml) fenugreek seeds, crushed
$\frac{1}{4}$ lb (125 g, $\frac{1}{2}$ cup) unsalted butter

Put the pieces of chicken into a large earthenware dish. Make 3–4 slashes down the bone and rub the lemon juice and salt well into each piece. Make the marinade: as you need roasted cumin seeds for both the marinade and sauce, put 2 teaspoons (10 ml) cumin seeds into a small iron frying-pan with no butter or oil. Place over a high heat and shake constantly. The seeds will slowly turn brown and pop around the pan. Remove and allow to cool slightly. Then grind in a mortar and pestle, or place in a small electric coffee grinder and grind finely. Divide the powder into two, reserving one half for the sauce. In a large bowl put 1 teaspoon (5 ml) cumin and add the onion and garlic. Place the nutmeg, ginger, cardamom seeds and green chilli in the electric coffee grinder or mortar and pestle, grind and add to the marinade, along with the chilli paste and yoghurt. Mix well and pour over the chicken; again mix well to thoroughly coat it. Place, covered, in the refrigerator for 24 hours, turning the chicken pieces occasionally.

Make up the sauce ahead of time, *except* for the butter and fenugreek, so that the spices can infuse their taste and aroma into the cream. In a bowl, pour all the ingredients *except the fenugreek and butter*, mixing well. Keep covered in a bowl in the refrigerator overnight. In a large saucepan, melt the butter, then add the sauce and stir constantly over medium heat until the butter is amalgamated into the sauce mixture. At the last minute add the fenugreek and heat the sauce slowly. Do not allow it to boil otherwise the fenugreek will turn bitter.

Preheat the oven to 450°F, 220°C, Mark 8. Remove the chicken pieces from the marinade, place in a baking pan and bake on the top shelf of the preheated oven for 25 minutes. Pour the sauce over the chicken pieces, sprinkle with chopped coriander (Chinese parsley) leaves and serve.

Preparation time: 45 minutes
Marinating time: 24 hours
Cooking time: 40 minutes

*Mushroom Pullao

8 oz (225 g, 1 cup) butter or margarine
3 small onions, sliced
10 oz (275 g, 1⅓ cups) long grain rice
salt and freshly ground black pepper
3 cardamom seeds
1–2 bay leaves
3 tablespoons (45 ml) chopped almonds
2 tablespoons (30 ml) lemon juice
1 lb (450 g) small mushrooms
3 tablespoons (45 ml) butter
a pinch of saffron or turmeric powder

Preheat the oven to 325°F, 170°C, Mark 3. In a large saucepan, melt 2 oz (50 g, ¼ cup) of the butter or margarine and sauté the onions until they turn a golden brown. Add the rice and the remaining butter or margarine and cook the rice, stirring frequently, until it has absorbed the fat. Season to taste with salt and pepper, then add the spices, bay leaves and the almonds and barely cover the mixture with boiling water. Put the lid on the saucepan and simmer very gently until the rice is tender.

In a saucepan, bring 4 fl oz (125 ml, ½ cup) water to the boil, add 1 teaspoon (5 ml) salt, the lemon juice, mushrooms and butter. Boil rapidly for 4–5 minutes. Remove the saucepan from the heat and drain the mushrooms.

When cooked, drain the rice into a large bowl and mix with the cooked mushrooms. Sprinkle the mixture with saffron or turmeric, put into an ovenproof dish and bake in the preheated oven for 5 minutes, so that the moisture will evaporate from the rice.

Preparation and cooking time: approximately 30 minutes

—— AFTER-THEATRE SUPPER ——
SERVES 6

*Curried Apricot Soup

———

*Vongole con Melanzane en Casseruola
(Clam and Aubergine/Eggplant Casserole)

Large Mixed Green Salad

———

Cheese and Biscuits

---

*Curried Apricot Soup

This is particularly good made from a pheasant too old to roast, or one which has been in the freezer a long time. It can be made with a chicken as well, but it will not have the more gamey taste.

1 lb (450 g) cooked and boned pheasant or chicken
4–5 whole, dried apricots, cooked and drained
1 pint (600 ml, 2½ cups) pheasant or chicken stock (broth)
2 tablespoons (30 ml) unsalted butter
1 tablespoon (15 ml) curry powder, or to taste
2 tablespoons (30 ml) plain (all-purpose) flour
16 fl oz (475 ml, 2 cups) double (heavy) cream
4 tablespoons (60 ml) chopped fresh mint

Cut up the pheasant or chicken and purée the meat with the apricots in a food processor or blender together with 8 fl oz (225 ml, 1 cup) stock (broth). In a large saucepan, melt the butter, add the curry powder, stir and cook until it becomes amalgamated, then add the flour. Stir and cook the roux until the rawness of the flour is taken out of the taste. Add the remaining stock (broth). Stir and cook until you have a creamy sauce, then add the game or poultry purée and mix thoroughly. You may prepare the soup up to this point ahead of time and refrigerate or even freeze it. When ready to serve, reheat, add the cream and heat again *but do not boil*, for approximately 10–15 minutes, until the mixture thickens. Sprinkle the mint on top of each serving.

Preparation time: if game or poultry is uncooked – 40 minutes
If game or poultry is already cooked – 10–15 minutes
Cooking time: 15–20 minutes

*Vongole con Melanzane en Casseruola

2 10-oz (275-g) cans clams
2 small aubergines (eggplants), diced
1 onion, chopped finely
3 tablespoons (45 ml) olive oil
12 oz (350 g, 2 cups) dry breadcrumbs
salt and pepper
3 tablespoons (45 ml) grated Parmesan cheese

Preheat the oven to 350°F, 180°C, Mark 4. Drain the canned clams, reserving the liquid. In a medium-sized saucepan bring some salted water to the boil and cook the aubergine (eggplant) for 10 minutes, then drain on kitchen paper towels. In a frying-pan sauté the onion in 2 tablespoons (30 ml) olive oil until it becomes soft and transparent, then add the clams, mix well and cook for 2 minutes. In a well-oiled deep gratin dish or shallow casserole, place a thin layer of breadcrumbs, then a layer of aubergine (eggplant) and a layer of clams. Season and repeat the layers until the ingredients are used up, then top with a layer of breadcrumbs. Pour in the clam juice, sprinkle with Parmesan and 1 tablespoon (15 ml) olive oil, and bake in the preheated oven for 45 minutes.

Preparation time: approximately 20 minutes
Cooking time: approximately 1¼ hours

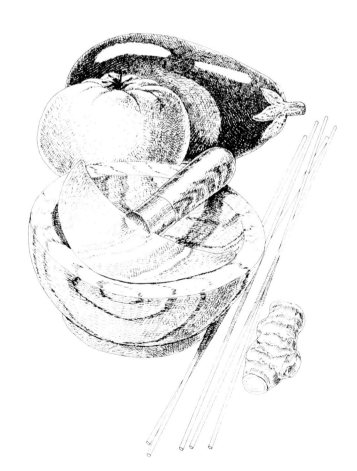

168

Alternative Menus

─── *DINNER* ───
Serves 4

*Seviche (Marinated Fish with Ginger and Coriander Sauce) (see page 136)

─────

Victoria's Veal Canigo with Potato Straws (see page 68)

French Beans with Paprika and Pine Nut (Pine Kernel) Butter (see page 103)

─────

*Kulfi (Indian Ice Cream) (see page 36)

─── *DINNER* ───
Serves 4

*Carciofi Forno (Cold Baked Artichokes) (see page 53)

─────

Sgombro con Salsa di Basilico (Baked Mackerel in Basil Sauce) (see page 62)

Yan Kit's Stir-fried Spinach in Bean Curd 'Cheese' Sauce (see page 101)

─────

Salad and Cheese

─── *DINNER* ───
Serves 6

*Seafood Cocktail (see page 27)

─────

Greek-style Quail with Salsa Victoria (see pages 24–5)

Belgian Endive and Watercress Salad

─────

*Hazelnut Crêpes Pralinées with Liqueur Sauce (see page 104)

LUNCHEON
SERVES 6

*Avocado Mousse (see page 40)

Red Mullet alla Livornese (see page 51)

Stir-fried Mangetout (Snow Peas) with Toasted Sesame Seeds (see page 66)

Fennel in Anchovies with Vinegar Sauce (see page 71)

Songos de Morangos (Spanish Strawberry Dreams) (see page 45)

DINNER
SERVES 4

*Gaspacho à Alentejana (see page 58)

Mutton Biryani (Indian lamb with Rice and Browned Onions) (see page 29)

Fried Bringals (Aubergine/Eggplant) (see page 36)

Dahi Pakodi
Spicy Yoghurt (see page 29)

---

*Strawberries in Wine (see page 55)

DINNER
SERVES 6

Asparagi all'Aglio
Asparagus with Garlic (see page 80)

Trotto al Forno (Baked Trout with Sardines) (see page 21)

Carciofi Fritti con Salsa (Italian Artichoke Fritters) (see page 25)

---

*Mixed Summer Berries of your Choice Tossed in Sugar

DINNER
SERVES 8

Austrian Eggs Czernin (see page 78)

Murg Tikka (Barbecued Chicken Cubes) (see page 44)

*Carrot Cosimber (see page 42)

Spinacci con Limone (see page 91)

Hot Stuffed Peaches with Zabaglione Sauce (see page 74)

DINNER
SERVES 2

Carciofi con Funghi (Artichokes stuffed with Mushrooms) (see page 138)

Lobster Marsala (see page 66)

Mixed Green Salad of your choice

---

*Mango and Kiwi Sorbet (see page 52)

SUNDAY LUNCH OR SUPPER
SERVES 4

Curried Pheasant (see page 134)

Kasha (see page 131)

*Raita (see page 51)

Mixed Green Salad and Cheese

─────── *DINNER* ───────
SERVES 4

*Mussel Soup (see page 129)

Iscas Lisbõa (Portuguese Liver and
Smoked Ham) (see page 137)

*Carrots in Orange Liqueur (see page
103)

Zucchini Frittata en Uova (Italian Fried
Courgettes, Zucchini, In Egg) (see page
48)

Cheese and Biscuits

─────── *DINNER* ───────
SERVES 6

*Fresh Corn Egg Flower Soup (see page
158)

Monkfish Delight (see page 18)

French Beans with Paprika and Pine Nut
(Pine Kernel) Butter (see page 103)

*Carrots in Orange Liqueur (see page
103)

*Ksheer Annam (Indian Rice Pudding)
(see page 94)

─────── *DINNER* ───────
SERVES 4

Austrian Eggs Czernin (see page 78)

Filetto di Sogliola Marinato (Fillet of Sole
in Vinegar Sauce) (see page 54)

Spinacci con Limone (see page 91)

*Glazed Carrots (see page 74)

*Torta di Nicciole Ciocolata (Chocolate
Nut Torte) (see page 69)

─────── *DINNER* ───────
SERVES 8

Gustaba (Kashmiri Meatballs) (see page
127)

*Mushroom Pullao (see page 167)

*Baked Aubergines (Eggplants) (see page
52)

Large Mixed Green Salad of your Choice

Cheese and Biscuits

─────── *LUNCHEON* ───────
SERVES 4

*Hot Green Pepper Soup (see page 60)

Minced Pheasant in Baked Potatoes (see
page 134)

Mixed Green Vegetable Salad of your
Choice

Cheese and Biscuits

───── *DINNER* ─────
SERVES 6

*Sopa de Avellanos (Hazelnut Soup)
(see page 161)

───────

Brazilian Pork Kebabs (see page 93)

*Mushroom Pullao (see page 167)

*Carrot Cosimber (see page 42)

───────

*Torta di Nicciole Ciocolata (Chocolate
Nut Torte) (see page 69)

───── *DINNER* ─────
SERVES 6

*Zuppa d'Ostrice (Oyster Soup) (see page
109)

───────

Kamargah (Kashmiri Spare Ribs of Lamb)
(see page 113)

Curried Corn Pudding (see page 122)

Palak Paneer (Spinach with Indian
Cream Cheese) (see page 54)

───────

*Lemon Squares (see page 58)

─ *SUNDAY LUNCH OR SUPPER* ─
SERVES 4

*Walnut Soup (see page 119)

───────

Turkey alla Cittadina (see page 115)

Garbanzos con Espinacas (Chickpeas with
Spinach) (see page 32)

───────

Mixed Green Salad and Cheese

───── *LUNCHEON* ─────
SERVES 6

*Sopa de Avellanos (Hazelnut Soup)
(see page 161)

───────

Cream di Granchi (Creamed Crab on
Toast) (see page 125)

Mixed Green Salad

───────

Cheese and Biscuits

───── *DINNER* ─────
SERVES 6

*Thai Lemongrass Soup (see page 126)

───────

*Osso Buco (see page 118)

Kasha (see page 131)

Mixed Green Salad

───────

Cheese

—————— *DINNER* ——————

SERVES 6

*Carciofi Forno (Cold Baked Artichokes)
(see page 53)

———

Petto di Anatra (Italian Breast of Duck)
(see page 74)

*Pilaf à la Grecque with Vegetables (see
page 120)

Belgian Endive and Watercress or Rocket
(Arrugula) Salad

———

Mixed Fruit Salad

—————— *DINNER* ——————

SERVES 6

Fernanda's Portuguese Baked Marinated
Pork Loin (see page 109)

Spanish Creamed Potatoes (see page 71)

*Yan Kit's Pickled Cabbage, Peking-style
(see page 84)

———

*Chocolate Mousse (see page 87)

———

The chocolate mousse will be a nice
sweet 'gout', but make it without the
meringue that was in the original recipe,
or it will be too rich and heavy.

—————— *DINNER* ——————

SERVES 6–8

*Hot Green Pepper Soup (see page 60)

———

Indonesian Pork Kebabs (see page 101)

*Lebanese Spiced Rice (see page 86)

Dahi Pakodi (Spicy Yoghurt) (see page
29)

———

Cheese and Biscuits

—————— *DINNER* ——————

SERVES 2

*Sopa de Avellanos (Hazelnut Soup) (see
page 161)

———

Baked Mackerel, Sauce alla Napolitana
(see page 139)

Potatoes All-i-oli (see page 42)

French Beans in Paprika and Pine Nut
(Pine Kernel) Butter (see page 103)

———

Cheese and Biscuits

—————— *DINNER* ——————

SERVES 4

*Carciofi Forno (Cold Baked Artichokes)
(see page 53)

———

Chinese Pork Chops (see page 130)

*Riso al Sugo d'Arancia (Spanish Orange
Rice) (see page 47)

Tao Gugi (Kashmiri Turnips) (see page
128)

———

Salad and Cheese

─────── *DINNER* ───────
SERVES 6

Kadhi (Gujarati Soup) (see page 117)
───
Stufato di Pesce al Forno (Baked Stuffed Haddock) (see page 77)

Zucchini Frittata en Uova (Italian Fried Courgettes, Zucchini, in Egg) (see page 48)
───
Mixed Fruit Salad of your Choice

or

Cheese and Biscuits

─────── *DINNER* ───────
SERVES 6–8

Hot Spinach and Chicken Liver Salad (see page 26)
───
Chinese Fish with Mandarin Sauce (see page 32)

Stir-fried Mangetout (Snow Peas) with Toasted Sesame Seeds (see page 66)
───
*Pear and Green Peppercorn Sorbet (see page 77)

*Almond Crisps (see page 55)

─────── *DINNER* ───────
SERVES 6

*Hot and Sour Soup (see page 165)
───
Yan Kit's Stir-fried Scallops in Oyster Sauce (see page 162)

Stir-fried Mangetout (Snow Peas) with Toasted Sesame Seeds (see page 66)
───
*Hazelnut Crêpes Pralinées with Liqueur Sauce (see page 104)

─────── *DINNER* ───────
SERVES 6–8

*Walnut Soup (see page 119)
───
*Veal Goulash (see page 111)

Kasha (see page 131) or Pilaf à la Grecque with Vegetables (see page 120)

Spinacci con Limone (see page 91)
───
Cheese and Biscuits

─────── *DINNER* ───────
SERVES 6

Caldo Verde (see page 121)
───
Eels alla Milanese (see page 120)

*Lebanese Spiced Rice (see page 86)
───
Cheese and Biscuits

─── *VEGETARIAN DINNER* ───
SERVES 4

Avial-Malayali
(Vegetable Curry) (see page 23)

*Mushroom Pullao (see page 167)

*Carrot Cosimber (see page 42)
───
*Seviyal Bakala Bath (Indian Vermicelli Pudding) (see page 33)

─── VEGETARIAN DINNER ───
SERVES 4

Pineapple Moddulu (see page 64)

Fried Bringals (Aubergines/Eggplants)
(see page 36)

*Carrot Cosimber (see page 42)

─────────

*Mango and Kiwi Sorbet (see page 52)
with *Biscotti di Mandorle (Almond
Biscuits) (see page 78)

─ SUNDAY NIGHT DINNER ─
OR QUICK LUNCH
SERVES 4

*Fresh Corn Egg Flower Soup (see page
158)

─────────

Quick Curried Prawns (Shrimp) (see page
147)

Rice

*Raita (with Palak) (see page 51)

─────────

Cheese and Biscuits

─── SUNDAY NIGHT SUPPER ───
OR QUICK LUNCH
SERVES 6

*Hot and Sour Soup (see page 165)

─────────

Polpette alla Napolitana with Agro Dolce
Sauce (Sweet and Sour Meatballs) (see
page 79)

Risotto (see page 146)

Large Mixed Green Salad

─────────

Cheese and Biscuits

Sauces and
Spice Mixtures

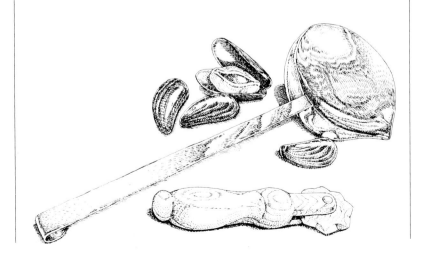

White Wine Fish Sauce

6 canned sardines
2 tablespoons (30 ml) olive oil
2 tablespoons (30 ml) plain (all-purpose) flour
8 fl oz (225 ml, 1 cup) fish stock (broth) or clam
    juice
juice of $\frac{1}{2}$ lemon
4 fl oz (125 ml, $\frac{1}{2}$ cup) dry white wine
1 tablespoon (15 ml) chopped fresh basil
salt and freshly ground black pepper
2 egg yolks

Soak the sardines in cold water for about 30 minutes, then drain, chop and rub them through a sieve or purée them in a food processor. In a saucepan heat the olive oil, stir in the flour to make a smooth roux, then the fish stock (broth) or clam juice. Cook until smooth and thick. Add the lemon juice, wine and the sardines, and simmer for approximately 10 minutes. Add the fresh basil, season to taste and gradually stir in the egg yolks.

Soaking time: 30 minutes
Preparation time: approximately 15 minutes
Cooking time: approximately 20 minutes

*Salsa Verde

For fish

1 medium-sized onion, grated
1 tablespoon (15 ml) finely chopped parsley
1 tablespoon (15 ml) capers
1 gherkin, chopped finely
3 anchovy fillets
1 tablespoon (15 ml) fresh white breadcrumbs
1 tablespoon (15 ml) good olive oil
juice of 1 lemon
1–2 tablespoons (15–30 ml) dry white wine

In a mortar and pestle or food processor, pound or mix the onion, parsley, capers, gherkin and anchovies until you achieve a smooth paste. Add the breadcrumbs and pound or mix again until they are thoroughly incorporated. Add the oil, mix well, then the lemon juice. Finally, add 1 tablespoon (15 ml) white wine. If you find it necessary to dilute the sauce further add another tablespoon (15 ml) white wine.

Preparation time: approximately 30 minutes

Sweet–Sour Game Sauce

$\frac{1}{4}$ lb (125 g) pine nuts (pine kernels), chopped
    finely
$\frac{1}{2}$ lb (225 g) pistachio nuts, skinned and chopped
2 oz (50 g) unsweetened chocolate
2 tablespoons (30 ml) sugar
4 fl oz (125 ml, $\frac{1}{2}$ cup) white wine vinegar
1 oz (25 g) mixed candied lemon and orange peel,
    chopped finely
2 tablespoons (30 ml) currants
3 tablespoons (45 ml) redcurrant jelly
8 fl oz (225 ml, 1 cup) pan gravy from meat
salt and freshly ground black pepper

In a medium-sized saucepan combine the ingredients and simmer for about 30 minutes, season to taste.

Preparation time: approximately 20 minutes
Cooking time: 30 minutes

*Red Wine Sauce

For meat and poultry

8 fl oz (225 ml, 1 cup) red wine
1 medium-sized onion, chopped finely
2 fl oz (50 ml, $\frac{1}{4}$ cup) red wine vinegar
pinch of rosemary
8 fl oz (225 ml, 1 cup) olive oil
1 clove garlic, chopped finely
pinch of cayenne pepper
salt

Mix all the ingredients together, pour them into an airtight jar and allow to stand for 24 hours before using as a basting sauce for meat and poultry. If kept in the jar, this will keep for weeks in the refrigerator.

Preparation time: 10 minutes
Standing time: 24 hours

*Orange Sauce

For a simple but tangy dessert, the following sauce can be used over hot or cold dessert crêpes, fritters, hot puddings or cold soufflés.

juice of 2 large sweet oranges
juice of 1 lemon
grated rind of 1 orange
1 oz (25 g, ¼ cup) icing (confectioners') sugar
2 tablespoons (30 ml) butter
flour
juice of 1 Seville orange

In a medium-sized saucepan, pour the sweet orange and the lemon juice, 15 fl oz (425 ml, scant 2 cups) water, grated orange rind and sugar. Roll the butter in some flour and stir into the sauce. Cook over a low heat, stirring, for 10–12 minutes. Just before serving, remove from the heat and stir in the Seville orange juice. Serve hot or cold.

Cooking time: approximately 12 minutes

*Almond Cranberry Sauce

Yields 2 pints (1.2 litres, 5 cups)

1 lb (450 g) sugar, granulated
12 oz (350 g, 4 cups) fresh cranberries, washed and sorted
4 fl oz (125 ml, ½ cup) apricot jam
2 oz (50 ml, ¼ cup) lemon juice
3 oz (75 g, ½ cup) toasted almond slivers

In a large saucepan combine the sugar and 8 fl oz (225 ml, 1 cup) water and bring it to the boil. Cook it for 5 minutes over medium heat. Add the cranberries and cook for an additional 3–5 minutes, or until the cranberries pop open. Remove the pan from the heat and stir in the jam and lemon juice. Chill, then add the almonds.

Cooking time: 15 minutes
Chilling time: 1 hour

Kahwah (Spiced Tea)

This unique Kashmiri tea is usually made in a samovar with live coals placed in the inner funnel and the ingredients in the outer chamber, but it can equally well be made in an ordinary Western teapot. We drank it continually while we were working in Kashmir, as often as we were offered it, and found it not only delicious but extremely refreshing.

1 teaspoon (5 ml) Japanese green tea
sugar to taste
pinch of ground cinnamon
2 cardamom pods
a thread of saffron
3–4 shredded almonds

Put the green tea into a saucepan, add 1¼ pints (750 ml, 1½ pints) water and bring to the boil. While it is boiling add sugar to taste. Then pour into a teapot and add the rest of the ingredients. Cover. Allow to stand for 5–10 minutes, then serve.

*Chaudfroid Verte

This is an interesting variation on an ordinary chaudfroid sauce, adding colour too. For chicken or fish.

10 oz (300 g, 1¼ cups) frozen chopped spinach
1 tablespoon (15 ml) capers
1 sweet and sour gherkin, chopped finely
salt and freshly ground black pepper
½ pint (300 ml, 1¼ cups) strong chicken stock (broth)
5 fl oz (150 ml, ⅔ cup) double (heavy) cream

In a medium-sized saucepan cook the spinach, capers and gherkin in 1 tablespoon (15 ml) water until they become soft. Mash to a purée and add salt and freshly ground black pepper to taste. Add the stock (broth), mix thoroughly, then strain. Return the sauce to the pan and stir in the cream, heating the sauce through but not allowing it to boil. Pour the sauce over a cold chicken or whole fish, and place in the refrigerator to chill.

Preparation and cooking time: approximately 20 minutes
Chilling time: 2 hours

*Sauce alla Borghese

For cold fish or meat

*4 anchovies, boned or 2-oz (50-g) can anchovy
    fillets, drained*
4 tablespoons (60 ml) good olive oil
*2 tablespoons (30 ml) fresh coriander (Chinese
    parsley) or Italian parsley, chopped finely*
1–2 shallots, chopped finely
1 oz (25 g, ⅓ cup) dried breadcrumbs
freshly ground black pepper
white wine, tarragon or shallot vinegar

Place the anchovies and the oil in a small
saucepan and cook for 6–7 minutes, pressing
continually with a fork to break up the fish. Pour
the mixture into a medium-sized bowl and add
the coriander (Chinese parsley) or parsley, the
shallots and breadcrumbs. Season with freshly
ground black pepper to taste but *no salt*. There is
ample in the anchovies. Slowly add the vinegar,
mixing continually until you achieve a creamy
consistency.

Preparation time: approximately 15 minutes
Cooking time: 6–7 minutes

*Tomato Sauce

2 lb (900 g) tomatoes, skin and seeds removed
3 tablespoons (45 ml) olive oil
1 medium-sized onion, chopped finely
1 clove garlic, chopped finely
5-oz (140-g) can tomato purée (paste)
salt and pepper
1 bay leaf
1 tablespoon (15 ml) dried oregano
1 teaspoon (5 ml) fennel seeds

In a deep saucepan heat the olive oil and brown
the onion and garlic. Then add the tomatoes, the
tomato purée (paste) and seasonings. Simmer for
1 hour or until the sauce has thickened.

Preparation time: 30 minutes
Cooking time: 1¼ hours

*Brown Sauce or Sauce Espagnole

Makes 1½ pints (900 ml, 4 cups)

4 oz (125 g, ½ cup) beef, veal or pork drippings
2 medium-sized onions, chopped coarsely
1 small carrot, chopped coarsely
2 oz (50 g, ½ cup) plain (all-purpose) flour
*3 pints (1.7 litres, 3¾ pints) hot brown stock
    (broth)*
3 sprigs parsley
1 stalk celery
1 small bay leaf
1 clove garlic, crushed
a pinch of dried thyme
*5 tablespoons (75 ml) tomato sauce or tomato
    purée (paste)*

Melt the drippings in a heavy saucepan. Add the
onions and carrot and cook until the onions start
to turn golden, shaking the pan to ensure even
cooking. Add the flour and cook the mixture,
stirring, until the flour, carrot and onions turn a
rich brown. Add 1¼ pints (750 ml, 3 cups) stock
(broth), the parsley, celery, bay leaf, garlic and
thyme, and cook the mixture, stirring frequently,
until it thickens. Add 1¼ pints (750 ml, 3 cups)
more stock (broth) and simmer the sauce slowly,
stirring occasionally, for 1–1½ hours, or until it is
reduced to about 1¼ pints (750 ml, 3 cups). As it
cooks, skim off the fat that rises to the surface.
Add the tomato sauce or purée (paste), cook for a
few minutes more and strain through a fine sieve.
Add 1¼ pints (750 ml, 3 cups) more stock (broth)
and continue to cook the sauce slowly for about 1
hour, skimming the sauce from time to time, until
it is reduced to about 1½ pints (900 ml, 4 cups).
Strain the sauce before using.

Preparation time: 10 minutes
Cooking time: approximately 3 hours

*Basil Honey Mustard

Makes approximately 2 lb (900 g)

4 tablespoons (60 ml) black mustard seeds
4 tablespoons (60 ml) white mustard seeds
white wine vinegar
clear honey (preferably Roumanian lime)
1 teaspoon (5 ml) good quality coarse sea salt
4 fresh basil leaves, bruised and chopped finely
olive oil (optional)

Grind together the black and white mustard seeds until they form a paste, (a small electric coffee grinder is ideal for this). Pour the paste into a bowl and add the vinegar until the seeds can absorb no more. Add an equal amount of honey, then the salt and basil. Mix well and leave to ferment for a few days before serving. If you find that the mustard is too strong for you, add a little olive oil. Store in a screw-top jar.

Preparation time: 10–15 minutes
Fermenting time: 3–4 days

*Garam Masala

Makes approximately 6 oz (175 g, $\frac{3}{4}$ cup)

2-inch (5-cm) piece cinnamon stick
$1\frac{1}{2}$ oz (40 g, $\frac{1}{4}$ cup) cardamom pods
2 tablespoons (30 ml) cloves
2 tablespoons (30 ml) cumin seeds
2 tablespoons (30 ml) black peppercorns
1 tablespoon (15 ml) coriander seeds

Combine all the ingredients in a dry heavy bottomed frying-pan, and cook over low heat, stirring constantly, until the spices have turned pale brown. Remove from heat and grind them, either in a mortar and pestle, or in an electric coffee grinder reserved for that purpose. Store the spice in an airtight container in the dark and away from heat. It should last a few weeks without losing its flavour.

Preparation time: approximately 20 minutes

181

Glossary of Chinese Ingredients

Bamboo Shoots are the young shoots of the tropical bamboo plant. They are available in cans, in chunks or sliced. It is more convenient to buy small cans, and use them up. Or, you can keep them in a screw-top jar filled with water, changing the water twice a week. They will keep in this manner for a week in the refrigerator.

Bean Curd also known as To-fu. The soybeans are puréed, then pressed into cakes 1 inch (2.5 cm) thick and 4 inches (10 cm) square. You can find them wrapped in plastic in the refrigerated section of Chinese supermarkets, and they will keep in your refrigerator for 1 week. The pressed version of bean curd, I freeze and use as necessary.

Black Beans (fermented) have an extremely powerful smell which affects the eyes. These salty black beans are used in small quantities for seasoning. Sold in plastic bags or jars, they will keep indefinitely in tightly shut screw-top jars.

Cellophane Noodles also known as vermicelli, are made from mung bean flour. They can also be used in Indian cooking and will keep indefinitely in the store cupboard. If you are using them in a soup, presoak them, but if frying them, there is no need for this.

Chili Paste with Garlic is useful for many cuisines. Sold in bottles. After opening the bottle, keep in the refrigerator where it will keep indefinitely. Also good in barbecue sauces for spare ribs.

Cloud Ears also known as tree ears or fungus. These must be soaked in hot water for approximately 30 minutes before using, and cleaned carefully. Used in soups, and with vegetables in meat and poultry dishes. Will store indefinitely kept in tightly topped jar in the cupboard.

Five-spice Powder is a combination of cinnamon, cloves, star anise, fennel, and anise pepper. Used as seasoning, it is sold in packages or jars.

Fresh Ginger Used in Chinese, Indian and Middle Eastern cooking. It is sold by weight. It will keep in the refrigerator for a few days as is, but will keep indefinitely if peeled, placed in a jar and covered with sherry. Seal the jar tightly and place in the refrigerator. To use fresh, it must *always* be peeled. Ground ginger is not a substitute.

Golden Lilies also known as golden needles. Dried lily flowers of a golden colour. Used to add flavour to meat, poultry dishes and soups. Sold in plastic bags. Keeps indefinitely in the cupboard.

Groundnut (Peanut) Oil is the best and healthiest oil to use in Chinese cooking as well as everyday cooking. Expensive.

Hoisin Sauce A spicy barbecue sauce used in many dishes, and the basis of the sauce used in Peking Duck. Sold in tins and jars. Once a tin is opened, if not used up, put the remaining sauce in a screw-top jar in the refrigerator.

Hot Pepper Oil Spicy oil used in Szechuan dishes. May also be used as seasoning in other cuisines. Sold in bottles.

Mushrooms (Chinese) Dried black-capped brown mushrooms which expand when soaked in hot water, which they must always be before using. Sold in plastic bags, they will keep indefinitely in a screw-top jar in the larder.

Oyster Sauce A thick flavoured sauce made from oyster extract and sold in bottles. Used for flavouring many Chinese dishes.

Sesame Seed Oil Very expensive. Should be used at the last moment in small amounts to bring out the 'fragrance' of the dish.

Sesame Seeds Sold in plastic bags. Can be kept indefinitely in a jar in the larder.

Shaohsing Wine A sherry-like wine (medium dry sherry may be substituted). Used as a seasoning in many dishes. Sold in bottles.

Soy Sauce Sold in bottles, light or thin, dark or thick, and very thick. The last one is used only in very special dishes. The dark or thick soy gives more colour than flavour, rather like gravy browning. The light or thin, is the best all-round sauce for most dishes. Keeps indefinitely.

Szechuan Peppers Brownish red peppercorns used in small amounts for their spicy fragrance, sometimes in tandem with coarse salt.

Vinegar Light rice vinegar is used in Chinese cooking, and may be used in salad dressings for everyday use as well. The red vinegar is used more as a dipping sauce.

Water Chestnuts Used as a vegetable with poultry and meat dishes as well as with other vegetables. Comes in cans. After opening, will keep in a screw-top jar in the refrigerator.

Sources and Further References

Behrens, Elsie, *Cooking the Spanish Way*,
  London, Spring Books, 1960

Daly, Dorothy, *Italian Cooking*, London, Spring
  Books, n.d.

Dar, Krishna Prasad, *Kashmiri Cooking*,
  Sahibabad, Vikas Publishing House PVT
  Ltd., 1977

Feng, Doreen Yen Hung, *The Joy of Chinese
  Cooking*, London, Faber & Faber, 1952

Gironci, Maria, translated and arranged by,
  Italian Recipes, London, Gaskill, Jones and
  Co., 1892

Hambro, Nathalie *Particular Delights*, London,
  Norman & Hobhouse, 1981

Manjón, Maite, *The Home Book of Portuguese
  Cookery*, London, Faber & Faber, 1974

Pruthi, J.S., *Spices and Condiments*, New Delhi,
  National Book Trust, India, 1976

Reejhsinghani, Aroona, *The Art of South Indian
  Cooking*, Bombay, Jaico Publishing House,
  1973

Roden, Claudia, *A Book of Middle Eastern Food*,
  Middlesex, Penguin Books Ltd., 1970

Serra, Victoria, *Tia Victoria's Spanish Kitchen*,
  translated by Elizabeth Gili, edited and
  adapted by Nina Froud, London, Nicholas
  Kaye Ltd., 1963

So, Yan Kit, *Classic Chinese Cookbook*, London,
  Dorling Kindersley Ltd., 1984

Solomon, Charmaine, *The Complete Asian
  Cookbook*, Sydney, Summit Books published
  by Paul Hamlyn Pty Ltd., 1976

Sorce, Rose L. *La Cucina. The Italian Kitchen*,
  London, The Cresset Press Ltd., 1955

Turner, Elsie, *Fifty Ways of Cooking a Pheasant*,
  London, Spottiswoode, Ballantyne & Co.
  Ltd., 1932